D1382786

The Introverted Actor

"This revolutionary book empowers quiet actors to leverage their strengths and navigate all aspects of the profession, from auditioning to networking. Highly accessible and well-researched, *The Introverted Actor* provides theatre educators and directors with a wealth of temperament-inclusive methods for the quiet actors in their casts. A seminal addition to teaching the art and craft of acting."
—Susan Cain, Co-founder of Quiet Revolution and Best-Selling Author of *Quiet, The Power of Introverts in a World That Can't Stop Talking*

"Roznowski, Conover, and Kasevich's groundbreaking book, "The Introverted Actor", will alter the way we perceive and value introversion in the theatre world. Utilizing data collected from over 500 interviews and surveys from student actors and theatre professionals, the authors construct a solid and convincing case that identifies and celebrates the strengths and contributions of all personality temperaments--extroverts, introverts, and ambiverts—can yield in actor training and the stage. The authors then proceed to offer practical approaches and techniques for student actors, theatre directors, and theatre professionals functioning in a world skewed in favor of the extrovert. This is pioneering work! After reading the authors' theories and their correlation to actor-training I immediately altered the way I deal with introverts and extroverts in the classroom. The results have been eye-opening and tremendously valuable. "The Introverted Actor", is a significant and indispensable text that has the potential to make anyone a better actor, director, and teacher."
—Deborah Jordan, Associate Professor of Theatre, *Program Head, Acting & Directing Jacksonville University, Jacksonville, FL*

"Deepening our understanding of the human experience is a core part of our work in the theatre, and this book helps us to do just that. The practical tools offered here can foster more meaningful engagement in the classroom and rehearsal room, not just for the introverts among us, but for everyone else too."
—Lauren Morris, Co-Director of the Apprentice Company, *Horizon Theatre Company, Atlanta, GA*

"The acting teachers of today and tomorrow need to be aware of hidden bias and inclusivity. Great acting teachers recognize not only various ways of knowing and learning, but also understand and adapt to the complex personalities and temperaments of their students. *The Introverted Actor* provides keen insight and excellent strategies to help teachers focus on this aspect of inclusive learning so they can reach out to all students. Every acting teacher should read this book and evaluate their approach to how they work with students!"
—Dennis Schebetta, Assistant Professor, *Skidmore College, Saratoga Springs, NY*

"This book is so needed! Reading it has actually been a cathartic experience for me. I wish this book existed when I was studying acting as it helped me redefine my perspective of myself. I love that this book reframes introversion as an asset instead of an obstacle to overcome. I hope this book gets widespread attention!"
—Dennis Corsi, NYC-based Professional Actor & Director

Rob Roznowski • Carolyn Conover
Heidi Kasevich

The Introverted Actor

Practical Approaches

palgrave
macmillan

Rob Roznowski
Department of Theatre
Michigan State University
East Lansing, MI, USA

Carolyn Conover
Department of Drama
Jacksonville State University
Jacksonville, AL, USA

Heidi Kasevich
Kase Leadership Method, Inc.
New York, NY, USA

ISBN 978-3-030-41606-5   ISBN 978-3-030-41607-2   (eBook)
https://doi.org/10.1007/978-3-030-41607-2

This Palgrave Macmillan imprint is published by the registered company Springer Nature Switzerland AG.
The registered company address is: Gewerbestrasse 11, 6330 Cham, Switzerland

Foreword

So, you're an introvert. Why go into acting? An introverted actor? It seems like an oxymoron. As an actor, your job is to stand in front of a crowd of people and present yourself as the center of attention. Your actor training involves immediate response, improvisation, and team-building that does not usually allow for the private processing and reflection time you so desperately crave. Your career requires constant auditioning and networking events where you must interact and socialize, leaving you drained and doubtful. Why do it?

You are an introverted actor. And there are lots of us! Don't feel like you don't belong because you don't fit into the "standard" extroverted model of the actor. There is an argument to be made that not only can (and do) introverts find success in this profession, but there are aspects of the introverted personality that enrich and strengthen acting work.

Do a quick search on the internet and there are many personal actor blogs or anecdotal online articles about being an introverted actor, but nothing that explores the situation in great detail. There is scant research examining such a seemingly incongruous match of temperament and profession. For this reason, the majority of this book will be first-person interviews from over eighty psychological experts, professional and student actors, educators, and directors who all work daily with both introverted and extroverted actors. We also collected data and stories from our over 400 international survey respondents about introversion and acting. Many of their insights and suggestions are quoted in full to offer a broader picture of this abstruse and neglected theatrical area.

As we avow numerous times throughout this book, not all introverts are alike. And individuality is to be celebrated. Introverts share certain traits, but they still remain vastly different from each other, and our book wants to embrace the idea of the individual introvert. However, we also generalize (as many books on the subject of introversion do) about what introverts prefer, need, and want. Such preferences are borne out of our findings in the survey and from other research adapted for the actor.

In addition, we acknowledge that distinctiveness and differences extend to the extrovert. Extroverted actors may thrive in solo analysis and connect to a rich interior life—traits more frequently associated with introverted actors. While the book will advocate for changes in training and professional theatrical practices to better support the introvert, it is not to diminish the contributions of the extrovert, but rather to place all actors on an equal footing. The necessary synergistic partnership between introvert and extrovert should be embraced and celebrated.

Our book aims for temperament inclusivity where introverts and extroverts can thrive in a variety of educational and work settings—ones that value and reward all types of learners. While this book labels actors through the lens of temperament, our goal in doing so is to effect change to create parity for introverts and extroverts in a field that has tended to favor the extrovert.

A note on tone: it is our goal that this book be accessible and useful to a variety of audiences, including actors, directors, educators, and students. In this, we have avoided an overly academic voice and attempted to keep the tone of the chapters clear, conversational, and informal, maintaining the theme and intention of our interviews. For this reason, a variety of pronouns are used throughout, shifting freely between "you," "we," and "they," as needed to provide the clearest meaning and most applicable perspective. Additionally, interviews have been edited and contextualized for length, clarity, and relevance.

A Bit About Us

So, a few people wanting to offer more study in the area of introversion and acting got together and wrote a book. These people are varied in terms of background and experience. We each have distinct personalities and different interests. We have different ethics, values, creative aesthetics, and senses of humor. We live all over the United States and have a variety of educational and professional training. But we identify in one common way. We are introverts.

Carolyn Conover is an Assistant Professor of Drama at Jacksonville State University in Jacksonville, Alabama. She holds an MA in English and an MFA in Theatre and is a professional actor and dramaturg. She has always struggled to find a balance between the alluring excitement of acting and character creation and her need to research, analyze, reflect, and decompress in quiet isolation, and to communicate this need without apology. She identifies as an introvert.

Heidi Kasevich is Founder of Kase Leadership Method and designs and delivers temperament-inclusive programs for schools and workplaces nationwide. As History Chair and Leadership Program Designer at schools in New York City, and Director of Education at Quiet Revolution, she made it her mission to set the stage for introverted students to learn and lead. She knew from her own childhood experiences that it can be painful to be told to "just come out of your shell." She holds a PhD in European History from New York University. She identifies as an introvert.

Rob Roznowski is a professor and Head of Acting and Directing at Michigan State University. He has performed nationally and internationally, but found his social anxiety was overwhelming in auditions and networking events. He found his rightful place out of the spotlight as director, educator, and writer. He identifies as an introvert.

Our book is written to appeal to and affect three interrelated audiences.

Actors, Both Student and Professional

To those of you who enjoy quiet reflection and analysis, and who need processing time …

To those of you who are constantly asked if anything is wrong when you are not talking …

To those of you who shut down when asked to improvise …

Educators and Directors

To those of you who try to draw someone out of their shell …

To those of you who don't go forward with an exercise until everyone has participated …

To those of you who think an actor isn't engaged when they aren't speaking …

For those of you who have, at times, thought, "Why did I go into this profession?" when confronted with ensemble-building exercises or a loud audition waiting room, those who understand the exhaustion of always "being on" ...

For those of you who feel like an outsider when everyone is socializing at a networking event, those who wish they could engage more like everyone else in rehearsal, those who dread making small talk at an audition ... we wrote this book for you.

Many professional "requirements" force introverted actors to behave in ways that do not honor their strengths. We'd like to help change that by acknowledging the subtle ways introverted actors contribute to the classroom and rehearsal space, and by making actor training more inclusive and egalitarian. We want introverts to be heard ... all the way to the back of the theatre!

ACKNOWLEDGMENTS

This book was inspired by a chapter about creating inclusive classrooms and studios for introverted actors written by Rob Roznowski for *Creativity in Theatre: Theory and Action in Theatre/Drama Education* (2018).[1] That chapter was edited by Suzanne Burgoyne. Her invaluable guidance helped narrow the focus, but there was so much more to explore. Along the way Dr. Heidi Kasevich, then the director for Susan Cain's Quiet Schools program, was interviewed for the chapter. That interview later turned into a residency at Michigan State University (MSU), with Heidi observing theatrical classes to make recommendations for more inclusive teaching. A trusted colleague, Carolyn Conover, has been a contributor to several books by Rob Roznowski and a major influence on pedagogical advances within those writings.

Special thanks must go to the numerous contributors and funding sources to assist with the project. Student assistance included Abbie Cathcart and Marshall Ross from Michigan State University, and Eric Gudgel, Brandon Pease, and Alia Stewart from Blackburn College. The MSU College of Arts and Letters Engaged Pedagogy Fund and other resources also supported this project. Our statistical buddy Dr. Dhruv Sharma from MSU's Center for Statistical Training and Consulting helped us examine the survey (and was extremely patient!), and he generously offered his time and expertise. We would also like to extend our thanks to Actor Wendy Hedstrom for introducing Rob to Susan Cain's book *Quiet: The Power of Introverts in a World That Can't Stop Talking* (Crown, 2012) and expanding his worldview;[2] Michael Rodriguez from MSU libraries for his mentorship; Dr. Karen Dillon for her review of our original book proposal; Rob Odorisio and Robbie Young for their awesome writing retreat; Amy Richardson for her help with the LAMDA interviews; Sherry Stevens for huge amounts of transcription; Andy Sloey of The Improv Shop in St. Louis, MO, as well as the members of Capital City Improv in Springfield, IL, for their generous insight; American Sharjah University in the United Arab Emirates for hosting a roundtable discussion on the subject; Andy Head for his keen and candid self-reflection; Joanne Magee for her compassion, insightful contributions, and invaluable feedback; Sean Patrick McGowan for his profound wisdom and selfless support; and Emmanuelle Roumain for her honest storytelling.

And finally, a very special thanks to Cameron Michael Chase, an MFA Acting candidate at Michigan State University who also teaches undergraduate courses in acting and theatre. As our research assistant, Cameron was instrumental in helping us to analyze and understand the numbers in our survey and assisted in writing the chapter exploring its results. He also contributed his own analysis to the self-awareness exercise in Chap. 3.

NOTES

1. Roznowski, Rob. "Reforming Theatrical Education from Its Extrovert-Based Model." In *Creativity in Theatre: Theory and Action in Theatre/Drama Education*, 105–20. Cham, Switzerland: Springer, 2018.
2. Cain, Susan. *Quiet: The Power of Introverts in a World That Can't Stop Talking.* Crown Publishing Group. 2012.

REFERENCES

Cain, Susan. *Quiet: The Power of Introverts in a World That Can't Stop Talking.* Crown Publishing Group. 2012.
Roznowski, Rob. "Reforming Theatrical Education from Its Extrovert-Based Model." In *Creativity in Theatre: Theory and Action in Theatre/Drama Education*, 105–20. Cham, Switzerland: Springer, 2018.

CONTENTS

LIST OF FIGURES

LIST OF TABLES

PART I

Acting and Introversion

CHAPTER 1

Foundations: Temperament Diversity

Origins and Definitions: Pressure to "Act Like an Extrovert"

Popular ideas concerning introversion and extroversion in twenty-first-century America are misleading. Oversimplification weakens the foundation of an understanding of our inborn temperaments. Common-sense/everyday notions of introverts in Western culture tend to have negative associations, including "slow," "passive," "unadventurous," "antisocial," and "loner." The extrovert, on the other hand, is seen as "dynamic," "alpha," "outgoing," "bold," and "charismatic." According to such popular notions, the former is not destined for leadership, but the latter shall rule our political—and theatrical—stages.

The pressure to "act like an extrovert" is real, and in many of our classrooms in America today, educators inadvertently set up conditions where extroverts can thrive, but introverts are left to try to act like extroverts in order to succeed. For instance, educators often define "participation" as quantity of speech, assigning a grade to the number of times students raise their hands in our classes. A teacher might pause just a few seconds before calling on students, and tell the more reserved to "come out of your shell." Under these conditions, extroverts are at an advantage because they tend to process information quickly. Introversion expert Lisa Kaenzig confesses: "People like me [an extrovert] are rewarded for being able to think quickly on their feet . . . [be] the first one to put their hands up, the one who can have a quick and witty response in a debate or in classroom

© The Author(s) 2020
R. Roznowski et al., *The Introverted Actor*,
https://doi.org/10.1007/978-3-030-41607-2_1

discussion."[1] Students with just a few close, meaningful friendships are encouraged to branch out and have a larger group of friends. As one student interviewed said, "You're expected to be doing something or going somewhere and are discouraged from spending time alone." And the educators themselves? Michael Godsey in "Why Introverted Teachers Are Burning Out" (2016) cites a study that shows 41% of teachers leave the profession within five years of entering it, a statistic associated with an emphasis on constant social interaction.[2] This pressure can take its toll on introverted students and teachers alike.

In their communities, introverted students are often shamed into feeling less than their extroverted peers, who are more likely to enjoy group work, crowded cafeterias, endless socializing, classroom discussions, and reward-motivated activities. They are often discouraged from spending time alone and reflecting, and made to feel "abnormal" for eating by themselves, staying in on a Saturday night, or even reading a book. These feelings can have further negative repercussions on their health, including lower self-esteem, stress, and anxiety. When they discover they fall on the introverted side of the spectrum, introverted students all too often lose confidence in their ability to lead.

It is not just our schools. Our workplaces tend to be crowded, noisy places, where the walls have come down, so it can be hard to find a place for privacy. Contemporary open office plans are designed to maximize the social experience: pods, hubs, and common spaces have replaced privacy areas and cubicles. Research assignments are merged with group projects and presentations, and there is an expectation for constant social and public interactions: meetings, brainstorming sessions, and even, in some parts of the country, games of ping-pong.

Why? The Origins of an Extroverted "Culture of Personality"

Many of the misconceptions surrounding introverts, at least in America, stem from a long history of valuing and expecting a specific kind of personality necessary for leadership, entertainment, success, and even happiness. In *Quiet: The Power of Introverts in a World That Can't Stop Talking* (Crown Publishing Group, 2012), Susan Cain connects the "extrovert ideal" in American culture—charming, charismatic, outgoing, action-oriented people who can talk to anyone—to the rise of the industrial and media ages, where it was often believed that you couldn't succeed in life unless you were a fast-talking salesman.[3] Cain relies on the groundbreaking research of cultural historian Warren Susman, who notes in *Culture as History* (Smithsonian, 1984) that as America began to shift from a nation of producers to one of consumers, collective ideas about the ideal self began to shift, too.[4] "Personality" replaced "character," and with this shift came an emphasis on cultivating an entertaining and bold personality so as to impress bosses and friends alike: self-sacrifice was replaced with self-expression; the work ethic with the leisure ethic; integrity with charm.

The charming traveling salesman had his counterpart in the dynamic actor, a larger-than-life personality who used his charisma in show business; the bright and bubbly actor was expected to constantly make a good impression and charm others with quick wit and a glitzy ability to think on their feet. Joanne Magee, theatre director at Little Red School House & Elisabeth Irwin High School (LREI), maintains that it was during the vaudeville era that America witnessed the rise of the actor as a charismatic extrovert who was "supposed to come out to sing and dance ... working hard to be a personality."[5] The transition from vaudeville performer to cinema actor further solidified the extrovert ideal in acting. Magee adds, "There was a time with the rise of movie making ... where vaudeville performers became movie stars ... and those actors needed to be glamorous wherever they went ... the life of the party who entertains every night." Sensationalized movie actors of the Hollywood star system were the next best thing to a royal family, as they cultivated personal brands in the quest to fill what Magee refers to as the "royalty gap." It's the cult of the charming, dynamic, and charismatic movie star that endures today.

At the same time American actors were moving from vaudeville stages to soundstages, a conflict was brewing among a trio of early-twentieth-century psychoanalysts—Sigmund Freud, Alfred Adler, and Carl Jung—that led to the birth of the ideas of "introversion" and "extroversion" as personality types. Soon after the inception of these new ways of categorizing human personalities, there was a negative label ascribed to those diagnosed as introverts, drawn to the internal world of thought and feeling, and the opposite for those deemed extroverts, drawn to the external world of people and activities. Briefly, here's how the story goes: Carl Jung, who is credited with defining introversion and extroversion in his 1921 groundbreaking work, *Psychological Types* (Rascher Verlag, 1921), emphasized heightened reflection or self-reflective introspection as the hallmark of the introverted temperament.[6] And his definition of extroversion? Merve

Emre, in her book *The Personality Brokers* (Vintage, 2019), maintains Jung took the theatrical notion of creating characters and used it to define the extrovert as someone who is constantly trying to fit into social expectations; his theory of extroversion is intimately connected to early-twentieth-century theatre culture.[7] Sophia Dembling in *The Introvert's Way* (2012) emphasizes that it was the notion of psychic energy—flowing inward for introverts and outward for extroverts—that was the hallmark of Jung's neutral and expansive definition.[8] Soon thereafter, however, as Marti Olsen Laney explains in *The Hidden Gifts of the Introverted Child* (2012), Freud, the most influential of the trio, began to use the term "introverted" in a negative way, going so far as to assert that the introvert's inward-turning nature constituted antisocial, narcissistic behavior.[9] Further, as Bernard Davidson, Ralph A. Gillies, and Allan Pelletier assert in "Introversion and Medical Student Education," (2015) Adler surmised that introverts experience feelings of low self-worth due to an excessive need for alone time.[10] Freud's negative reaction, coupled with Adler's notion of the introverted inferiority complex, served as the crucible for a rise in prejudice against introverts.

Let's fast forward to the 1950s and 1960s, when, as Cain maintains, the rise in the use of anti-anxiety drugs can be traced to diagnoses of introversion as a pathology. Almost as if it were an affliction, in a society that prized verbal fluency and assertiveness over introspection and reticence, those who did not fit in were treated with medication. By 1956, one out of every twenty Americans had tried the anti-anxiety drug Miltown, for the "disorder" of not fitting in.[11] Cain maintains in "Shyness: Evolutionary Tactic?" that as recently as 2011, the *Diagnostic and Statistical Manual*, the DSM-IV, or so-called "psychiatrist's bible of social disorders," came close to pathologizing introversion as a disorder and adds that introversion, along with its cousins, sensitivity and shyness, were considered second-class personality traits.[12]

What Does It *Really* Mean to Be an Introvert? Extrovert? Ambivert?

So much recent research explores this topic, but we will focus on a few salient points to get you oriented and equipped to better relate with your colleagues, directors, professors, and scene partners. Let's pick up where we left off with Carl Jung, and a spirited and talented American mother-daughter team devoted to Jungian psychology, Isabel Briggs Myers and Katherine Briggs. They were passionate about the idea of connecting workers and spouses to their ideal matches in the office and at home, and their Indicator was designed to fulfill the promise of using inborn gifts as a route to what they called "personal liberation," or satisfying jobs and happy marriages. They capitalized on Jung's inward-outward energy model of introversion-extroversion to develop what has today become a widely popular psychometric test. The Myers-Briggs Type Indicator (MBTI), a simple distillation of Jung's psychological types, affirms that introverts gain energy from turning inward and private reflection, whereas extroverts gain their energy from turning outward and social interaction. The Indicator is used by almost all Fortune 500 companies and 200 million people a year. The MBTI is so popular today as a psychometric test that in the many interviews we gathered for this book, the focus on how energy is gathered, spent, and restored was a common theme. Witness actor and educator Andy Head's testimonial:

> The best example of what an introvert and extrovert are in my mind is that an extrovert receives energy being around people and an introvert spends energy being around people. I classify myself as someone who can be around a group of people, but it's something I have to work at doing. It's tiring for me, and I don't want to do all the time … Growing up, we moved around a lot, and it was always hard to make new friends. Maybe someone would take pity on me and become my friend, but I wasn't the one going out and trying to find friends. I got good at being by myself.[13]

While this idea of personal isolation related to introversion is a common one, there is so much more to what it really means to be an introvert or an extrovert than is revealed in the MBTI Type Indicator. When taken multiple times, the MBTI can help you gain the self-awareness needed to honor your true self as an introverted actor and/or to create temperament-inclusive environments for introverted and extroverted actors. Yet the self is exceedingly complex, and the essence of what it means to be an introvert does not simply revolve around energy gained from solitude. One of the dangers of the binary MBTI definition of introversion/extroversion is that introverts can be stereotyped as antisocial. As Adam Grant asserts in "Say Goodbye to the MBTI, the Fad That Won't Die," (2019) introversion and extroversion have more to do with the way our brains process the things we see and hear (also known as neocortical arousal) than it does with a preference for interacting with people; thus, the idea that extroverts get energy from social interactions while introverts get energy from private reflection doesn't hold. In reality, both introverts and extroverts enjoy spending time with people, and talking with others can energize introverts and extroverts alike.[14] That said, introverts prefer to socialize with a few close friends in one-on-one conversations, and extroverts tend to thrive in bigger groups and stay connected with large numbers of people.

DEFINITIONS: SENSITIVITY TO STIMULATION AND SENSITIVITY TO REWARDS

For the purposes of this book, we will be working with a common definition of introversion/extroversion that combines sensitivity to stimulation with sensitivity to rewards. This definition is linked to the outcome of a groundbreaking study by Susan Cain's Quiet Revolution and UPenn's Scott Barry Kaufman in 2014: they teamed up to develop an Introversion/Extroversion (I/E) assessment that focuses on two key elements of our biogenetic natures—sensitivity to stimulation from the environment and sensitivity to the reward value of gaining information—and the preferences that emerge from our neurobiology.[15,16]

That said, let's also acknowledge that adolescents and adults alike often self-identify as individuals who fall somewhere along a continuum of introversion/extroversion. As Harvard Business School behavioral scientist and author of *Sidetracked* (Harvard Business Press, 2013) Francesca Gino affirms, many people exhibit both introverted and extroverted tendencies.[17] Those who fall in this more central point on the spectrum are referred to as "ambiverts." Some researchers, such as Professor of Management and Psychology at The Wharton School, Adam Grant, contend that almost two-thirds of people don't feel as though they lean in one direction or the other.[18] There are many possible reasons for self-identifying as an "ambivert." Throughout your life, your inborn temperament interacts with the environment, including your family, cultural norms, and other markers of your identity. And personalities shift over time: as you grow and change, you may come to equally enjoying solitude and social attention. Finally, while our introverted/extroverted traits are part of our inborn nature, we can and do engage in free traits to choose who we want to be in our public/professional lives.

Let's look at the more recent science about the biological underpinnings of introversion/extroversion. Beginning with King's College's Professor of Psychology Hans Eysenck's seemingly simple "lemon juice test" in 1967, a multitude of studies show that, at their most basic, introversion and extroversion have to do with our sensitivity to social and sensory stimuli from the outside world: crowds, bright lights, and loud noises—or even the taste of tart lemon juice.[19] Eysenck hypothesized that humans seek just the right level of neocortical arousal, the speed and amount of the brain's activity. According to a summary of his findings in Psychologist World's "Lemon Juice Introversion Test," Eysenck discovered that introverts experience higher levels of neocortical arousal in the brain than their extroverted counterparts, and they are driven to reduce outside stimulation as a way to find their "sweet spot" between quiet, on the one hand, and social activity, on the other. In his 1967 study, Eysenck showed that when tasting a stimulant such as lemon juice, the "energy-in" introverts salivated more than the "energy-out" extroverts. Fast forward ... from lemon juice in the 1960s to coffee in the twenty-first century. Does coffee affect introverts and extroverts in the same way? Do they equally get a jolt that makes them more alert and ready to tackle the day? Alas, no, as coffee is a stimulant that can be experienced as an overload by the introvert. In the process, that cup of java might actually lower introverts' performance rather than enhance it.

Later, in 1979, Jerome Kagan demonstrated that sensitivity to environmental stimuli—or high reactivity—is present from birth and endures throughout adulthood.[20] Kagan's study began with babies as young as four months of age. About 20% of these infants exhibited signs of distress when exposed to environmental stimuli, such as the sounds of popping balloons or the sight of a mobile swaying overhead. This distress manifest physically as the babies cried, arched their backs, and kicked their legs. These kinds of physical responses are examples of high reactives. Think of the children in their strollers at the supermarket who are so agitated by the lights and noise that they cry incessantly. Or the toddler who hides under the rocking chair at his own birthday party because the clown invites him on stage in front of the thirty guests wildly cheering him on; he simply cannot take the sensory overload. Kagan's longitudinal study revealed that the 20% who were high reactives as babies were more likely to develop into introverted teens. In 1999, Carl Schwartz (Kagan's colleague and protégé), Human Specialist at the Developmental Neuroimaging & Psychopathology Research Laboratory at Massachusetts' General Hospital, used fMRI machines to show that the high or low reactive temperament does not disappear in adulthood.[21] In particular, the high reactives were still more sensitive to pictures of unfamiliar faces even into their early twenties. In Quiet Revolution's podcast about the ways in which neurobiology shapes temperament, Schwartz's numerous studies affirm that highly reactive two year olds, those more sensitive to novelty, will continue to behave in a similar manner at age twenty-one. In other words, the two-year-old introvert who clings to his caregiver's side at a family gathering will mature into an adult who, by nature, prefers to decline an invitation to a networking event after a long week of auditions.[22]

Based on the sensitivity to outside stimuli, introversion reveals a pattern of avoiding social attention and taking time to warm up to what is new or different. Consider, as Marianne Szegedy-Maszak writes in "As Noise Rises, So Do the Dangers," (2005) that too much stimulation for an introvert can literally feel like Florence Nightingale's 1959 description of "noise," which she likened to severe sensations of pain.[23] What is their response to this sort of acute discomfort? Introverts tend to regulate their reactivity to the environment by acting in a variety of different manners: they may become shy (afraid to speak up or take action, as they are worried about what others might think of them), reflective (turning inward), anxious, or timid.[24]

A more cautious reaction to strangers leads to the second most important way to understand how our brains are wired as introverts or extroverts: sensitivity to rewards in the environment. Reward is connected to the neurotransmitter dopamine, released in response to anticipated pleasures. As Jennifer Granneman affirms in "Why Introverts and Extroverts Are Different: The Science," (2015) introverts and extroverts have the same amount of dopamine in their brains, but the dopamine pathway is more active in the brains of extroverts, so they will feel more energized than introverts at expectation of rewards: making friends with a stranger on the subway, winning a medal in a soccer game, or being cast in a role.[25] Ashton, M. C., Lee, K., & Paunonen, S. V., in their 2002 research on the central feature of extroversion, suggest that extroversion represents a high-intensity strategy for gaining social attention.[26] In this way, and as Scott Barry Kaufman affirms in the Scientific American Blog Network (2014), "Will the Real Introverts Please Stand Up?"[27] the key consequence of the extrovert's reward sensitivity is the desire to gain positive attention from friends and strangers alike, which may be affiliated with, but not limited to, such behaviors as planning a party or telling a joke. So, when extroverted actors volunteer first to share their monologues with the class, they are likely experiencing a dopamine rush!

In her book *The Introvert Advantage* (2001), Marti Olsen Laney maintains that while extroverts prefer to use the neurotransmitter dopamine, introverts prefer a different neurotransmitter called acetylcholine.[28] These neurotransmitters are connected to the two different sides of our nervous system: the sympathetic side (the rest and digest side) and the parasympathetic side (the fight, flight, or freeze side). While both neurotransmitters are associated with pleasure, we are more prepared for contemplation with the former, and readier to take action and make quick decisions with the latter. Yet, for the introverted third to half of the population in America today, that contemplative side can often be misinterpreted.

Enduring Misconceptions of Introverts

We are all susceptible to the ways in which our minds are automatic association-making machines. In addition to the work of understanding personality differences and the ways in which our culture values one type over the other, we have to bring attention to our own unconscious biases. Particularly when it comes to introversion.

Imagine two actors waiting in the lobby for an audition. One is stretching in the center of the room and doing vocal warm-ups before running lines out loud. The other is sitting alone in the back, wearing earbuds and quietly reading lines from a script. Which actor is more experienced? More dedicated? There is no right answer to this question, yet often we affiliate the first actor—the "extrovert"—with "experience and dedication" and the second actor—the "introvert"—as lacking these qualities. Do we know anything about either of these individuals, their experience, or their abilities? No.

This scenario illustrates the way the mind makes automatic associations. As Banaji and Greenwald affirm in their book *Blindspot: The Hidden Biases of Good People* (Bantam Books, 2016), when the mind encounters any information, related information instantly comes to mind.[29] In this, we make quick assumptions about people based on traits we think we recognize. We might assume behavior implies certain characteristics we see in ourselves or in people we know. In fact, back in 1922, Walter Lippman first coined the term "stereotype" to describe the way we conjure up images to categorize individuals we meet.[30] The catch: these categories often consist of negative traits, and such unfavorable judgments are pervasive. That's the bad news. The good news? These automatic associations are *malleable*. We can unlearn them simply by pausing before we make judgments: "You can control it, once *you think about it*."[31] So, when we take time to truly understand another's personality, we are more likely to find ourselves in a judgment-free zone—one that is not dependent on outward appearances.

Despite this effort, there is still a long list of words that linger in our collective unconscious when we learn that our friends, colleagues, or scene partners are introverts. Let's explore the three most prevalent myths regarding introverts: they are shy; they are antisocial; they are slow. In examining and disrupting these biases, we set the stage for temperament-inclusive cultures where both introverts and extroverts can thrive.

1: Introverts Are Shy

It's commonplace today to equate introversion with shyness, even though they are not the same thing. To the outside world, they can appear the same—as someone who is not speaking up or who is retreating to the sidelines. But, it is important to distinguish between the two as we gain an awareness of ourselves and others. To put is simply: "I have a fear of messing up" does not spring from the same source as "I am tired from always having to make high-energy choices." The first has to do with social anxiety (shyness), and the second with overstimulation (introversion). But they are often both assumed to be affiliated with introversion.[32] In her article "Unconscious Discrimination: How to Defeat Four Hidden Teacher Biases" (2018), Fuglei cites a 2011 study divulging that children deemed "quiet and shy" were given lower ratings on intelligence and academic ability in comparison to those described as "average and talkative."[33] In extreme cases, both introversion and shyness are pathologized as mental disorders, and psychiatrists may prescribe anti-depressants known as SSRIs or encourage cognitive-behavioral therapy to cure these "sick" patients. In contrast, in her *New York Times* piece "Shyness: Evolutionary Tactic?" Susan Cain explores the gifts and talents of introverts (or "sitters") in the animal kingdom and invites us to consider the great loss to our society when we medicate those deemed "unfit": the shy, the introverts, and the shy introverts.[34] In fact, the introvert's "look before you leap" mentality is the perfect complement to that of the extroverts (or "rovers"), who tend to "just do it!" We are stronger together.

Both introverts and extroverts alike can be "shy." A shy extrovert and a shy introvert may simply appear to be similarly "quiet," but given their natural preferences for stimulation and rewards, they go through different experiences. It is quite possible that shyness might be an even more painful experience for extroverts, who tend to seek social attention, socialize in larger groups, and thrive at processing their thoughts out loud. With such an innate tendency to interact with others, it might be a difficult experience to hold back from social interactions out of the fear of what others might think. One actor we interviewed for a roundtable session devoted to "Introversion and Acting" at a theatre festival in the United Arab Emirates (UAE) described shy extroversion this way: "We assume that an extroverted person won't have stage fright because he'll want to be on display all the time. I've found the opposite is true. Extroverts sometimes have more stage fright. It does seem to be a strange paradox that someone quiet (or introverted) would want to be a performer." An understanding of the difference between introversion and shyness can help us to unpack what this actor describes as a "strange paradox."[35]

It is important to note that, over time, an introverted performer may actually become more shy. Why? The more introverts, with their tendency to take time to think and their need for quiet recharging times, are counseled to "just speak up" or "just come out of your shell," the more likely they are to fear what others think of them. In this way, an introverted actor might get stage fright simply because they feel something is wrong with them: "I will never be the first to raise my hand, so I won't succeed."

Further, the social pressure to be seen as effortlessly perfect, in a witty and charming way, can serve as fertile ground for the fear of revealing oneself in public. The anxiety that fuels shyness could also be the result of social trauma, such as the internalization of the expectation to be more outgoing in school, as Ellen Hendriksen points out in her article "The Four Differences Between Introversion and Social Anxiety."[36] Although Laurie Helgoe notes in a 2019 article in *Psychology Today* that such social anxiety may be more common among introverts than extroverts, this does not mean that all introverts necessarily experience social anxiety.[37] In fact, there can be calm extroverts, anxious extroverts, calm introverts, or anxious introverts. Further, anxiety exists along a spectrum, with diverse manifestations, such as panic attacks, the reticence to volunteer to go first, or insomnia.

Declaring one's true nature can help normalize conversations about introversion/extroversion and shyness. We can begin to reframe negative language that is often automatic. "I am shy" becomes "I take it all in and don't miss a thing" or "I'm internally aware."

2: Introverts Are Antisocial

Multiple studies have found that a person's actual influence is often over-looked for "airtime," or the amount of time he or she talks. As Cain mentions in *Quiet*, talkative people have been rated as smarter, better-looking, and more desirable as friends.[38] In addition, the need to recharge alone can make introverts more susceptible to "loner" labels.

An interview with an introverted actor at our UAE roundtable discussion begins to lead us from myth to reality: "I've never thought of introversion as a dislike of people. In fact it's the opposite. I've always been fascinated by people … I'm more sensitive to … (social) cues." Yet this actor was often labeled as "antisocial." It is important to note here that if a self-declared introverted actor is also a "highly sensitive person," as per Elaine Aron's important research into this type, they are more likely to be extremely empathic.[39] In her book *The Highly Sensitive Person* (Broadway Books, 1997), Aron notes that about 70% of highly sensitive persons (HSPs) are introverts. And while no data exists about how many of those HSPs are actors, since actors traffic in emotion, it does seem a natural fit for some introverted actors to have a connection to empathy.

Another actor from a UAE roundtable shares how directors often mis-interpret a lack of nodding and/or smiling as "difficult" behavior. The actor recounts: "I end up having a conversation with the director because they'll give me a note, and my face looks like I hate everything they said or I disagree with it, and it's truly not. It's me sitting and processing; taking a moment to internalize what they said so I can apply it." This actor has experienced what many introverted actors experience on a regular basis: the misinterpretation of reflection time for impertinence or a lack of interest in being with others.

The reality? Introverts do like to socialize. They just socialize differently than extroverts. Introverts prefer to be in the company of close friends. They might have a fabulous time at a big party, but after a couple of hours, they may feel the need to recharge their batteries in solitude. According to William Pavot, Ed Diener, and Frank Fujita in their 1990 "Extraversion and Happiness" study, introverts spend about the same amount of time with others as do extroverts.[40] Such energy can come from one-on-one conversations, small-group interactions, or performing in front of an audience. According to Leon F. Seltzer in "Inside Every Introvert Is an Extrovert," (2019) standup artists Johnny Carson, Steve Martin, and Woody Allen (who all self-identify as introverts) experience a profound sense of gratification and joy from the social experience of performing.[41] The trick is knowing when and how to recharge your batteries.

Introvert expert Lisa Kaenzig echoes these words in an interview: "One of the biggest issues is this idea that introverts are checked out or not paying attention."[42] Kaenzig adds, "She seems like she's not really with me. I don't know that she's paying attention in class." The student who appears disengaged might simply need time to restore. This need to recharge after socially demanding situations is amplified for actors who find themselves in long performance runs or traveling shows. One example from our UAE roundtable admits that it's all about lifestyle:

> I was on the road for two years with a company for eleven months a year, constantly living in hotels and vans. I love performing and working, but I could feel my person being eviscerated. It's that intense. It was very difficult. It's hard to find people who understand that. If you're introverted, and isolate yourself more, people think you should come out more in order to feel better, but that makes it worse.

The whole process can be simply exhausting. Let's replace the word "antisocial" with the following phrases: "I am comfortable being alone"; "I need time to recharge."

3: Introverts Are Slow

Introverted actors are often attuned to their environments and to other people. In this, they apply a combination of the character strengths of prudence and perspective that can sometimes be mistaken for hesitation or slowness. This approach is markedly different from that of extroverts, who tend to talk out their ideas with others as soon as those thoughts emerge and who tend to excel at talking rather than listening. In extrovert ideal cultures, the lack of volunteering, the "hands-down" approach of the introvert during group work can easily be interpreted as disengagement.

Prudence is unrelated to current notions that tend to connect this trait with fearfulness. Derived from the Latin *prudentia*, meaning sagacity or expertise, prudence involves an approach to decision making whereby you take time to consider right and wrong—all possible consequences of your actions. You can indeed be a prudent risk taker! Prudence goes hand in hand with perspective. The Values in Action Institute on Character describes the character strength of perspective as the ability to weigh options before making decisions.[43] In order to give great advice, the listener is fully present with his/her counterpart during a conversation, paraphrases to confirm understanding, and is open to validating emotions in a non-judgmental way. It's a paradox Amy Cuddy describes in her book *Presence* (Back Bay, 2018), as she links power with the trust that grows as we truly and authentically listen to our colleagues, partners, and ensemble members.[44]

LREI theatre director Joanne Magee states, "When you call on introverted actors to speak – with preparation time – they have incredible points to make. They are not daydreaming."[45] They are, more often than not, sitting with their thoughts and listening to others before sharing their ideas. The fuel for this style is reflective pausing. This can be thought of as preparation time to turn inward, consider possibilities, and rely on your inner compass; or time to turn outward, observing and attempting to fully understand the meaning of a counterpart's words. A pause can provide the context needed to nurture the introvert's proclivity for cautious risk-taking. As Los Angeles-based actor and writer Emmanuelle Roumain states, "I take the time to ask clarifying questions before responding."[46] In this example, the "reflective pause" involves open communication between actor and director.

This duo of prudence and perspective strengths can be cultivated by introverts and extroverts alike. Together, they serve as the foundation for cognitive empathy, our ability to identify and understand other people's emotions. As Daniel Nettle points out in "Psychological Profiles of Professional Actors" (2006), empathy allows the actor to get into the skin of the character in ways that are both vulnerable and sensitive.[47] Introverted New York actor Carol Schultz celebrates, "I've always tried to live by that wonderful Stanislavski quote, 'Infect your partner! Infect the person you are concentrating on! Insinuate yourself into his very soul, and you will find yourself the more infected for doing so.'"[48] Or, as Los Angeles actor and writer Sean Patrick McGowan reassures, "One of the greatest projects we have as humans on earth is to engage in our empathy and to experience, as fully as possible, what other people's experiences are, so we can understand and respond with informed compassion."[49]

A critical part of engaging in empathy is getting to know when your friend, colleague, or scene partner is stepping outside of their comfort zones, and offering support to help this person achieve their goals.

Adaptability and Comfortable Stretching

As Adam Grant explains in the second episode of his WorkLife podcast (2018), adaptability is a personality trait just like introversion/extroversion, and it comprises about 40% of our identity.[50] In the podcast, Grant interviews Brian Little, Cambridge University fellow of the Well-Being Institute and Director of the Social Ecology Research Group in the Department of Psychology. Little's wide-ranging research in *Human Natures and Well Being, Me, Myself and Us* and *Who Are You Really? The Surprising Puzzle of Personality* (2019) points to the idea that both free and fixed traits coexist in our complex selves.[51] Additionally, some of us, regardless of our inborn introversion or extroversion, may be "high self-monitors." Such high self-monitors, according to Snyder's self-monitoring scale, adapt themselves to situational norms in a flexible way.

When we engage in free traits, or tendencies expressed by individual choice, we can override our biogenetic natures. In other words, when in different situations, the high self-monitor can act like a different person—the introvert can "extrovert" or the extrovert can "introvert." For example, when introverted actors engage in animated, dynamic, enthusiastic rehearsal with an ensemble, but then desperately need to recharge alone, they are "acting out of character,' which, as Little maintains, can be a noble act. Although some actors may feel "fake," they should know this feeling does not necessarily mean they are acting in a disingenuous manner. Rather, this adaptability allows them to thrive in the highly social or public demands of life—and in the theatre.

It is dedication to our "Core Personal Projects," as Little maintains, that drives us to step outside our comfort zones and enables us to stretch with authenticity.[52] In other words, while we are born with certain personality traits, we can and do flex beyond our perceived comfort zones in the service of meaningful, manageable projects related to our professions and our loved ones. Introverted acting students can learn to be the first to speak up in ensemble work; extroverted actors can stretch to deeply listen to others during networking events. When done in the service of our passions, such stretching brings us joy and we don't need to negate our biogenetic natures in the process.

According to Little's 2017 article "How Our Projects Shape Our Personalities – and How We Can Use Them to Remake Who We Are,"[53] there are many different kinds of Core Personal Projects, ranging from the grandiose to the mundane. We choose to engage in Core Personal Projects from one of the following categories, with the most frequently listed first:

- Occupational/Work: Take an improv class.
- Interpersonal: Have coffee with ensemble members.
- Maintenance: Go to the library to check out a book related to your part.
- Recreational: Take a hike after the show closes.
- Health/Body: Gain 15 pounds for your role.
- Intrapersonal: Manage anxiety before and during auditions.

Note that such goals should be chosen carefully, with advanced planning. One 1985 study by Janet Polivy and Peter Herman of the University of Toronto warns that setting unrealistic goals can result in "false hope syndrome."[54] Whether it is a goal for an audition, a rehearsal, or a networking event, it takes a unique combination of timing and realistic assessment of consequences in order to fully actualize our potential and avoid burnout.

Rubber Band Theory

In order to preserve your authenticity while stretching, you need to pursue your Core Personal Projects while still honoring the 50% of your nature that is inborn. We need to respect our limits, flexing in ways that are comfortable, avoiding both the undo stress and the self-negation that can occur when we try to be someone we are not. How can we do this?

As Susan Cain writes in her book *Quiet*, think of yourself as a rubber band: you can flex when you want to, but if you are pulled too far, you will snap.[55] In these moments of stretching, self-awareness is vital. Acting outside your comfort zone to fulfill others' expectations of what it means to be "successful" or stretching in the service of someone else's goal for your life can lead to severe health problems, including anxiety and compromised immune functioning. If you place too much attention on your likeability, you may be at risk for compromising authenticity for the sake of social status. Lauren Smith, in her essay "When the Need Arises: Acting the Introvert in Order to Teach" in the book *An Introvert in an Extrovert World: Essays on the Quiet One* (2015), believes she would not be able to engage in such a dynamic manner with her students if she were not so self-aware.[56] As an introvert, she takes the breaks she needs in order to run classes that feel, at times, as though she is hosting her own cocktail party. Ms. Smith often reminds herself that teaching is her Core Personal Project, and in so doing, she liberates herself to stretch in comfortable ways.

Setting Boundaries

A "Free Trait Agreement" is one way to manage our energy as we step outside our comfort zones. Dr. Brian Little suggests we can prevent burn-out by setting boundaries in an informal, yet contractual way with our friends, partners, castmates, and even our directors.[57] Such agreements acknowledge that we will each act out of character some of the time, but for the rest of the time, we will honor each other's needs for either calm (for the introvert) or excitement (for the extrovert). For example, when a self-proclaimed "extreme" extrovert wants to go out every night after rehearsal, they can work out a schedule with their introverted friend in the cast, who favors leaving rehearsal immediately to go home and process their notes. Their Free Trait Agreement might be: *half the time we'll go out, and half the time we'll go home*. The ultimate goal is to help one another find our sweet spots between social activities and alone time—our productive zones of stimulation. Planning ahead on a daily, weekly, or monthly basis is advisable. At the core of any such agreement lies self-awareness, a deep understanding of temperament diversity and empathy. These agreements allow us to honor our authentic selves and flex in ways that protect our well-beings.

Recharging: The "Restorative Niche"

Comfortable stretching can be achieved only when we are aware of our own needs for recovery time. Dr. Little has coined the term "restorative niche" for that place where we go to return to our true selves in order to recuperate after flexing outside our comfort zones. This could be a solitary time of breathing and stretching for the rehearsal-bound introverted actor, or a loud cast party for an extroverted actor who has spent the day memorizing lines alone in their apartment. In a 2005 article, "Personal Projects and Free Traits," Little writes that "for a biogenic introvert who has been protractedly acting out of character as a 'pseudo-extravert,' the best restorative niche would be one of solitude and reduced stimulation."[58]

So, energized introverts at cast parties will need to retreat to the side-lines or head home after a couple of hours in order to recharge their batteries. Honoring the need for solitude after a performance or ensemble work is essential for the well-being of introverts. Extroverts, on the other hand, may need to seek further stimulation from people—even after that cast party—to feel at their best.

The next chapter examines some integral and intertwined aspects of introversion and acting. It analyzes general acting practices in relation to the introvert's temperament as a way to explore, expose, and examine why an introvert would choose acting as a profession. What is their basic motivation? The chapter also begins to align introverted strengths with areas of acting in which introverts excel.

Notes

1. Kaenzig, Lisa. Personal interview. 15 Dec. 2018.
2. Godsey, Michael. "Teaching: Not for Introverts." The Atlantic. Atlantic Media Company, January 25, 2016. https://www.theatlantic.com/education/archive/2016/01/why-introverted-teachers-are-burning-out/425151/
3. Cain, Susan. *Quiet: The Power of Introverts in a World That Can't Stop Talking*. Crown Publishing Group, 2012.
4. Susman, Warren I. *Culture as History: The Transformation of American Society in the Twentieth Century*. Washington, D.C.: Smithsonian Inst. Press, 2003.
5. Susman, Warren I. *Culture as History: The Transformation of American Society in the Twentieth Century*. Washington, D.C.: Smithsonian Inst. Press, 2003.
6. Jung, C. G. *Psychological Types*. Rascher Verlag. Zurich. 1921.
7. Emre, Merve. *The Personality Brokers: The Strange History of Myers-Briggs and the Birth of Personality Testing*. Toronto: Vintage Canada, 2019.
8. Dembling, Sophia. *The Introverts Way: Living a Quiet Life in a Noisy World*. New York: Penguin Group, 2012.
9. Laney, Marti Olsen. *The Hidden Gifts of the Introverted Child*. New York: Workman, 2006.
10. Davidson, Bernard, Ralph A. Gillies, and Allen L. Pelletier. "Introversion and Medical Student Education: Challenges for Both Students and Educators." *Teaching and Learning in Medicine* 27, no. 1 (February 2015): 99–104. https://doi.org/10.1080/10401334.2014.979183
11. Cain, Susan. *Quiet: The Power of Introverts in a World That Can't Stop Talking*. London: Viking, 2013. 29.

12. Cain, Susan. "Shyness: Evolutionary Tactic?" The New York Times. The New York Times, June 25, 2011. https://www.nytimes. com/2011/06/26/opinion/sunday/26shyness.html
13. Head Andy. Personal interview. 15 Aug. 2018.
14. Grant, Adam. "Say Goodbye to MBTI, the Fad That Won't Die." LinkedIn. Accessed November 21, 2019. https://www.linkedin.com/ pulse/20130917155206-69244073-say-goodbye-to-mbti-the-fad-that-won-t-die
15. Kaufman, Scott Barry. "How to Change Your Personality." The Atlantic. Atlantic Media Company, July 30, 2016. https://www.theatlantic.com/ health/archive/2016/07/can-personality-be-changed/492956/
16. Kaufman, Scott Barry. "The Real Science of Introversion (and the Rest of Personality)." *Scientific American Blog Network*, Dec. 7, 2015. https:// blogs.scientificamerican.com/beautiful-minds/the-real-science-of-introversion-and-the-rest-of-personality/
17. Gino, Francesca. *Sidetracked: Why Our Decisions Get Derailed, and How We Can Stick to the Plan.* Boston, MA: Harvard Business Review Press, 2013.
18. Grant, Adam. "5 Myths About Introverts and Extroverts." Quiet Revolution, September 23, 2015. https://www.quietrev. com/5-myths-about-introverts-and-extroverts/
19. Eysenck, Sybil B. G., and H. J. Eysenck. "Salivary Response to Lemon Juice as a Measure of Introversion." *The Measurement of Personality*, 1976, 87–93. https://doi.org/10.1007/978-94-011-6168-8_10
20. Kagan, Jerome, and Nancy C. Snidman. *The Long Shadow of Temperament.* Cambridge, MA: Harvard University Press, 2009.
21. Schwartz, Carl E., Nancy Snidman, and Jerome Kagan. "Adolescent Social Anxiety as an Outcome of Inhibited Temperament in Childhood." *Journal of the American Academy of Child & Adolescent Psychiatry* 38, no. 8 (1999): 1008–15. https://doi.org/10.1097/00004583-199908000-00017
22. Schwartz, Carl, and Susan Cain. "Quiet Revolution." *Quiet Revolution* (blog). Panoply, June 15, 2016.
23. Szegedy-Maszak, Marianne. "As Noise Rises, So Do the Dangers." *Los Angeles Times*, November 28, 2005. https://www.latimes.com/archives/ la-xpm-2005-nov-28-he-noise28-story.html
24. Davidson et al. "Introversion and Medical Students."
25. Granneman, Jennifer. "Why Introverts and Extroverts Are Different: The Science." Quiet Revolution, December 21, 2015. https://www.quietrev. com/why-introverts-and-extroverts-are-different-the-science/
26. Ashton, Michael C., Kibeom Lee, and Sampo V. Paunonen. "What Is the Central Feature of Extraversion? Social Attention versus Reward Sensitivity." *Journal of Personality and Social Psychology* 83, no. 1 (2002): 245–52. https://doi.org/10.1037/0022-3514.83.1.245

27. Kaufman, S. B. (2014, June 9). Will the Real Introverts Please Stand Up? *Scientific American Blog Network*. https://blogs.scientificamerican.com/beautiful-minds/will-the-real-introverts-please-stand-up?
28. Laney, Marti Olsen. *The Introvert Advantage*. New York: Workman Publishing, 2001.
29. Banaji, M. R., and Anthony G. Greenwald. *Blindspot: Hidden Biases of Good People*. New York: Bantam Books, 2016.
30. Lippman, Walter. *Public Opinion*. Place of publication not identified: Brace and Company, 1922.
31. "Managing Bias." Managing Bias Facebook. Accessed November 21, 2019. https://managingbias.fb.com/
32. "Shy, Introverted, Both, or Neither (and Why Does It Matter)?" Quiet Revolution, October 5, 2015. https://www.quietrev.com/are-you-shy-introverted-both-or-neither-and-why-does-it-matter/
33. Fuglei, Monica. "4 Hidden Teacher Biases & How to Defeat Them." Portland, September 7, 2018. https://education.cu-portland.edu/blog/classroom-resources/unconscious-discrimination-avoiding-teacher-biases/
34. Cain, Susan. "Shyness: Evolutionary Tactic?"
35. "Introversion and Acting." *American University of Sharjah Theatre Festival*. February 4, 2019.
36. Hendriksen, Ellen. "The 4 Differences Between Introversion and Social Anxiety." Quiet Revolution, May 20, 2016. https://www.quietrev.com/the-4-differences-between-introversion-and-social-anxiety/
37. Helgoe, Laurie. "Revenge of the Introvert." Psychology Today. Sussex Publishers. Accessed November 21, 2019. https://www.psychologytoday.com/us/articles/201009/revenge-the-introvert
38. Cain, Susan. *"Quiet."*
39. Aron, Elaine. *The Highly Sensitive Person: How to Thrive When the World Overwhelms You*. S.l.: Broadway Books, 1997.
40. Pavot, William, Ed Diener, and Frank Fujita. "Extraversion and Happiness." *Personality and Individual Differences* 11, no. 12 (1990): 1299–1306. https://doi.org/10.1016/0191-8869(90)90157-m
41. Seltzer, Leon F. "Inside Every Introvert Is ... an Extrovert." Psychology Today. Sussex Publishers. Accessed November 21, 2019. https://www.psychologytoday.com/us/blog/evolution-the-self/201405/inside-every-introvert-isan-extrovert
42. Kaenzig, Lisa. Interview.
43. "Perspective." Perspective | Character Strength | VIA Institute. Accessed November 21, 2019. https://www.viacharacter.org/character-strengths/perspective
44. Cuddy, Amy Joy Casselberry. *Presence: Bringing Your Boldest Self to Your Biggest Challenges*. New York: Back Bay Books, 2018.

45. Magee, Joanna. Interview.
46. Roumain-Yang, Emmanuelle. Interview. 30 April 2019.
47. Nettle, Daniel. "Psychological Profiles of Professional Actors." *Personality and Individual Differences* 40, no. 2 (2006): 375–83. https://doi.org/10.1016/j.paid.2005.07.008
48. Schultz, Carol. Personal interview. 20 Jan. 2019.
49. McGowan, Sean Patrick. Personal interview. 13 April 2019.
50. Grant, Adam. "WorkLife." *WorkLife* (blog). TED, 2018. https://www.ted.com/podcasts/worklife
51. Little, Brian R. *Me, Myself, and Us: The Science of Personality and the Art of Well-Being.* New York (N.Y.): Public Affairs, 2014.
52. Little, Brian R., and Admin. "Personal Projects and Free Traits: Personality and Motivation Reconsidered." Dr. Brian R., December 24, 2014. https://www.brianrlittle.com/articles/personal-projects-and-free-traits/
53. Little, Brian R. "How Our Projects Shape Our Personalities – and How We Can Use Them to Remake Who We Are." ideas.ted.com. ideas.ted.com, August 15, 2017. https://ideas.ted.com/how-our-projects-shape-our-personalities-and-how-we-can-use-them-to-remake-who-we-are/
54. Polivy, Janet, and C. Peter Herman. "Dieting and Binging: A Causal Analysis." *American Psychologist* 40, no. 2 (1985): 193–201. https://doi.org/10.1037/0003-066x.40.2.193
55. Cain, Susan. *"Quiet: The Power of Introverts in a World That Can't Stop Talking.*
56. Smith, Lauren. "When the Need Arises: Acting. The Introvert in Order to Teach." In *An Introvert in an Extrovert World: Essays on the Quiet Ones.* 135–146. Cambridge Scholars Publishing, 2015.
57. Little, Brian R. "Acting Out of Character in the Immortal Profession: Toward a Free Trait Agreement." Dr. Brian R. Little, October 30, 2014. https://www.brianrlittle.com/articles/acting-out-of-character-in-the-immortal-profession-toward-a-free-trait-agreement/?doing_wp_cron=1574365982.8035399913787841796875
58. Little, Brian R. "Personal Projects and Free Traits: Personality and Motivation Reconsidered." *Social and Personality Psychology Compass* 2, no. 3 (2008): 1235–54. https://doi.org/10.1111/j.1751-9004.2008.00106.x

References

Aron, Elaine. *The Highly Sensitive Person: How to Thrive When the World Overwhelms You.* S.l.: Broadway Books, 1997.
Ashton, Michael C., Kibeom Lee, and Sampo V. Paunonen. "What Is the Central Feature of Extraversion? Social Attention versus Reward Sensitivity." *Journal of Personality and Social Psychology* 83, no. 1 (2002): 245–52. https://doi.org/10.1037/0022-3514.83.1.245.

Banaji, M. R., and Anthony G. Greenwald. *Blindspot: Hidden Biases of Good People.* New York: Bantam Books, 2016.

Cain, Susan. *Quiet: The Power of Introverts in a World That Can't Stop Talking.* Crown Publishing Group, 2012.

Cain, Susan. "Shyness: Evolutionary Tactic?" The New York Times. The New York Times, June 25, 2011. https://www.nytimes.com/2011/06/26/opinion/sunday/26shyness.html

Cuddy, Amy Joy Casselberry. *Presence: Bringing Your Boldest Self to Your Biggest Challenges.* New York: Back Bay Books, 2018.

Davidson, Bernard, Ralph A. Gillies, and Allen L. Pelletier. "Introversion and Medical Student Education: Challenges for Both Students and Educators." *Teaching and Learning in Medicine* 27, no. 1 (February 2015): 99–104. https://doi.org/10.1080/10401334.2014.979183.

Dembling, Sophia. *The Introverts Way: Living a Quiet Life in a Noisy World.* New York: Penguin Group, 2012.

Emre, Merve. *The Personality Brokers: The Strange History of Myers-Briggs and the Birth of Personality Testing.* Toronto: Vintage Canada, 2019.

Eysenck, Sybil B. G., and H. J. Eysenck. "Salivary Response to Lemon Juice as a Measure of Introversion." *The Measurement of Personality,* 1976, 87–93. https://doi.org/10.1007/978-94-011-6168-8_10.

Fuglei, Monica. "4 Hidden Teacher Biases & How to Defeat Them." Portland, September 7, 2018. https://education.cu-portland.edu/blog/classroom-resources/unconscious-discrimination-avoiding-teacher-biases/

Gino, Francesca. *Sidetracked: Why Our Decisions Get Derailed, and How We Can Stick to the Plan.* Boston, MA: Harvard Business Review Press, 2013.

Godsey, Michael. "Teaching: Not for Introverts." The Atlantic. Atlantic Media Company, January 25, 2016. https://www.theatlantic.com/education/archive/2016/01/why-introverted-teachers-are-burning-out/425151/.

Granneman, Jennifer. "Why Introverts and Extroverts Are Different: The Science." Quiet Revolution, December 21, 2015. https://www.quietrev.com/why-introverts-and-extroverts-are-different-the-science/.

Grant, Adam. "5 Myths About Introverts and Extroverts." Quiet Revolution, September 23, 2015. https://www.quietrev.com/5-myths-about-introverts-and-extroverts/.

Grant, Adam. "Say Goodbye to MBTI, the Fad That Won't Die." LinkedIn. Accessed November 21, 2019. https://www.linkedin.com/pulse/20130917155206-69244073-say-goodbye-to-mbti-the-fad-that-won-t-die.

Grant, Adam. "WorkLife." *WorkLife* (blog). TED, 2018. https://www.ted.com/podcasts/worklife. December 24, 2014. https://www.brianrlittle.com/articles/personal-projects-and-free-traits/.

Head Andy. Personal interview. 15 Aug. 2018.

Helgoe, Laurie. "Revenge of the Introvert." Psychology Today. Sussex Publishers. Accessed November 21, 2019. https://www.psychologytoday.com/us/articles/201009/revenge-the-introvert.

Hendriksen, Ellen. "The 4 Differences Between Introversion and Social Anxiety." Quiet Revolution, May 20, 2016. https://www.quietrev.com/the-4-differences-between-introversion-and-social-anxiety/.

"Introversion and Acting." *American University of Sharjah Theatre Festival.* February 4, 2019.

Jung, C. G. *Psychological Types.* Rascher Verlag. Zurich. 1921

Kaenzig, Lisa. Personal Interview. 15 Dec. 2018.

Kagan, Jerome, and Nancy C. Snidman. *The Long Shadow of Temperament.* Cambridge, MA: Harvard University Press, 2009.

Kaufman, Scott Barry. "How to Change Your Personality." The Atlantic. Atlantic Media Company, July 30, 2016. https://www.theatlantic.com/health/archive/2016/07/can-personality-be-changed/492956/.

Kaufman, S. B. (2014, June 9). Will the Real Introverts Please Stand Up? *Scientific American Blog Network.* https://blogs.scientificamerican.com/beautiful-minds/will-the-real-introverts-please-stand-up?

Kaufman, Scott Barry. "The Real Science of Introversion (and the Rest of Personality)." *Scientific American Blog Network,* Dec. 7, 2015. https://blogs.scientificamerican.com/beautiful-minds/the-real-science-of-introversion-and-the-rest-of-personality/

Laney, Marti Olsen. *The Hidden Gifts of the Introverted Child.* New York: Workman, 2006

Laney, Marti Olsen. *The Introvert Advantage.* New York: Workman Publishing, 2001.

Lippman, Walter. *Public Opinion.* Place of publication not identified: Brace and Company, 1922.

Little, Brian R. "Acting Out of Character in the Immortal Profession: Toward a Free Trait Agreement." Dr. Brian R. Little, October 30, 2014. https://www.brianrlittle.com/articles/acting-out-of-character-in-the-immortal-profession-toward-a-free-trait-agreement/?doing_wp_cron=1574365982.8035399913787841796875.

Little, Brian R. *Me, Myself, and Us: The Science of Personality and the Art of Well-Being.* New York (N.Y.): Public Affairs, 2014.

Little, Brian R. "Personal Projects and Free Traits: Personality and Motivation Reconsidered." *Social and Personality Psychology Compass* 2, no. 3 (2008): 1235–54. https://doi.org/10.1111/j.1751-9004.2008.00106.x

Little, Brian R. "How Our Projects Shape Our Personalities – and How We Can Use Them to Remake Who We Are." ideas.ted.com. ideas.ted.com, August 15, 2017. https://ideas.ted.com/how-our-projects-shape-our-personalities-and-how-we-can-use-them-to-remake-who-we-are/.

"Managing Bias." Managing Bias Facebook. Accessed November 21, 2019. https://managingbias.fb.com/.

McGowan, Sean Patrick. Personal Interview. 13 April 2019.

Nettle, Daniel. "Psychological Profiles of Professional Actors." *Personality and Individual Differences* 40, no. 2 (2006): 375–83. doi:https://doi.org/10.1016/j.paid.2005.07.008.

Pavot, William, Ed Diener, and Frank Fujita. "Extraversion and Happiness." *Personality and Individual Differences* 11, no. 12 (1990): 1299–1306. doi:https://doi.org/10.1016/0191-8869(90)90157-m.

"Perspective." Perspective | Character Strength | VIA Institute. Accessed November 21, 2019. https://www.viacharacter.org/character-strengths/perspective.

Polivy, Janet, and C. Peter Herman. "Dieting and Binging: A Causal Analysis." *American Psychologist* 40, no. 2 (1985): 193–201. https://doi.org/10.1037/0003-066x.40.2.193.

Roumain-Yang, Emmanuelle. Interview. 30 April. 2019.

Schultz, Carol. Personal Interview. 20 Jan. 2019.

Schwartz, Carl, and Susan Cain. "Quiet Revolution." *Quiet Revolution* (blog). Panoply, June 15, 2016.

Schwartz, Carl E., Nancy Snidman, and Jerome Kagan. "Adolescent Social Anxiety as an Outcome of Inhibited Temperament in Childhood." *Journal of the American Academy of Child & Adolescent Psychiatry* 38, no. 8 (1999): 1008–15. https://doi.org/10.1097/00004583-199908000-00017.

Seltzer, Leon F. "Inside Every Introvert Is...an Extrovert." Psychology Today. Sussex Publishers. Accessed November 21, 2019. https://www.psychologytoday.com/us/blog/evolution-the-self/201405/inside-every-introvert-isan-extrovert.

"Shy, Introverted, Both, or Neither (and Why Does It Matter)?" Quiet Revolution, October 5, 2015. https://www.quietrev.com/are-you-shy-introverted-both-or-neither-and-why-does-it-matter/.

Smith, Lauren. "When the Need Arises: Acting. The Introvert in Order to Teach." In *An Introvert in an Extrovert World: Essays on the Quiet Ones.* 135–146. Cambridge Scholars Publishing, 2015.

Susman, Warren I. *Culture as History: the Transformation of American Society in the Twentieth Century.* Washington, D.C: Smithsonian Inst. Press, 2003.

Szegedy-Maszak, Marianne. "As Noise Rises, so Do the Dangers." *Los Angeles Times,* November 28, 2005. https://www.latimes.com/archives/la-xpm-2005-nov-28-he-noise28-story.html.

CHAPTER 2

Introversion and Acting

For many, when we think of the stereotypical actor, it is a version of a spotlight-loving extrovert who seeks attention and becomes the star of every interaction, no matter the size of the audience. Examining the definition of the word "theatrical" uncovers synonyms like "histrionic," "overdone," "melodramatic," "exaggerated"—all these terms point to a larger-than-life personality type more closely associated with the extrovert. So where does the introvert fit in? How does the introvert thrive and succeed in what appears to be an extroverted profession?

In the book *Careers for Introverts and Other Solitary Types* by Blythe Camenson (2006) several careers are mentioned as a possible "perfect fit" for the introverted personality.[1] They include security guard, forest ranger, and mail carrier. In another book to help introverts find occupations matching their temperament, author Laurence Shatkin, in *200 Best Jobs for Introverts* (2008), suggests jobs like embalmer, crossing guard, and the clergy.[2] Shatkin notes, "One of the cornerstones of modern career development theory is the idea of person-environment fit, sometimes called congruence. The idea is that people will be most satisfied with their work and most productive if the work environment fits their personality" (11). Both of these books, devoted to finding careers for introverts congruent to their temperaments, seem to operate under the impression that introverts want to be left alone, with minimal human interaction. Nowhere, in either book, is the profession of acting for the introvert even considered,

© The Author(s) 2020
R. Roznowski et al., *The Introverted Actor*,
https://doi.org/10.1007/978-3-030-41607-2_2

possibly because interaction with another is the basis of acting. So, why the disconnect?

The question is quite simple: why do introverts act? This is a governing question we will return to throughout the book. Psychology professor Dr. Brent Donnellan suspects introverted actors "have other motivations and personality traits that want to be expressed that are even stronger than their introversion. They have a need for creativity or expression that outweighs any tendency to pull back."[3] Introverted actors are not alone. Many people find they must stretch certain aspects of their personality in order to find or experience something they love. Donnellan continues, "This happens in a lot of careers. There may be several elements of your personality that fit with your career but one that doesn't. People have to overcome that [one that does not fit] in order to throw themselves into a career." With a gamut of personality traits, some outweighing others, the motivation for the introvert to choose acting begins to make sense, but the choice can still be confusing.

PSYCHOLOGY

As stated in our introduction, research examining the introverted actor is scarce. One article from 1940 called "Personality Traits of Drama School Students" from the *Quarterly Journal of Speech* studied college and high school students interested in drama and found the drama school students showed a greater tendency toward extroversion and, on a specially designed questionnaire, indicated and admitted to being considered exhibitionists, egotists, and out of the norm.[4] Daniel Nettle's 2006 article "Psychological Profiles of Professional Actors" compared the personalities and cognitive styles of 191 different actors to those typically seen in the general population and found most actors scored higher as extroverts than their comparison groups.[5] Nettle's belief is that the environment and temperament of actors most closely align with those of extroverts, offering traits like empathy and openness as chief contributors to an actor's overall thought process. The article goes on to suggest that elements of risk, scrutiny, and ease with a lack of control central to the work of an actor would seem to align more closely with the typical risk-taking temperament of the extrovert, concluding that a more extroverted actor might even experience a stronger sense of reward through connection with both the audience and their fellow ensemble members. While this article supports the extrovert ideal of the actor, little other research examines the introverted actor in great detail. There are many acting texts with mentions of introversion and extroversion, including Kevin Page's excellent *Psychology for Actors: Theories and Practices for the Acting Process*, but none of these sources examines the introverted actor in training and professional practices.[6]

Unpacking the theory that extroverts have a higher propensity for entering the acting field requires a more nuanced examination. Psychology professor Dr. Brent Donnellan agrees, noting, "Perhaps some people who score low [on the Big Five personality Test] on extroversion (how much a person is energized by the outside world) score high on 'openness to new experiences' (the drive for cognitive exploration of inner and outer experience), and possess a curiosity, creativity, and interest in expressing themselves. It's those folks, who have a high level of 'openness' but aren't the most outgoing, that find their way into acting."[7] In other words, actors (whether introverted or extroverted) may share a high percentage of "openness," and when seen from a Big Five perspective, there is a common bond connecting this personality trait and acting.

Dr. Richard Lucas, a psychology professor at Michigan State University, was asked this question in an interview: there's a supposition in the book that there are two motivations for going into the business of acting—one is to connect to an audience, and the other is to experience another person's life through the exploration of a character—do you see those corresponding to introversion and extroversion? Dr. Lucas responded, "The first one seems closely linked to extroversion, and the other one might be [linked to] introversion. But it also might be something more like 'openness.'"[8] Dr. Lucas again looks at the less reductive and more detailed approach to such a question. He explains that an actor might score low in extroversion and have a desire to think about what it might be like to be another person or immerse themselves into another character's life. That tendency could be correlated with levels of "openness." As you will see in the upcoming survey results in Chap. 4, when placed in opposition to "connecting with an audience," the majority of introverted actors self-report an inclination for "becoming another" as their driving motivation to pursue acting.

Dr. Brent Donnellan sees a correlation to the idea of introversion and playing another character perhaps as a means of testing the waters and pushing the boundaries of traditional introverted behavior.[9] He posits, "the potential to try on new elements of the self or play a role that is completely separate from your own personality is probably attractive to a lot of people, to see what life would be like if they were extroverted or what life would be like if they were motivated by a great deal of power." The idea of introverted actors finding ease in typically difficult or challenging situations may be attractive to some, where acting becomes the tool introverted actors use to explore circumstances or interactions they might otherwise try to avoid on their own. Donnellan highlights the allure of acting for the introvert as a combination of both escape and experience. For example, an actor who is often uncomfortable in social situations might be attracted to the idea of playing a character who is outgoing and poised. The idea of experiencing a temperament different than the one you were born with could attract either extroverts or introverts. But does it?

To most laymen, the very act of being an actor—being "center stage" and "in the spotlight"—implies an extroverted personality comfortable with being the focus in a crowd. It is only natural that many believe actors are extroverts. Even the offstage behavior can seem extroverted, where the affectionately named "theatre dorks" sit at their group table laughing at their shared jokes and trying on silly voices. (Horrible generalizations, we know, but public perception is important.) Even backstage behavior can veer toward extroversion. A respondent for a survey we conducted for this book (covered in Chap. 4) notes, "There's a definite culture that theatre people are loud. Little things, such as playing music in the dressing room pre-show, chatting on breaks during rehearsals in big groups … frustrate me greatly."[10] This respondent corroborates that, culturally, actors are thought of as boisterous. But that very respondent is in fact an introverted actor.

The stereotype of the extroverted actor permeates our culture. Professional actor and self-defined introvert Molly Ringwald, featured on Susan Cain's website quietrev.com, wonders how introversion and acting can work together when an actor is expected to be "on" all the time?[11] She admits the pressure and anxiety introverts often feel can seem like a contradiction to the demands of the work. Professional actor and educator Andy Head agrees, noting the common misconception that "people assume if you are in the theatre or on the stage, then the rest of your life you want to be in that same kind of spotlight."[12] How many introverts give up on their passion for acting because they believe this profession belongs to the extroverts?

There are many successful introverted actors. It may offer surprise, and perhaps relieve some, to learn that many actors self-identify as introverts.

Dr. Lisa Kaenzig, an expert on introversion and gifted students, also subverts the stereotype of the extroverted actor, noting, "A lot of actors are introverts. Julia Roberts is a classic example of that. Actors spend time reading through their script, memorizing their lines, getting inside their heads. And these are strengths of introverts."[13] Kaenzig recognizes that acting has some elements that reward the introvert. She suggests that the introverted actor has numerous strengths that contribute to their successful work as actors, but because these are often less flashy or captivating than the other, more public aspects of acting, they are somehow forgotten or minimized. Though perhaps not as immediately dazzling, Kaenzig notes that introverted actors have an advantage in numerous ways: "With the ability to examine an internally alive idea in the sense of having an active imagination, being comfortable living in your own head, it makes sense that an actor might also be more of an introvert. It plays to quite a few of their strengths." Before we examine those strengths in more detail, let's first examine the introvert's motivation for becoming an actor.

To Become Another

As noted, one of the suppositions of this book is that, generally, introverts may be drawn to acting in order to portray another. In both the survey and personal interviews, this view was supported. One reason for this attraction may be that the introvert has a deep connection to their own interior life and this bond could result in an innate ability to understand another—including the creation of another character.

Broadway actor Matthew Marks states acting can be about hiding inside the actions and thoughts of another, confessing that when he is not on stage, he is much more stressed and concerned about how his words and behavior might be interpreted by others.[14] He also tends to overanalyze and fret over personal interactions, but when he is on stage, "it's a way of hiding; especially when I'm in character, it's great to be that person." Scripted lines of dialogue and living in the "skin" of another might release some of the anxiety and self-judgment that can affect some introverts in social situations. Marks continues that acting even allows him to be the kind of person he often wishes he could be. Marks goes on to note there is difficulty in being himself onstage, but in his current Broadway show, each night in front of 1100 people, he is not nervous because he is playing another. Like so many other introverted actors, Marks finds freedom, courage, and calm in playing a character.

Linda Mugleston, a self-defined introverted actor who has appeared in nearly a dozen Broadway musicals, describes how she got into acting: "I had an affinity for it. I had an ability for it. There are times when I can be extroverted when it's needed, but my set point is definitely introversion. I love the idea of going into another character and living in another person's shoes. That's why I do it ... I love being in character."[15] Mugleston's story parallels many other introverted actors. She understands the freedom that comes with playing someone so different from herself. Mugleston noted she is currently playing a role on Broadway in which the character is stronger and more outspoken than she is in real life. Mugleston understands that while they are not part of her everyday self, when it is necessary for the character and storytelling, she is capable of summoning those strong and outspoken personality traits more often associated with extroversion. Whether we are introverts or extroverts, we can relate to the idea that, at times, we must mobilize those irregular (for us) qualities depending on the situation. In this mobilization, introverted actors engage in a kind of personality code-switching that allows them to become other, more extroverted characters. For the introverted actor, the access to different qualities and behaviors happens more regularly and, ideally, on command, not to lose themselves, but to become another. The freedom and exploration that comes with this kind of character work is not escapism, but rather, it is an opportunity to be somebody else, even for a few hours; to rage, or to be silly, and then to return to a set point where you live most naturally.

Pearl Theatre Resident Acting Company member Carol Schultz defines her largest motivation for entering acting as "the desire to fully inhabit someone other than myself. Introspection is an aid in that. You are able to learn everything you can about this other person and become that person."[16] Rather than the focus on the self, which may cause the introvert anxiety, Schultz suggests relying on a basic tenet of acting—always focusing on the other. Putting focus on the scene partner provides temporary relief for the introvert from constant self-reflection. That loss of self-consciousness, while living freely in the mindset of another character, can be liberating to introverts.

Whether an introvert's motivation to act is to become another character or to access untapped daily emotions, introverted actors are still working within a very public forum—either on stage or on set. Regardless of the venue, there is always the presence of some kind of audience, whether a group of individuals who have gathered to watch the performance or a collection of fellow cast and crew members observing the shot. Are those "audiences" negatively impacting the introverted actor, whose energy might be depleted from crowds? Why do introverts act?

At a theatre festival held in the United Arab Emirates (UAE) with a collection of international actors and artists, this exchange was recorded as part of a roundtable session as research for this book.[17] The dozens of international actors in the room shared their ideas on introversion and acting:

Actor 1:   It does seem a strange paradox that someone quiet would want to be a performer, but when I was young and started to perform, I found a power shift in that. People knew I was quiet, but the fact that I wanted to perform and share this thing made them see it must be important to me; I must've been holding on to this for a long time.

Actor 2:   There is a distinct difference between ... [having] to get up and tell my personal story ... that makes me want to cower in a corner ... and being able to be a different person ... then I'm fine. I'm okay with that professional mask. I'm wearing it right now, and that is okay with me. I have developed an extroverted persona professionally, but personally, introversion can paralyze me from publicly talking about my personal story.

Actor 3:   As an introvert, we are given a script ... we're given a safe community. We're given rules of engagement. We have this scripted community that makes us feel safe. For some introverts, the idea of visiting or playing an extrovert is a fun exploration, knowing we don't have to put ourselves in situations we would never really put ourselves in.

Actor 4:   Growing up, I was desperately shy. If somebody spoke to me, my cheeks would burn, and I didn't want to talk. I wanted to be in the crowd. Going on to do drama at school allowed me not to be myself. That is fantastic because, in a way, I can't fail...it's not you and nobody is going to comment on who you are and your personality. You don't have to put yourself out. You're playing somebody else.

Actor 5:   [Acting] is a safety net, and no one can blame you if you use the acting. If anyone comments on your personality, you can say, "no, that's just because I'm acting. It's not really me." Whatever you do is justified because acting is a form of extroversion.

In this collection of testimonials from the UAE festival roundtable, actors sometimes equate social anxiety and shyness with introversion. As noted in Chap. 1, those qualities aren't necessarily introverted traits, but the theme of an introvert losing the self to play another seems to cross international boundaries. This collection of artists from around the globe found common ground related to their motivation for entering the field of acting as introverts.

Instant Community

As hinted at by one of the roundtable actors, another motivation for introverts to discover and embrace acting may be the instant community created, with its rule-based safety of the rehearsal process where all participants work toward a common purpose. The ideas of community and safety are main motivators for so many, both introverts and extroverts, who gravitate toward this art form. Broadway actor Matthew Marks shares his story of how he found acting very early, which may be similar to many readers:

> The first show I did was *The Sound of Music* in community theatre. I was nine years old. It made me feel safe. I knew exactly what was going to happen, when it was going to happen, and that always, to this day, has made me feel very safe. Whether it was from [the worry that] someone was going to call me "faggot" on my way to lunch in school, or people making fun of me or pushing me around. Especially when I was really young, theatre was protected. They were like-minded people; we all liked to do the same thing, and we all liked to sing and dance, and everyone accepted me.[18]

Marks lands on something in his story that is very important to the introvert—the idea of safety in a world where everyone is assigned a task or role. There are rules about how to engage in this community. There is a clear hierarchy. And it is composed of like-minded people all working toward the same goal. All of these reliable elements favor introversion. While earlier data suggests that artists have a higher percentage of openness to new ideas, introverts also seek out regimented regularity.

Even with strict scheduling, that same sense of community can also be draining for an introvert. From post-rehearsal get-togethers and cast parties to pre-show group warm-ups, mandated conviviality and socialization can take a toll on the introvert. Remember the actor from Chap. 1 who worked on a touring company on a two-year contract?[19] To this actor, the constant community and close professional and personal quarters were exasperating, making him go so far as to say, "I love performing and working, but I could feel my person being eviscerated." For many introverts, the idea of forced and seemingly unending social and creative interaction can be depleting. Additionally, under the extreme circumstances of touring, performing, and living with the same company, an actor might begin to feel as though they can never restore to a place they feel comfortable: "It's hard to tell people who don't understand. If you're introverted, you might isolate yourself more. Then people think you should socialize more in order to feel better, but that makes it worse." For many introverted actors, there is a tradeoff between getting to ply their craft and the downside of a compulsory community. Imagine how many introverts chose not to make that sacrifice for the community but rather decided to stay home.

Despite some of the downsides to the community, it still draws many to acting. The overwhelming sense of finding your tribe, having an equal partnership with others, and the sheer act of collaboration draw so many to this field where introverts and extroverts work together in a community structure. Its appeal is undeniable.

CONNECTION

Sometimes the motivation for entering into acting can be simply one of wanting to connect with others. While in many cases, an introvert craves solitude, sometimes that isolating choice can be overwhelming. The safety of theatre allows for escape into a group setting away from the introvert's quiet interior life. Rehearsals give the introvert a literal safe and scheduled "play date" with others.

For some introverted actors, their craft is a chance to shed their sometimes overwhelming connection with the inner voice to which they are, so often, closely linked. The work offers the introvert a place where rules and regulations are adhered to strictly with rehearsal calendars, daily calls, and Equity breaks. It is in these moments of planning, organization, structure, and reflection that the introverted actor can thrive and interact comfortably with others.

Theatre offers another protective element most other public forums do not: the script. Scripted interaction or dialogue can reduce an introvert's dislike of impromptu interactivity. When asked to speak extemporaneously, introverts can sometimes get tripped up and retreat into their heads, causing them to appear distant or even unprepared. But the script provides the dialogue and dictates the exchange, allowing for interactivity using the playwright's words. Actor Matthew Marks agrees: "I'm a creature of habit, so scripted interaction does help … knowing exactly what the other person is going to say and not worrying about how to respond."[20] Of course, anxiety about small talk is not purely the domain of the introvert, but the script does provide a freeing relief from having to examine and over-analyze conversations.

While there are many more motivations for why an introvert might feel called upon to act, we cannot deny the enduring stereotype that actors are inherently extroverted—the histrionic actor who loves to entertain, thrives as the center of attention, makes big bold choices, and craves the spotlight. But this is only one aspect of being one kind of actor. Much of the work actors do corresponds with the strengths of an introvert. Rather than trying to overcome your introversion in order to become an actor, we say, embrace the introverted gifts that make you a different kind of actor—one who understands introversion and how it can positively impact your acting.

Access to Vulnerability

All actors are brave. Performing on stage or on screen for public scrutiny, with the hope of helping people better understand their own lives, is a courageous act. For some extroverts, the connection to the audience empowers and galvanizes them. This may be the case for the introverted actor too; though the transaction between actor and audience may be a bit more nuanced.

As mentioned earlier, each actor is unique, and actors fall across the spectrum of ambiverts, extroverts, and introverts. There are extroverts who enjoy their time alone. There are introverts who love big crowds. Extroverts who value private reflection. Introverts who occasionally love being the center of attention. LA actor and writer Sean Patrick McGowan understands the differences between "performing" and "acting," where performing is much more concerned with public behavior in social situations, such as "performing" at a party.[21] Acting, on the other hand, is a much more intimate process, one McGowan describes as mining the very private aspects of interior life. For McGowan, acting comes with a willingness "to be discovered and seen for parts of you that many people are unwilling to have seen." This vulnerability requires a level of trust in the self and a willingness to freely offer the "solemn gift" of yourself to the audience, or as McGowan puts it, "your privacy, your imagination, and your insanity." To some extent, it involves trust in the audience, as "to truly let someone see you, you have to trust them." Trust, comfort, and bravery are all necessary for the introverted actor when on display in front of an audience.

Broadway actress Linda Mugleston similarly suggests the acting process is an opportunity to "crack yourself open a little bit and live your life a little bit more fully, and perhaps be more vulnerable. And when the show is done, that closes back up again."[22] The act of sharing such intimacy can be overwhelming, but when an introverted actor is highly empathic, that empathy might allow them greater access to vulnerability and connection when performing.

"Empathy" or "sensitivity" and the introverted actor make great sense, as actors traffic their work dealing in emotion. As noted earlier, it may appear some of these introverted interviewees fall into Elaine Aron's definition of highly sensitive people or HSP explored in her book *The Highly Sensitive Person* (Broadway Books, 1997).[23] It is also important to note that extroverts can also be highly sensitive.

Professional actor Andy Head shared a personal story of how introversion negatively impacted his desire to connect, both onstage and off:

It's harder to meet and work with new people in a way that feels open and vulnerable ... for me, the offstage part is the harder one. I worked at a summer Shakespeare Festival, and it ended up being a difficult experience for me because I felt like I wasn't connecting with anyone outside of rehearsal. That started to influence rehearsal. All of my introverted qualities rushed in ... I didn't represent myself in a good way at all because I was feeling those [overwhelming] feelings of being an introvert.[24]

The desire to connect, but lacking the skill set to do so, can result in a daunting internal battle. The struggle between personal and professional availability for the actor is an interesting conundrum. An actor may want to remain personally invulnerable, but the discipline of acting comes with the job requirement of accessing vulnerability in performance. The ability of an actor to read a script and empathize with the character means they may be able to use that empathy as a stepping stone to vulnerability in performance.

LISTENING

The act of listening is key to many major acting theorists, and introverts are known for their keen ability to listen. This act of listening can allow introverts to become theatrical repositories for the stories they collect. What the introverted actor does with the stories is also important. Marks notes, "[Actors are] really storytellers. That's the crux of what we do. For an introvert to be a storyteller, they're taking an important part of themselves they've internalized, and sharing it."[25] The transaction of listening to another and sharing it with an audience is important to an actor's success. Access to a library of stories, when used with the power of observation, is an unstoppable combination for an actor.

OBSERVATION

An actor observes human behavior to assist in their pursuit of living truthfully onstage, so it stands to reason that an introverted actor, who watches and observes life regularly, has collected an array of rich life observations to choose from when creating a character. The skill of observing everyday life allows the introverted actor to transform into a myriad of characters. Actor Molly Ringwald explains that this power of observation connects an introvert to the human condition and allows them to understand why people do what they do.[26] For her, this type of observation also provides added levels of empathy, sensitivity, and depth of understanding. Tapping into the skill of observation also instills a comfort with taking time to sit in silence and think; to sit in the question of the character, rather than jumping in right away to embodiment. Ringwald posits these are all skills more inherently rooted in an introverted actor.

An adaptation of the observation exercise from Chap. 5 can be used to examine your skills of observation. Spend some quiet time observing others in order to empathize with another, expand your ability as an actor to portray differing temperaments and to have a higher awareness of the ways in which you interact with the world in relation to your own thought processes. Observe first as an introvert and then as an extrovert. Having self-awareness about the way we think and observe as actors can allow us to become more thoughtful observers of the human condition. It's all in the analysis.

PROCESSING TIME

For the actor, the skill of analysis can be defined and incorporated in a variety of ways, from sitting in silence and pondering the motivation for a character's action, to the time spent justifying every line of dialogue, to scoring a script with rich and detailed given circumstances, moments before, and backstory. A deep analysis of the script guides an actor's choices, and this cerebral approach might be seen as the domain of the introverted actor. These reason-based, analytical skills need processing time to allow thoughts to marinate using the storytelling, listening, and observational skills related to human behavior. Most introverted actors have expressed a deep affinity for this part of the actor's process, and for many, the secluded time spent analyzing, reading, and researching a script is the best part of acting. So, be proud of your analytical skills. They are the well from which all other parts of acting spring.

Lest this book be thought of as a chastising rebuke of the extrovert, we remind you of our charge in the introduction: we respect and appreciate extroverted actors. These different approaches to the art make the process unique to each individual and make the act of collaboration with actors of a variety of temperaments so interesting. The interchange of introvert and extrovert working together can deeply affect each other. So, rather simply, both introverted and extroverted actors are valuable to the process.

DELIBERATE PRACTICE

This concept will be covered in more detail in Chap. 5, but when elaborating on introverted tendencies that benefit the actor, this concept could not go unreported. As you learn more about the concept of deliberate practice, you will see how introverts thrive on the repetition a rehearsal process offers. Introverts tend to excel in crafting, refining, and perfecting their work, which is exactly how standard theatrical rehearsals are run.

EMBODIED PERFORMANCE

Nearly all that is written in this chapter seems to examine the inner workings of the introvert's mind. And most of the strengths ascribed to the introverted actor seem entirely head-centered. But that is only one half of the actor's toolkit. How then does an introverted actor work physically? In the upcoming survey results chapter, we provide first-hand information about how an introverted actor might approach physical work, but this aspect of the craft of acting is so essential, it seems important to begin to address it here.

More often than not, actors may dismiss a performance or rehearsal by saying, "I was in my head too much." Being "in my head" is a common phrase heard in many acting classes and rehearsal halls. For actors, this phrase is a negative one, and most likely means they were watching their performance and critiquing it with negative self-talk or remembering the adjustments the director previously gave them. But for the introverted actor, being "in your head" is a common-place occurrence and, when acknowledged and managed accordingly, can be considered a strength. Connecting to a character's inner monologue, assessing the situation in the moment, empathizing with a partner, and observing and analyzing are all positive ways of working "in your head."

It is when this internal work overtakes the external work that the introverted actor may be in trouble. One actor at the UAE festival notes, "As an introverted person, I find the inner monologue for the character first, then I can understand who this person is…but physicality and all the external stuff is hard for me."[27] This actor is allowing the head to overtake the physical life of the character. So, while the actor is expertly connecting to the psychology of the character, those choices do not manifest in physical, holistic acting.

Another introverted actor at the same festival had a different point of view and found their introversion was a benefit to physical character creation, revealing the physical work helped them to dig deeper into their character's internal life, as one easily connected with and influenced by the other. This actor went on to praise what they saw in their introverted classmates, commending their "physical bravery to break down [a character] internally first and then blossom outwards."[28] The idea of mindful practice here is another way to allow introverts to access their connection from internal to external choices.

Most probably think of the introverted actor as working from the inside out. It makes sense, as the introvert's processing skills assist in exploring the psychology of the character and then letting that exploration affect the body. However, introverted actors can and do have access to a mind/body connection. There are many highly physical introverted actors who are adept at connecting internal analysis to external transformations. If you are an introverted actor, your progress in physical or external work is merely an aspect of your actor toolkit to continue to monitor, train, and observe. The goal for all actors, no matter the temperament, is to become a holistic, embodied artist.

The goal of this chapter is the analysis of introverted strengths and the ways in which those strengths can inform and assist the introverted actor toward success. We believe that self-awareness can bring the introverted (and extroverted) actor to a place of understanding, where their personality style is a gift. In the next chapter, we offer ways to have a greater self-awareness of your traits and analyze how they affect your work as an actor.

NOTES

1. Camenson, Blythe. *Careers for Introverts & Other Solitary Types*. New York: McGraw-Hill, 2006.
2. Shatkin, Laurence. *200 Best Jobs for Introverts*. Indianapolis, IN: JIST Pub., 2008.
3. Donellan, Brent. Personal interview. 1. Dec. 2018.
4. Golden, Alfred L. "Personality Traits of Drama School Students." *Quarterly Journal of Speech* 26, no. 4 (1940): 564–75. https://doi.org/10.1080/00335634009380595.
5. Nettle, Daniel. "Psychological Profiles of Professional Actors." *Personality and Individual Differences* 40, no. 2 (2006): 375–83. https://doi.org/10.1016/j.paid.2005.07.008.
6. Page, Kevin. "Psychology for Actors," September 2018. https://doi.org/10.4324/9781351130950.
7. Donnellan, Brent. Interview.
8. Lucas, Richard. Personal interview. 15. Jan. 2019.
9. Donnellan, Brent. Interview.
10. Anonymous respondents. "Introversion Survey." Qualtrics survey. Michigan State University, 2019
11. Ringwald, Molly, and Susan Cain. "QUIET PODCAST: Episode7." *Quiet: The Power of Introverts with Susan Cain*, Panoply, podcasts podcasts.apple.com/us/podcast/episode-7-molly-ringwald-hollywoods-introvert/id1065074566?i=1000364998124
12. Head, Andy. Personal interview. 15. Aug. 2018.
13. Kaenzig, Lisa. Personal interview.15 Dec. 2018.
14. Marks, Matthew. Personal interview. 10 Jan. 2019.
15. Mugleston, Linda. Interview.
16. Schultz, Carol. Personal interview. 20 Jan. 2019
17. "Introversion and Acting." *American University of Sharjah Theatre Festival.* February 4, 2019.

18. Marks, Matthew. Interview.
19. "Introversion and Acting," Sharjah.
20. Marks, Matthew. Interview.
21. McGowan, Sean Patrick. 13 April 2019.
22. Mugleston, Linda. Interview.
23. Aron, Elaine, N. *The Highly Sensitive Person*. Broadway Books. 1997.
24. Head, Andy. Interview.
25. Marks, Matthew. Interview.
26. Ringwald, Molly. Podcast.
27. "Introversion and Acting," Sharjah.
28. "Introversion and Acting," Sharjah.

References

Anonymous respondents. "Introversion Survey." Qualtrics survey. Michigan State University, 2019

Aron, Elaine N. *The Highly Sensitive Person*. Broadway Books. 1997.

Camenson, Blythe. *Careers for Introverts & Other Solitary Types*. New York: McGraw-Hill, 2006.

Donellan, Brent. Personal interview. 1. Dec. 2018.

Golden, Alfred L. "Personality Traits of Drama School Students." *Quarterly Journal of Speech* 26, no. 4 (1940): 564–75. https://doi.org/10.1080/00335634009380595.

Head, Andy. Personal interview. 15. Aug. 2018.

"Introversion and Acting." *American University of Sharjah Theatre Festival*. February 4, 2019.

Kaenzig, Lisa. Personal interview. 15 Dec. 2018.

Lucas, Richard. Personal Interview. 15. Jan. 2019.

Nettle, Daniel. "Psychological Profiles of Professional Actors." *Personality and Individual Differences* 40, no. 2 (2006): 375–83. https://doi.org/10.1016/j.paid.2005.07.008.

Page, Kevin. "Psychology for Actors," September 2018. https://doi.org/10.4324/9781351130950.

Marks, Matthew. Personal interview. 10 Jan. 2019.

McGowan, Sean Patrick. 13 April 2019.

Mugleston, Linda. Personal Interview. 20 Jan 2019.

Ringwald, Molly, and Susan Cain. "QUIET PODCAST: Episode 7." *Quiet: The Power of Introverts with Susan Cain*, Panoply, podcasts podcasts.apple.com/us/podcast/episode-7-molly-ringwald-hollywoods-introvert/id1065074566?i=1000364998124

Schultz, Carol. Personal interview. 20 Jan. 2019.

Shatkin, Laurence. *200 Best Jobs for Introverts*. Indianapolis, IN: JIST Pub., 2008.

CHAPTER 3

Self-Awareness

So far, several components of this book examining introversion in acting have had an intentional implication of heightened self-awareness. How self-aware are you of your temperament and its predisposition? The ability to self-analyze is then used for the actor in myriad ways. How do I best audition? How can I feel comfortable making conversation in the rehearsal studio? How does introversion affect my relationship with an audience? Do I create characters with a similar temperament to my own? If so, how can I break that pattern? These are all beautiful questions, and they are answered only through self-analysis (and some help from this book). But as stated in the introduction, each introvert's, nay, each person's, journey to becoming the actor they want to be is an individual one. Thus, the coping strategies and concepts we suggest are to be personalized and synthesized through your own self-awareness.

In the book *The Happy Introvert: A Wild and Crazy Guide for Celebrating Your True Self* (Ulysses, 2009),[1] author Elizabeth Wagele defines the introverts' creative process: "The introverted process takes place in the psyche beyond the reach of conscious knowing, resulting in fresh ways of seeing, feeling, and thinking. Out of this, practical, innovative, or imaginative new directions may emerge. Some feel they help the introverted process along by turning their backs on the world and finding stillness" (89). Having a keen awareness of how the introvert creates allows the actor to be aware of the insularity of the process, to be aware of times to include others or to spend time in thought. That knowledge

© The Author(s) 2020
R. Roznowski et al., *The Introverted Actor*,
https://doi.org/10.1007/978-3-030-41607-2_3

impacts the way in which you approach any role. But in order to have an awareness of the creative process, you must first discover if you are indeed an introvert.

In our numerous interviews for the book, we asked actors and experts how they knew they were introverts. Some noted they just felt it, were self-identified, or had been repeatedly told by friends or family. However they arrived, they knew they were introverts. Several actors reported their first realization they were introverted came from taking a personality test. Take a few minutes to take an updated introversion/extroversion personality assessment. It can be as simple as a quick, ten-question preference quiz available online, or it can be a more complicated, in-depth one that examines and analyzes your entire personality.

At the UAE theatre festival, several actors talked about their experiences with such tests:

Actor 1:   I've taken multiple tests across my life, in both professional and personal environments. Even my job required it. But my questions were different because it pertained to my job, not who I am in my personal life. But the results were the same.

Actor 2:   I've taken Myers-Briggs type indicators [at least] thirteen times, and I've always gotten the same results.

Actor 3:   Twenty years and the results are always inevitable.

Actor 4:   I've never taken a quiz, but I know I'm an introvert just by knowing myself; maybe other people perceive me in a different way, but [I know] what I'm like.

Actor 5:   I've taken tests, but I don't think they're always reliable because they're more like, "What kind of pizza do you like?" I can't be the only one who feels that way. We already know whether or not we're an introvert or an extrovert.[2]

Your reactions to such testing may align with one of the above statements. People can enjoy such examinations or find them as innocuous as a "Which Disney Princess Are You?" online quiz. Some find the classification and labeling of personality types destructive, unnecessary, or even unhealthy, while others find comfort and reinforcement in the repeated pattern of results. In a book that aims for temperament inclusivity, we ask that you consider where you currently fall on the introvert/extrovert spectrum and the preferences that go along with your innate temperament.

You may or may not have taken such tests in the past, and perhaps it has been a few years since you last took a Myers-Briggs test (probably the most widely accepted testing platform to determine introversion and extroversion).[3] And, yes, there is debate among experts on the validity of this test, but we are going to advocate for taking this psychometric test—multiple times through different lenses. Because our life experiences keep us ever-evolving, it is very possible your results have also changed and evolved. So, for the best application of the exercises in this book, we ask that you take the Myers-Briggs test or a free variation of it. And, if you want to examine the role of introversion in your acting work in even more depth, consider taking the test four times.

THREE SELVES (FOUR TESTS)

Most people have two versions of themselves—a personal and a professional self. The personal self may be much less formal than the cultivated, professional self you present to the world. The separation between our private and public selves seems fairly obvious. Psychology professor Brent Donnellan applies this dual concept to academics, stating that even if a teacher tends to self-identify as an introvert, the nature of their work demands a more extroverted professional persona, admitting, "teaching large lectures is a context that asks for [extroversion]. It's not something we're too comfortable doing, but we want to be good at our jobs, so we adopt the persona of a fairly extroverted, outgoing lecturer in order to teach and do the things we love."[4] In your journey to self-awareness, what adaptations are you making for the professional self from the private self? Take the personality test two times, once as your personal self and the next as your professional self. Record those results and compare them for any sort of discrepancy or synergies. Did you find you are more extroverted and assertive at work than you are in your personal, everyday life? These distinctions will assist you in finding a deeper self-awareness and can even help you find comfort in understanding varied ways in which you interact with the world. You may find there are few or no differences. Thus, part of your self-awareness might mean you discover little adaptation between your personal and professional selves.

In considering how we change and adapt our personalities to our given circumstances, the larger question becomes one of authenticity. Do I feel authentic and honest in my professional self? Using the example above, after teaching in a large lecture hall or interacting in a similar public setting, do you need time to recharge because you were working outside your comfort zone?

Many of us make adaptations for our careers or passions. We may have to make those adjustments in order to find success. This is also true of the introverted actor, and for many introverted actors, authenticity is key. Sometimes the personal introversion muddies the demands of the professional and necessary social interaction. How then can an actor best restore, following a professional situation that often drains energy from an introvert? Andy Sloey, improv artist and educator, describes his way of restoring: "I don't like being in front of or around large groups of people. [It] makes me uneasy and nervous. However, if that's flipped, and I'm leading a class or hosting a show, it's easy to flip the switch to be 'on.' But that flipping draws energy; so, if I'm teaching multiple classes, by the end of the day, I'm wiped, and my brain is shot. I'm ready to go home and play video games ... that's mostly how I restore."[5] Finding a specific way back to balance is personal and requires self-awareness.

Indian actor Kavya Misra describes the challenge to balance her personal and professional selves and discover a professional persona that would give her more confidence speaking in public.[6] Numerous interviewees shared such stories of attempts to stretch into professional levels of ambiversion or extroversion, with professional expectations long favoring the traits of the extrovert, and introverted actors striving to reverse their introversion in order to make a good impression or build the best connections to get the role. But these expectations may undercut the creative and professional contributions introverted actors bring to the craft. In an industry built on an extroverted ideal, should all actors be expected to interact with the same level of professional behavior? Are introverted actors treated with equity in the audition room and rehearsal hall? Why are quiet actors considered moody or aloof? Why are actors who choose not to attend a cast gathering labeled as antisocial or uncooperative members of the ensemble? How many introverted actors have failed the extrovert-favoring interview section of the audition? These questions permeate our profession and warrant careful examination to finally consider how both the professional and personal expectations often placed on actors inherently put introverts at a disadvantage. Ultimately, we ask: should the introverted actor have to change the fundamental traits of their personality in order to be successful in this profession? Or, should the profession make adaptations that favor both temperaments? Or is it somewhere in the middle? We think it is. Gradual adaptations from both actors and educators.

We can't expect actors to change their bio-genetic core, nor can we expect the profession to move away from many of its accepted and fundamental practices. But slight modifications can be made by both parties.

For some introverts, their professional life offers a version of themselves that transforms from introvert to extrovert. Indian actor Shafali Jirial admits the more extroverted parts of her personality are present, but because they are hidden, the switch must be assessed through self-awareness.[7] Jirial reveals her work on stage is the perfect vehicle for accessing her more extroverted, professional self: "On the stage, I am not the person you see. I don't know how I get this confidence when I am [acting]. To begin is a bit difficult for me; therefore, I try to push myself. Talking to myself or writing helps me to open my heart, especially for something I love." Jirial has a way of revving up for her theatrical interactions, and, in that process, she has created a version of an extroverted professional self accessible through acting. A thoughtful comparison of test results between personal and professional selves might reveal tactics for adaptation and compromise between the two types. These are the first two of the four recommended personality tests. The latter two focus even more carefully on the work of the actor.

While many careers see tensions between personal and professional selves, the actor is unique. The actor also creates variations of the self, or even creates an entirely new self, in the creation of characters. This new "character self" certainly uses selected elements of the actor's personal self as the basis for a character. This is largely done through identification and assimilation. But each new character also makes unique demands on the actor that move beyond the use of only the personal self. Characters possess their own unique needs from the given circumstances of a script, and often these circumstances far exceed an actor's personal experience. Playing a war-mongering tyrant, or a meticulous and officious pastry chef, or a powerful and supernatural being, all likely exceed the actor's personal self. All roles require some room for pretense and imagination in order for the actor to invest in a different time period or character reality. We begin with our personal identification and then adapt our physical, vocal, and psychological behaviors to meet the demands of the script. All this requires an adaptation of the self. (The book *Roadblocks in Acting* (2017) should be examined for a more in-depth analysis of these concepts.[8])

Regardless of how we approach the work of acting, this necessary adaptation may be subtle or extreme. Whether you believe acting is less about creating distinct differences and more about finding similar aspects in yourself and enhancing them, whether you think acting requires more personal connection and less overt transformation, or whether you identify as a personality actor or character actor (for more on these distinctions, the book *Embodied Acting: What Neuroscience Tells Us About Performance* (2012) by Rick Kemp offers clear definitions): no matter your entrance into creating a character, some form of adaptation and transformation occurs.[9]

Is it easy for introverts to play extroverted characters? And vice versa? As actors, we like to believe we can play anything. But is that entirely true? Can the reserved introvert play a bombastic attention-seeking salesman? And conversely, can the gregarious extrovert portray a pensive writer richly connected to their interior life?

In a 2019 *New York Times* review of the film *A Beautiful Day in the Neighborhood* starring Tom Hanks as beloved children's television personality Mr. Rogers, critic A. O. Scott argued that Tom Hanks was miscast.[10] His reasoning was that Hanks was a natural-born extrovert and therefore could not tame his energy to play the quiet and introverted Mr. Rogers. Scott rather alarmingly compares Hanks's extroverted energy to that of a friendly Labrador Retriever and classifies Mr. Rogers' introverted energy as feline and more melancholic. While you may notice some extrovert bias in these classifications, this critic appears to believe it is difficult for extroverted actors to capture the proper energy or temperament of an introvert. You may also question the assertion in the review that there are few other mass-media celebrities as introverted as Daniel the Striped Tiger.

We posed the question of whether an actor of one temperament can accurately portray a character of the opposite temperament to psychology professor Brent Donnellan, who surmised that the thrill to work outside the borders of your temperament is clear and compelling.[11] Donnellan uses the example of the excitement and fun an actor might experience in playing a villain character. In playing nefarious or despicable characters, actors are often asked to explore and embody behaviors, beliefs, and attitudes that are "bad" or unorthodox. And many find this thrilling. Of course, everyone has the capability for bad behavior, but we don't regularly express it. Donnellan suggests playing these roles is a fascinating opportunity to understand the motivations of this behavior and a safe way to explore characters outside their own temperaments. So, the excitement for acting and becoming another is clear, but does one personality type have an advantage over the other?

Donnellan notes, for introverts, especially people uncomfortable in social situations, acting provides an outlet for fun and safe exploration of untapped personalities. Donnellan also posits extroverted actors might find it difficult to "rein in all that energy and activity … In contemporary society, there's such a push to be extroverted, whereas if you already are extroverted, trying to rein that in would be a more demanding role." Donnellan is, of course, merely hypothesizing, but the argument is an interesting one: the powerful and bold energy of the extrovert forced into a more reserved role can be just as challenging.

Psychology professor Rich Lucas is a bit more pragmatic about the question.[12] He notes this adaptation might, in some ways, occur when individual actors attempt to change their personalities and find it difficult to do so. Sometimes actors find they can't portray these counter-characters because they are so antithetical to their natural tendencies. So, an introverted actor might want to play an extroverted character, but they may not be entirely successful because of an ingrained resistance to the embodiment of that type. Can one truly inhabit the temperament of another so differently wired, even when it is their profession? Lucas does give extroverted and introverted actors hope in the freedom of exploration that comes with playing the opposite, even for a limited amount of time. Most actors enjoy the stretch of playing someone so different from who they are normally. It is perhaps what drew many introverts to acting in the first place.

At the UAE festival, actors were asked a similar question, "Is it easy for an introvert to play an extrovert?" Their responses were varied:

Actor 1:   It's easier because as an introvert, if you want to play yourself, you're going to aim for perfection, and you can never get to that. Playing the idea of the extrovert, you can play it as you see it from other people.

Actor 2:   As an introvert, you're going to be intimidated showing a part of yourself, if your character's introverted too. Taking on an extroverted character lets you put aside your personal introversion and put on this other show. That doesn't seem as scary [because] you're not putting yourself completely out there.

Actor 3:   I notice spillover from one into my life. I've played a lot of really boisterous or extroverted characters, and I enjoy doing that, and for a bit after the show, there's an extroverted spillover. I'm still more likely to engage and joke in that time after because that personality is still in me, and I find that exhilarating.

Actor 4:   I'm extroverted. Doing the opposite, playing an introverted
character, is more fun because I get to have the thought, I sit
in silence, and I get to just exist, which is one of the hardest
things to do on stage, but it's also one of the most exhilarating.
That bleeds over because after a show, people try to talk to
me ... and I take more time to myself.[13]

The first UAE actor suggests playing a character of a similar temperament would be more frustrating to an introvert because they would never
achieve perfection, while playing a character of a different temperament
would reduce the need for perfection (knowing it is such a different
approach). While there is no proof of this, it is an interesting theory.

The other actors from the UAE were split over which type might be
easiest to play, and our interviews concluded the same: some noted it
might be more fun, others that it would be challenging, while still others
that it would be freeing. Even the final extroverted actor noted playing an
introvert has profound personal reverberations.

LA actor and writer Sean Patrick McGowan gives a philosophical
response, reframing the question: "Would I rather play someone with circumstances similar to my own, or wildly different to my own? Of course,
I would rather play someone who is different ... but I am trying not to
think about it (in this way). No matter who it is, they are me, and you
need to start from that."[14] What becomes clear, hopefully, is that an understanding of the opposite temperament must be researched and understood
by the actor.

We ask you, can you adapt yourself and your personality to honestly
portray a character who has a different temperament than yourself? And if
so, how drastic are those changes? As always, you can rely on self-awareness,
and you can seek the feedback of your friends, directors, or critics. But
additionally, you can rely on the personality tests you have already taken
twice (as personal and professional self). For this third examination, take
the introversion/extroversion test again, this time in "character." Take the
test in the mindset of a character you recently played in which you felt
particularly successful. Success can be based on a teacher's feedback, an
audience's laughter, or your personal pride, but put yourself back in the
mind and circumstances of that role and answer the questionnaire as that
character might. Record those findings alongside your results for personal
and professional self and begin to examine patterns or similarities across
various categories. Look for large disparities between percentages. How

similar is this character to your personal or professional self? How extreme or subtle is your adaption from your personal self?

Finally, take the test one last time, this time as a character you created that you felt was not successful. Use the same barometers from before to make this determination (critics, director personal pride, etc.). We've all had those roles that, for whatever reason, didn't feel right or didn't feel connected or authentic. Usually, we like to forget these roles. Here, we ask you to go back into that character and take the test one last time.

Following each step, you will have four sets of numbers to compare. The first two sets are to compare your personal and professional selves. Have you cultivated a more extroverted version of yourself for business or professional purposes? What do the percentages reveal about your adaptation and evolution? The last two findings compare two characters you've created, with opposite degrees of success. These results should also be compared with each other. Why did one role succeed while the other was a struggle? Do the percentages reveal a pattern in the types of character personalities you have portrayed? More broadly, how do those two roles compare with your personal and professional selves? Did you successfully portray someone with a different temperament than your own? Did you feel more successful in playing roles very similar to your personal self? The test will most likely contain other categories for examination, but for the purposes of this book, we will concentrate mainly on the question of introversion and extroversion between the three selves of the actor: personal, professional, and character.

EXAMPLE COMPARISONS

Two of the contributors to this book took the tests four times so we could share and analyze their results. Their information is included in the following tables (Tables 3.1 and 3.2).

Some analysis on these results follows.

From Carolyn Conover

Self—I knew I'd be an INFJ. I have been my entire adult life, every time I've taken this test. It has come to be a source of pride for me, though, because we are so rare! I've also finally stopped apologizing for being an introvert. The 71% Turbulent, for me, is quantitative evidence of how much I work to avoid conflict.

Table 3.1   Carolyn's results[15]

Carolyn Conover	Mind	Energy	Nature	Tactics	Identity
Self INFJ-T The advocate	Extroverted- Introverted 96% introverted	Intuitive- Observant 51% intuitive	Thinking- Feeling 69% feeling	Judging- Prospecting 79% judging	Observant- Turbulent 71% turbulent
Professional ISTJ-A The logistician	56% introverted	54% observant	58% thinking	68% judging	59% assertive
Character + M'Lynn from *Steel Magnolias* ESTJ-A The executive	86% extroverted	77% observant	67% thinking	67% judging	61% assertive
Character - Marquise de Merteuil from *Les Liaisons Dangereuses* ESTJ-A The executive	93% extroverted * Yep, I am the polar opposite of Merteuil!	56% observant *Most similarity here in "Others" and all the opposite of my self-identification	85% thinking *It's amazing that so many of these results reveal a stark contrast to my self-identification!	72% judging *Interesting that Prospecting doesn't appear in any of my approaches!	74% assertive *All three "Others" are opposite from my natural self.

Professional—I was very surprised to see my results were almost evenly split down the middle. This reveals how much I am working to balance what I know my personality tends toward and what I know is probably best for my responsibilities at work as a teacher, mentor, director, and colleague. According to the analysis, this is one of the most abundant types,

Table 3.2 Cameron's results[16]

Cameron Michael Chase	Mind	Energy	Nature	Tactics	Identity
Self INTJ-T The advocate	Extroverted-Introverted 74% introverted	Intuitive-Observant 56% intuitive	Thinking-Feeling 64% feeling	Judging-Prospecting 81% judging	Observant-Turbulent 60% turbulent
Professional INTJ-T The advocate	51% introverted	52% intuitive	57% feeling	86% judging	56% turbulent
Character + Stanley Stubbers from *One Man, Two Guvnors* ENTP-A The debater	86% extroverted	66% intuitive	61% thinking	72% prospecting	61% assertive
Character − Kenneth from *A Memory of Two Mondays* ISTP-T The virtuoso	72% introverted *Almost identical introversion scores as personal self.	68% observant *The character I struggled with lives far away from my personal and professional self.	65% thinking *Interesting that I am feeling but my characters are thinking.	68% prospecting *Similar response to the last column. Remains a difference between me and characters.	83% turbulent *I like that there is variety across characters and selves.

so I wonder if many of us who are introverts are attempting this balance in our professional lives.

M'Lynn—This makes clear sense to me, since this character is a controlling mother who wants to keep her daughter safe, even at the risk of smothering her. She also feels most people make the wrong decision when they don't seek out her advice first. And even though she has a good heart and the best of intentions, her need to be in control and not to reveal any of her own vulnerabilities can push people away.

Mertuil—The main features that made this character a struggle for me were her selfish and arrogant nature, her calculated nastiness, and her mercurial tendencies. All of these attributes were difficult for me to tap into and embody because they are so foreign to me. Like M'Lynn, Merteuil is a controlling person, but her nefarious motivations and unbridled confidence and certainty, as well as her overtly sexual tactics, were all challenging.

From Cameron Michael Chase

Self—These results were very close to what I was expecting. As I continue to grow and learn more about introversion and extroversion, I expected to find my percentage to be a little closer to 50, but 74% still makes sense to me. I agree with much of the written analysis of the personality type, too.

Professional—The same personality type as my personal self. Again, this was what I expected to happen, only to a smaller degree. I was anticipating ENTJ or ENTP. With that, the level of introversion dropped nearly 25% and is right in the middle now at ambiversion. Feeling dropped a bit as well, which is also true because I try to keep emotional-based decisions from entering the workplace as much as possible.

Stanley—The opposite in almost every possible way, aside from still being fairly intuitive. It is fascinating to see how a character so different from me is one that I was so successful at playing. My gut tells me this is because of the level of transformation. It is someone so different from me, and I can become someone else in a safe place.

Kenneth—While still an introvert, he is quite different from who I am, which might be why it was a difficult character to connect with. My immediate response is that we are both introverts, so I should know who this character is, but that is just one piece of the puzzle. The ways we take in and view the world around us are very different. I follow my intuition and logic to make my decisions, while Kenneth is more of an observer. That is highlighted in the play's second half when he becomes much more reactive and less of an instigator. We see him stop and observe the life around him, and then the introvert kicks in, and he doesn't want to share his thoughts or feelings anymore. He lets feelings, emotions, or passion lead his actions in the first half when he is more rational and pessimistic.

Examining and comparing these results offers some interesting insight as to how actors, both student and professional, can so drastically adapt their ingrained personality traits to embody and discover a completely opposite character, often to great success. Both actors comment that the result of the introverted personal self was no surprise, underscoring the importance of honest and unapologetic self-awareness when approaching the initial test. This self-awareness and personality identification serve as an important foundation against which the other three tests should be compared. In both examples, the professional self reached a more balanced middle ground that perhaps allows the actors to function in a more public and collaborative manner. Both actors comment on the necessity of these adaptations in their work as educators, corroborating Dr. Donnellan's earlier example of the academic lecturer personality adopting a more extroverted approach.

In terms of the latter two tests exploring the personalities of two characters, the tests yielded one fascinating point: three of the four roles reveal highly extroverted characters possessing vast percentage variations from the actor's personal selves. This might indeed provide some early, quantifiable evidence to our ongoing question of whether or not introverted actors can successfully and authentically portray extroverted characters. The interesting difference between the character Cameron succeeded with (a strongly identifying extrovert) and the character he struggled with (an introvert) perhaps could point to the idea of the mask necessary for an introvert to feel safer onstage. The score for both the character he struggled with and his personal self are within 2% of each other—making this character very similar on this scale to Cameron himself. Of course, the other categories offer more wide-ranging differences, but the introversion score is what is primary to our purposes. Through further self-analysis beyond these numbers, these actors could compare the other categories and examine synergies or issues related to the characters they felt most successful versus those with which they struggled. This simple exercise can allow actors to examine more closely how their temperament affects their work and will allow them to set goals for future roles.

Stretch Goals

Many introverts recognize or have an interest in cultivating a more ambivert-like professional self but have little understanding or capacity for such a transformation. A change this drastic cannot happen overnight, and even more, we must ask ourselves if forcing this transformation is necessary, healthy, or even possible. Introversion is related to the dopamine reward system in the brain. Our neurochemistry is an important part of our introversion and is related to our authentic core. In other words, we are born this way, and our introversion is hard-wired into our brains. But that's only half of who you are; the other half is who you want to be, and this may involve stretching outside of what is comfortable to become the opposite—more extroverted if you're an introvert, or more introverted if you are an extrovert. Many introverts feel the need to make this adaptation because we live in such a social world, and theatre is often a highly social discipline.

Many reported trying to adopt an extroverted persona but subsequently retreating from it, feeling inauthentic or drained afterward. Finding a solid coping strategy within this business is a key element in finding and maintaining a satisfying sense of authenticity. Having a clear sense of self-awareness offers another coping strategy, one that asks the question, "Am I pretending to be someone I am not in order to be accepted in this extroverted environment?" Many introverts prefer smaller crowds and a small posse of trusted and valued friends, perhaps supporting a greater sense of authenticity and less pressure to maintain the professional self in larger groups.

While some have done so through trial and error over many years, LA actor and writer Emmanuelle Roumain-Yang, who self-identifies as an introvert, reports she has developed a facility for interacting at parties that honors her true self: "Even if I don't know anyone at a party, I feel comfortable talking to people. But I'm also introspective … I have to sit with my thoughts for a while before sharing them."[17]

Think about stretch goals like baby steps, consciously working a bit outside your comfort zone. In this, we are aware of how much stimulation can be taken from the outside world and then slightly push that boundary. These goals can be set for an entire production or even one rehearsal, in whichever way seems manageable and achievable. In the book *The Genius of Opposites: How Introverts and Extroverts Achieve Extraordinary Results Together* (2016), author Jennifer Kahnweiler writes, "When you step out of character or use traits that aren't as comfortable, you stretch and grow. Your 'opposite muscle' will inevitably get stronger" (43).[18] In experimenting with these adaptations and boundaries, many introverts experience a sense of failure or disappointment when they attempt to change their personalities so drastically in one moment or for one event, usually when they attempt to act fully as an extrovert. Trying to immediately become an alpha or be the life of the party inevitably leads to feeling inauthentic and can cause an introvert to shut down and burn out. In some extreme cases, putting these demands on an introvert, either from external or internal stimuli, can even cause an increase in anxiety or depression.

Setting small, achievable, and realistic stretch goals can lead to successful pathways toward the professional self to which you aspire, and indeed, this professional self may include a higher level of extroversion. Your wish may be to engage more in the social aspects of rehearsal or on set. Rather than ignoring your introversion completely, a realistic stretch goal may be to accept every third invitation to join the group. It may be to make conversation with your fellow actors on breaks in rehearsal. An achievable stretch goal would be to prepare discussion topics you feel comfortable sharing so you have those to bring to the conversation. It may mean, at your next audition, you engage longer with the casting director and ask questions of them to promote a friendlier version of yourself. Stretch goals can help you prepare for a myriad of possibilities where you are cultivating a more social, yet still authentic, version of your professional self.

Coping strategies are equally important after experimenting with stretch goals. Introverts are sensitive to stimulation from the outside world; self-awareness helps us gauge how much stimulation we can sustain in one instance. This outside stimulation can range from demanding or unexpected social interactions, to simply a distracting or alarming level of noise. Any of these stimulants cost time away from an introvert's home base. There are as many ways to recharge as there are individual introverts. Recharging can be as simple as solitude and space from all that stimulation. After completing a stretch event, no matter how small it might seem, there is also a need for processing time that allows the introvert to take some time to honor the reflective pause and consider what has just happened. Was your stretch goal effective? Did it feel authentic? Can you do the same thing again? Can you devote more time to the next go-round, or does it need to be less? Following recharge and reflection time, you might feel more motivated to go back out and engage with others and the world.

Each introvert is individual and the idea of self-awareness remains at the core of this work. Individuality is respected, and actors can gain solace in understanding there are other introverts out there like them. Numerous interviewees thanked us for taking on this project because they have felt so alone as introverts in this profession, feeling out of the norm and not fitting into what was expected. In the next chapter, we will explore general findings from a survey about introversion and acting. Our purpose for sharing these results is to help introverted actors see where they align with the findings and where they diverge, all with the ultimate goal of gaining ownership and confidence of their place in this profession.

NOTES

1. Wagele, Elizabeth. *The Happy Introvert: A Wild and Crazy Guide for Celebrating Your True Self.* United States: Ulysses Press, 2009.
2. "Introversion and Acting." *American University of Sharjah Theatre Festival.* February 4, 2019.
3. "Myers-Briggs Type Indicator." Official Myers Briggs Test & Personality Assessment | MBTI Online. Accessed November 22, 2019. https://www.mbtionline.com/
4. Donnellan, Brent. Personal interview. 1 Dec. 2018.
5. Sloey, Andy. Personal interview. 16 May 2019.
6. Misra, Kavya. Personal interview. 10 Feb. 2019.
7. Jirial, Shafali. Personal interview. 15 Feb. 2019.
8. Roznowski, Rob. *Roadblocks in Acting.* London: Palgrave, 2017.
9. Kemp, Rick. *Embodied Acting What Neuroscience Tells Us About Performance.* London: Routledge, 2012.
10. Scott, A.O. 'A Beautiful Day the Neighborhood' Review: Be My Friend, *NY Times.* 22 Nov. 2019 https://www.nytimes.com/2019/11/21/movies/a-beautiful-day-in-the-neighborhood-review.html
11. Donnellan, Brent. Personal interview.
12. Lucas, Richard. Personal interview. 15 Jan. 2019.
13. "Introversion and Acting," Sharjah.
14. McGowan, Sean Patrick. Personal interview. 13 April 2019.
15. Conover, Carolyn. "Introversion Self-Study." *Introversion Self-Study,* n.d.
16. Chase, Cameron Michael. "Introversion Self-Study." *Introversion Self-Study,* n.d.
17. Roumain-Yang, Emmanuelle. Interview. 30 April. 2019.
18. Kahnweiler, Jennifer B. *The Genius of Opposites: How Introverts and Extroverts Achieve Extraordinary Results Together.* Oakland, CA: Berrett-Koehler Publishers, 2016.

REFERENCES

Chase, Cameron Michael. "Introversion Self-Study." *Introversion Self-Study,* n.d.
Conover, Carolyn. "Introversion Self-Study." *Introversion Self-Study,* n.d.
Donnellan, Brent. Personal Interview. 1 Dec. 2018.
"Introversion and Acting." *American University of Sharjah Theatre Festival.* February 4, 2019.
Jirial, Shafali. Personal interview. 15 Feb. 2019.
Kemp, Rick. *Embodied Acting What Neuroscience Tells Us about Performance.* London: Routledge, 2012.
Lucas, Richard. Personal Interview. 15 Jan. 2019.

McGowan, Sean Patrick. Personal Interview. 13 April 2019.

"Myers-Briggs Type Indicator." Official Myers Briggs Test & Personality Assessment| MBTI Online. Accessed November 22, 2019. https://www.mbtionline.com/.

Misra, Kavya. Personal interview. 10 Feb. 2019.

Kahnweiler, Jennifer B. *The Genius of Opposites: How Introverts and Extroverts Achieve Extraordinary Results Together.* Oakland, CA: Berrett-Koehler Publishers, 2016.

Roumain-Yang, Emmanuelle. Interview. 30 April. 2019.

Roznowski, Rob. *Roadblocks in Acting.* London: Palgrave, 2017.

Scott, A.O. 'A Beautiful Day the Neighborhood' Review: Be My Friend, *NY Times.* 22 Nov. 2019 https://www.nytimes.com/2019/11/21/movies/a-beautiful-day-in-the-neighborhood-review.html.

Sloey, Andy. Personal interview. 16 May 2019.

Wagele, Elizabeth. *The Happy Introvert: A Wild and Crazy Guide for Celebrating Your True Self.* United States: Ulysses Press, 2009.

CHAPTER 4

Survey Results

In preparation for the writing of this book, we crafted a survey to receive feedback and gain clarity in relation to some of the suppositions held by the authors related to the introverted actor. The survey was widely distributed and helped guide our interview questions and the ultimate focus of the book. The results reveal some interesting connections related to the education and professionalization of introverts in the acting field. To match the tone and spirit of the rest of the book, the analysis here will be less academic and more accessible to read and digest. We use the layout of the survey to guide the chapter.

Through a research data and survey program called Qualtrics, we created a thirty-one-question survey that was distributed to actors and acting educators alike. We relied on our diverse and international connections in the profession, targeted major acting schools and universities around the globe, and shared the survey on various online actor sites (such as *BroadwayWorld*, *Backstage*, and *Playbill*). Over 400 people completed the survey, and the results were fascinating.

The survey began with a short introduction that stated, "The purpose of this survey is to identify the best methods to reach both introverted and extroverted actors." The program allowed respondents to begin the survey if they had already self-identified as an extrovert, introvert, or ambivert. If they were unsure of their temperament, two pre-survey online testing programs were offered for the respondents interested in gaining clarification related to their personality type before taking the survey. The first pre-survey option was a quick ten-question questionnaire from Susan Cain's quietrev.com site called "The Quiet Revolution Personality Test";[1] the other option was a more detailed, eighty-one question test from psychologytoday.com called the "Extroversion Introversion Test."[2] With a clear self-definition and categorization, the respondents then began our survey.

The survey was divided into three sections. The first section was devoted to gathering broader general impressions of the respondents and their motivations and ideas about acting and its relationship to introversion. The second section was devoted to actor training and the third to the acting profession. These categories mimic the structure of this book.

GENERAL INFORMATION

Question #1: What Best Describes You?

In the chart in Fig. 4.1 you can see the majority (143) of those who responded were professional actors, followed closely (123) by student actors. The rest of the respondents were comprised of non-professional actors and actor educators. These categorizations were the only options for selection as we wanted to target a specific audience for this survey.

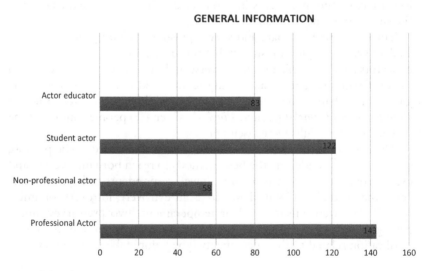

Fig. 4.1   Question #1

Question #2: What Is Your Gender?
As you can see from the chart in Fig. 4.2, the majority (253) of respondents were female-identifying. We have no scientific reason for this slightly disproportionate number (56%) of females responding based on the globe's rather even distribution of gender. There is no proof that a majority of female-identifying actors populate the field of acting. We felt that, though the percentage of female over male respondents was slightly higher than the world's average, this did not have any deep impact on the overall survey results.

Question #3: What Is Your Age?
As you can see from the chart in Fig. 4.3, there is a distribution of ages of respondents that more heavily favors a younger demographic. We acknowledge this statistic is related to our heavy distribution to educational institutions. We were encouraged that there were representatives from each age range offered to give a broader perspective.

Question #4: What Is Your Country of Origin?
While most of our results could be traced back to the United States, we received responses from thirteen other countries, including the United Kingdom, India, Colombia, Australia, and South Africa. The international component was important to get a broader view of introversion and acting.

Fig. 4.2 Question #2

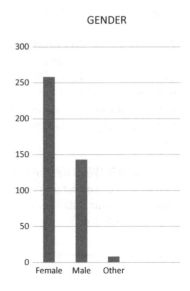

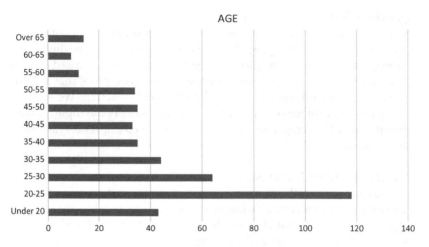

Fig. 4.3   Question #3

Question #5: What Race Do You Identify As?
The majority of our respondents self-identified as "white" or "Caucasian." There were many who identified themselves as "black" or "African American," as well as many "Hispanic" or "Latinx." A minority of respondents identified themselves as "Asian," "Pan-Asian," or "Hindu." While race does not influence temperament, culture does influence personality style, as covered in the later chapter on cultural comparisons.

Question #6: Do You Identify as an Extrovert, Introvert, or Ambivert?
We asked each participant to tell us how they identify themselves. Of the over 400 respondents, 39% identified as introverts, 14% as extroverts, and 47% ambiverts. We believe we had fewer extroverted respondents because the title and subject of this book were included in the introduction to the survey, thereby self-selecting some respondents who may have felt excluded by the subject.

Question #7: Why Did You Go into Acting?
(While there are certainly more options, choose the one that most closely aligns with your initial motivation.) "To become another" or "Connection with an audience."

The question offered only two options and began to examine the differences between introverts and extroverts in their relationship with acting. The first choice was "To become another" and the second choice was "Connection with an audience." We understand those options were reductive and limiting, but our goal was to seek out a clear reason for an actor's motivation for going into the field. Our fear was that if we gave too many options, we would dilute the major overall research question related to introversion. As expected, over two-thirds (67%) of introverts chose "To become another" while only 20% of extroverts selected this option. The second option "Connection with an audience" was selected by 80% of extroverts and only 33% of introverts. Our ambiverts were divided nearly equally, with 49% choosing "To become another" and 51% choosing "Connection with an audience." This supports the supposition in this book that introverted actors have an affinity for the kind of acting that allows for transformation and the safety of the mask of the character when performing. Many of our interviewees also support this claim.

Question #8: Do You Describe Yourself as a More Internally Aware Actor or Physically Aware Actor?
In this question, we wanted to examine the belief that introverts have keen access to their internal awareness. A majority, 79%, of our introverts labeled themselves as more internally aware, while 53% of extroverts labeled themselves as such. This connection of extroverts to internally aware acting could be a byproduct of the majority of our respondents' training in the United States, who may have been trained in an "outside-in" method where the "internals" (the character's psychology) are examined in order to affect the externals (character's physicality). The ambiverts self-identified as 59% internally aware and 41% physically aware.

Question #9: When Approaching Character Building, Do You Find You Make Most Progress Through Thoughtful Solo Analysis or Group Exploration?
The answer was definitive for over two-thirds of introverts, who chose "solo analysis" (69%). Extroverts and ambiverts both fell in the middle range, both identifying about 50% for "solo analysis" and "group exploration." In this question, we were examining the idea that an introvert needs time to analyze in a private fashion.

Question #10: Why?
In this simple follow-up question, we wanted to gain information from the respondents as to why introverts might prefer solo work to group work. Some of their responses included:

- Group work makes me self-conscious.
- It helps to do my character work alone. I also get time to make my character's story.
- I feel other's views as a hindrance. It's not that I don't respect their views. I should be able to approach a character's psyche. I can take guidance or help from others, but in the end, it's only me building the character. For me, acting is a personal thing. It starts within and ends within.
- I enjoy both, but I usually need time alone for personal realization beforehand.
- I love analyzing the history of the character and their backstory, and while I love group exploration as well, I work better on my own most of the time.
- I prefer solo analysis because I like to have ideas to bring to the table before I work with others. I like to give my character and their motivations some thought first. However, I am very willing to throw some of my ideas out the window if I find a different choice plays better off the group dynamic
- Solo work gives me an opportunity to flesh things out fully in my head and make sure my motivations are clearly outlined without the distraction a group can give.
- I get to focus on my own material without distractions or the need to please other people in the room.
- Though I love making discoveries in the rehearsal process, I find I'm at my most creative in finding new discoveries when I'm doing research on my own.
- The basis of my characters come from within, not from others.
- I am insecure at times, as most actors are, and do well by myself where I feel less judged!
- It allows me to be alone with my thoughts and bring them into a safe space to play. It's more organized for me.[3]

In these responses and many others from the survey, you can see that introverts have a proclivity for working alone. Their love of research and analysis fits well with this beginning stage of building a character. This does not mean to say that introverts cannot thrive in group work or that extroverts cannot enjoy research alone.

Other introverts also noted the need for group work:

- Collaboration sometimes opens more doors of discovery for me … but I also need time on my own to flesh things out.
- If I do too much solo analysis, I end up trapped and moving in circles. Groups force me to put my character into the context of society and relationships.
- I appreciate feedback and various perspectives to further explore my own thoughts. Working with a group also heightens my energy, and I find more good ideas.
- So much of my character is built on how they interact with others in their world. Some solo analysis is helpful to bring into the room, but the real magic happens when I begin discussions and explorations with my scene partners. They also help me define the rules of the world of the play.[4]

These responses show a measured understanding that group work can benefit the introvert. The responses also reveal the reality that group work is a necessity in theatrical training.

Question #11: Does Introversion or Extroversion Affect Your Work/Study as an Actor?

In this question, we wanted to examine whether introverts understand how their biological traits might impact their chosen profession. Only 26% of introverts responded "No," introversion has no impact on their work as an actor, with 39% reporting "Yes" and 35% responding "Maybe." It appears that introversion might be a benefit to acting. Extroverts identified with 42% "Yes," 27% "No," and 31% "Maybe. Ambiverts answered 37 % "Yes," 27% "No," and 36% "Maybe." We intentionally did not imply whether the impact referenced in the question was negative or positive, and therefore, it is imagined that extroverts may have selected "Yes" because their gregariousness positively impacted their time in rehearsal. Or introverts may have believed that their introspective nature was a benefit while rehearsing a play. Whether positive or negative, introversion and extroversion seem to have an impact on the life of an actor.

Question #12: How?

In this response, we were seeking concrete examples of the ways introversion can impact an actor. We got a plethora of responses. We have distilled the main themes of these responses below. As we hypothesized, it appears that many introverted actors see their introversion as a strength to character development, self-awareness, empathy, and connection to partner, but see its potentially challenging impacts on ensemble building, improv, and risk-taking in the rehearsal process. Several comments highlighted the introvert's need to decompress and find quiet after the demands of the work. It is also important to see all three types (introverts, extroverts, and ambiverts) highlight the strengths of their own self-identified temperament. Some examples of responses to this question include those from ambiverts:

- I am an ambivert, so when I need my space, I take it, and when there has to be team work, we do it together.
- Being an ambivert, I make lots of bonds and friendships with my co actors and directors. I also become a good actor by working on myself.

From extroverts:

- Sometimes it gets tough to find the "silent" introverted aspects of my character when I am such an extroverted person.
- Being an extrovert makes going from cast to cast and forming new friendships and bonds easy and exciting, and makes me look forward to reuniting with my cast every day, instead of having to brace myself for that social environment. However, I do not think it affects my literal acting work in the preparation and performance of my character.

From introverts:

- I sometimes need more time, especially during show weeks, to decompress after intense interactions.
- As a more introverted actor, it can make me anxious to try new things on the spot. However, if it is a scene or class I am more confident in already or I trust my classmates, the anxiety is lessened.
- My introversion makes me hesitant if I feel unprepared. It can also hold me back in social situations that limit my experience in life, giving me more fear of being wrong in the rehearsal room.

- Sometimes it is hard to make yourself work if you feel socially drained, but you do it anyway because that is what you are training for.
- Being around a large cast makes me feel uncomfortable and unimportant. Especially if everyone is loud and talking over each other. I like to hear each person speak and have an intention.
- I sometimes have to remind myself it is okay to put myself out there and take big risks.
- It can feel difficult to keep up with all the extroverts. Their ability to charge amidst people gives them a great advantage, especially in shows that have large casts.
- I am more comfortable around my cast or group depending on how well I know them or how much time I have spent with them.
- In a new crowd, I initially don't feel comfortable, but bit by bit I start to feel able to act.
- I prefer to work alone until performance because dealing with people can be draining.
- It was something I had to consciously address in acting classes and auditions. Once I was in the process, my introversion felt like a strength.[5]

The variety of responses from introverts, extroverts, and ambiverts all display a keen self-awareness of who they are, what they need, and how they operate. We shared a majority of introverted responses, as that is the focus of this book. Many of the struggles mentioned by the introverts in the survey will be covered in upcoming chapters.

ACTOR TRAINING

Question #13: Do You Believe Current Actor Training Favors Extroverted or Introverted Students?
In our most pointed question so far, we sought to examine if there was an implicit and/or explicit bias related to favoring extroversion in actor training, and the results were overwhelming. An astounding 95% of introverts, 90% of extroverts, and 88% of ambiverts selected current actor training favors extroverted actors. Let's restate the fact that all types of actors in our survey overwhelmingly believe current actor training benefits extroverts. That staggering statistic could encourage many educators to re-examine their approaches to training in the classroom. In the upcoming

section, we will showcase methods that favor extroverts and offer solutions for creating actor training with parity for all learners.

Question #14 and Question #15
We asked our survey respondents to choose the most extroverted and introverted aspects of actor training. While the examples were overwhelmingly divided between improv for extroverts and analysis for introverts, the respondents' follow-up responses offered further examples of what activities, and even some methodologies, they felt were exclusionary in the acting studio.

Extroverted Aspects of Actor Training:

- There are times in acting classes where everyone is forced to improvise in front of everyone else, and if you don't, you are seen as not fully participating. It takes a lot of energy for me to improvise, and if I am not full of energy on any given day, I find participating in that activity difficult.
- Actors are asked to make changes on the spot, which is something we will see in callbacks in the professional world as well, but it can be jarring to do a scene/song differently without having time to process a note.
- We are expected to build ensemble and close, warm relationships immediately.
- Doing artistic work in front of an audience before feeling prepared.
- Giving feedback in class in a bold, charismatic way without much mental preparation or reflection time.
- Making big physical choices.
- Physical touch and treating someone as an intimate partner when you have just met.
- The studio favors those who volunteer and speak up.
- You are forced to be silly, awkward, and not polished. Those moments are totally vulnerable; you are asked to be different in front of a group.
- Everything is loud as hell all the time. While I've been able to break the mold, it is often the loud and quirky people who are often the ones cheered on by their peers … A quirky/energetic/silly actor who is unfocused gets applauded for getting up in front of a class while a focused person is seen as no fun.

- Actor training relies so heavily on the willingness to fail, but if the environment hasn't been built up to support each person, it can quickly become toxic. An actor may be willing to fail, just not in front of their peers.
- You have to be in the room, interact, aim to understand, and work, not just with another character, but with another actor. This is the extroverted essence.[6]

As you can glean, these responses cover a large swath of actor training, from creating instant relationships when introverts have not had the necessary preparation time, to the pressure to "make big choices," to asking introverts to act silly when their reasoning skills make them ask, "Why?"

Introverted Aspects of Actor Training:

- I love the internal reflection used in Stanislavski to draw out emotions you have already felt. You have to look inside yourself and recall past events that only you experienced; no one else can tell you what you felt in that moment.
- We are often told to work on our scenes and songs outside of class, which gives introverts a chance to try new things without an audience.
- Script analysis and character development are very personal and often begin with an individual rather than a group. Though some of these ideas are shared with the collective, they are conceived individually.
- Research and character development. Reading of source materials and history and discovering backstories for complex characters.
- Warming up and preparing for a rehearsal or performance can be invigorating.
- The focus on inner monologue and justification for the internal character
- Being able to look at yourself and admit your faults and work on them. And truly push yourself to be more vulnerable
- Being self-aware and taking care not only of your body, but also your mind, your thoughts, and overall wellbeing ... This awareness requires introspection.
- Good acting training balances out introversion and extroversion. It addresses intuitive and subtle ways of transforming. It favors allowing yourself to be changed by the material rather than imposing yourself on the material; this is a more introverted place to be, and a better place for the actor to work from.

- Acting is getting to know your character; the best way to do that is to be alone with them.[7]

In these responses, introverts offer numerous examples that align with solo research and preparation that allows for time to delve deeply into their character. As mentioned in Chap. 2, this is a strength of the introvert.

Question #16: What Is the Part of an Acting Class You Look Forward to Most?
In this question, we wanted to see if introverts had a preference for learning within the acting classroom. The results seen in Table 4.1 are revealing, with introverts favoring solitary activities like script and character analysis. The extroverts tend to prefer to work in groups.

Question #17: What Do You Feel When Asked to Improvise in a Class or in a Rehearsal? (0 = No Stress and 10 = Very Stressed)

The respondents were then asked to gauge their level of stress in relation to this acting classroom staple where actors must come up with dialogue and have little to no pre-planning. Table 4.2 reveals that 43% of introverts chose greater stress levels (numbers 8–10) related to improvisation. Only 10.8% of extroverts acknowledged higher stress related to improvisational activities.

Question #18: What Strategies Have You Employed to Find Success in the Classroom Related to Extroversion or Introversion?
In this question, we were seeking concrete ways to assist with creating parity within the acting studio space. Patterns regarding self-awareness, perseverance, and trust quickly emerged. The following suggestions consider

Table 4.1 Question #16

	Introverts	Extroverts	Ambiverts
Warm-up and improv exercises	6%	14%	8%
Script and character analysis	45%	23%	28%
Coaching in front of others	13%	20%	15%
Working with a partner	15%	18%	26%
Presenting final work	16%	14%	14%
Working in a group	5%	26%	8%

Table 4.2   Question #17

	Introverts	Extroverts	Ambiverts
0 (No stress)	1.7%	2.7%	3.7%
1	5%	5.4%	7.5%
2	5%	16.2%	12.7%
3	10.7%	10.8%	9%
4	6.6%	13.5%	9%
5	12.4%	18.9%	10.4%
6	7.4%	13.5%	8.2%
7	8.3%	8.1%	9.7%
8	12.4%	5.4%	11.25%
9	13.2%	2.7%	9.7%
10 (much stress)	17.4%	2.7%	9%

the strengths of both temperaments and mirror some of the ideas and strategies we share within the upcoming educational chapters:

- Trust the process. Trust that everyone in the room is feeling the same way. There is no reason to be afraid.
- Assuring myself that my voice is worthwhile and I know what I'm talking about
- Prepare what I need outside of class to adapt to what is being required in class
- For extroverted classrooms, I find success by letting go of the idea of people judging me and learning to play in the space and revel in the feedback. In introverted classrooms, I take the time we are given by ourselves to focus and recharge.
- The most critical elements to growing as an actor are learning to listen and learning to tolerate taking risks, and there is no better way to develop this than learning improv. Especially for introverts who might be averse to social risk-taking, or for extroverts who might not listen as well to their partners.
- As an introvert, I try to work with people I have not worked with before, that way I am getting out of my comfort zone. As an actor, your comfort zone can blind you from discovery and creation.
- I find comfort in the fact that my classes are a safe space, and that everyone is probably feeling the same way. I won't get the results I want if I don't push myself

- Improv alone can still be scary, but as long as I have fellow actors to help out, it comes down to trust.
- I've ended up as an actor because it gets me out of my own head, and out of my own little world, to create characters and worlds collaboratively. As soon as it's over, I'm back to my retiring self. But in the classroom or rehearsal or on stage, I look forward to being fearless. That's my chance to move forward as an artist.
- Get to know your peers. Once you know the people you are working with, it takes a lot of fear away. You know you can be silly because you know the people around you will also let go and have fun.
- As a teacher, I try to find ways to honor both extroverts and introverts. I allow a little more room and space for the introverts (as I am one myself!). I also sometimes go around the circle and ask for a response from everyone. Sometimes introverts want to speak but need to be invited.
- Learn how to wear both hats. Sometimes extroversion gets the job done and sometimes it's introversion. Actors certainly benefit from experiencing both perspectives. This helps make them diverse learners and portray genuine characters on stage.[8]

This last response points to the inclusive practices called for in this book where both introverts and extroverts are necessary for success in training. This respondent typifies the balanced and fair approach for creating a studio where the work of both types of learners is valued.

PROFESSIONAL LIFE

The next set of questions regarding rehearsal and performance can affect both students and professional actors. We did not divide up responses related to professional or student actors in this section; it seemed unnecessary, as most actor training programs mimic professional standards related to auditions, rehearsals, and other activities.

Question #19: How Do You Like to Work in Rehearsal? Pre-Planned Choices or Create Choices in the Room?
The introverts responded, identifying that 59% preferred creating choices in the room. We would assume that introverts (mirroring trends from the past questions) would more likely choose "pre-planned choices," since they were spending so much time in their solo analysis. We then realized

the language related to "pre-planned choices" could have a negative connotation, since it is supposedly antithetical to an actor's goal of "being in the moment." So, with that in mind, the unexpected introverts' percentage makes more sense. Additionally, 72% of extroverts and 68% of ambiverts also chose "Create choices in the room."

Question #20: Ensemble-Building Exercises Cause (0) No Stress or (10) Much Stress
In this question (Table 4.3), we were again testing the concept of ensemble-building, team, or group activities. As more fully explained later in this book, these traditional, and often mandatory, group activities can sometimes leave introverts feeling undervalued. In this table, we were most interested in the two-thirds of extroverts who chose no or minimal stress (numbers 0–3) in this question. This vast difference between introverts and extroverts clearly shows that temperament in the classroom has an impact on actor training.

Question #21: When Working in an Ensemble Setting, What Do You Do When a Director Asks for One or More People to Take Charge of the Group?

In Table 4.4 you can note the variety of options respondents had to choose from related to this question. The extroverts' column reveals much of what could be thought of as the "extrovert ideal," whereby the loudest and first to volunteer are rewarded for that behavior.

Table 4.3 Question #20

	Introverts	*Extroverts*	*Ambiverts*
0 (no stress)	4.7%	5.1%	9.6%
1	14%	30.8%	14.1%
2	10.1%	33.3%	17.0%
3	15.5%	5.1%	11.9%
4	10.1%	5.1%	9.6%
5	10.9%	5.1%	12.6%
6	10.9%	5.1%	5.9%
7	5.4%	7.7%	6.7%
8	3.9%	0%	4.4%
9	2.3%	0%	4.4%
10 (much stress)	12.4%	2.6%	3.7%

Table 4.4 Question #21

	Introverts	Extroverts	Ambiverts
Volunteer immediately	22%	49%	25%
Volunteer to help but not lead	46%	45%	56%
Avoid eye contact	14%	0%	8%
Stand in the back and wait to be asked to join	18%	6%	10%

Question #22: What Do You Do During Breaks in Rehearsal?
In Table 4.5 you will note the variety of options respondents had to choose from related to the time spent in rehearsal where the focus was not on the craft of acting but rather personal time during mandated breaks. In the rehearsal chapter, there are strategies employed by some of our interviewees that can shed more light on this data. However, the percentage (62%) of extroverts who relax and socialize, in comparison to the top choice of introverts, which involved sitting alone and reviewing notes, elucidates the differences between the way these groups approach the rehearsal process.

Question #23: What Is the Part of Rehearsal You Look Forward to the Most?
This question (Table 4.6) was created to see if there was a major difference in the way introverts and extroverts approached the rehearsal process. What we discovered was that even greater than the differences between these two personality traits was the idea that most actors are possibly more "open to new experiences" or openness related to one of the Big Five personality traits. An actor's connection to openness is a theory posited by one of our psychology contributors and makes sense, since people with a high level of openness are often described as creative, imaginative, and curious—all traits often used to describe actors. As you can see, all actors, no matter the classification, gravitated to the "New choices and discoveries" option.

Question #24: What Part of the Performance Do You Look Forward to Most?
Similar to past questions, the options were limited but did contain some interesting aspects related to introversion (Table 4.7). It is clear that the first choice for introverts ("The discoveries made over a long run") matches their analytical bent. Similarly, the extroverts' first choice ("Working with fellow actors") also matches what is generally believed about their personality. The nearly identical percentages in relation to the

Table 4.5   Question #22

	Introverts	Extroverts	Ambiverts
Immediately go to your phone	12%	6%	9%
Sit alone and review notes	33%	19%	22%
Network with others	1%	11%	6%
Ask questions in private	7%	0%	6%
Leave the space or look for isolation	20%	2%	9%
Relax and socialize	26%	62%	49%

Table 4.6   Question #23

	Introverts	Extroverts	Ambiverts
Table work	9%	13%	5%
Blocking	11%	2%	7%
Tech and dress rehearsals	14%	15%	11%
New choices and discoveries	55%	49%	57%
Socializing	0%	8%	5%
Creating an ensemble	11%	13%	15%

Table 4.7   Question #24

	Introverts	Extroverts	Ambiverts
Opening night	3%	4%	5%
The energy of the audience	30%	34%	36%
The stakes of performance	9%	6%	10%
The discoveries made over a long run	31%	19%	21%
Working with fellow actors	26%	38%	28%

energy of the audience should dispel any thoughts that introverted actors can't connect or relate to strangers in an audience, but rather thrive, like ambiverts and extroverts, in front of a crowd.

Question #25: What Strategies Have You Created to Assist in Success During Rehearsal and Performance Related to Extroversion or Introversion?
Many of the respondents' useful and varied answers to this question are contained in a later chapter on rehearsals.

Question #26: Before an Audition, How Do You Behave/Interact with Others Auditioning?
The results of this question show the stark differences between introverted and extroverted actors. The percentage (3%) of introverts who engage, socialize, and network at auditions is very similar to the percentage (only 6%) of extroverts who actively avoid others (Table 4.8). These differences offer clear examples of the different ways in which introverted and extroverted actors operate in a shared audition space.

Question #27: Networking with Others at Auditions Causes (0) No Stress or (10) Great Stress?
In Table 4.9, you can see a steady rise in stress for introverts as the numbers in the table grow. This is a clear indicator that, for introverts, networking and stress are inextricably linked in many professional settings. Look closely at number 10, where a majority of introverts identified themselves as having great stress, an experience shared by zero respondents who self-identified as extroverts.

Question #28: Auditioning in a New Environment for New People Causes (0) No Stress or (10) Great Stress?
Auditions are a naturally stressful situation where a job is on the line, so some amount of stress is expected. You can see introverts, extroverts, and ambiverts alike all acknowledge this fact. But if you look at the higher numbers related to great stress (numbers 8–10), 44.8% of introverts rate their stress in these categories, while only 16% of extroverts experienced these high levels. Despite the wide fluctuation across all numbers here, the greater stress levels reveal a relationship between introverts and stress at auditions (Table 4.10).

Question #29: What Strategies Have You Employed to Aid in Your Success at Auditions Related to Extroversion or Introversion?
In this question, our goal was to gain ideas to help actors in a naturally stressful situation. Many of the respondents' answers to this question are contained in a later chapter on auditioning.

Table 4.8 Question #26

	Introverts	Extroverts	Ambiverts
Engage, socialize, network	3%	36%	10%
Casual greetings and work on your material	66%	58%	74%
Actively avoid	31%	6%	16%

Table 4.9 Question #27

	Introverts	Extroverts	Ambiverts
0 (no stress)	2%	6.4%	6.4%
1	2%	6.4%	4.8%
2	4.1%	19.1%	8.4%
3	6.1%	25.5%	10.2%
4	6.1%	6.4%	9.6%
5	11.6%	14.9%	18.7%
6	12.2%	6.4%	9%
7	14.3%	4.3%	10.8%
8	15%	8.5%	15.1%
9	6.1%	2.1%	3.0%
10 (much stress)	20.4%	0%	4.8%

Table 4.10 Question #28

	Introverts	Extroverts	Ambiverts
0 (no stress)	0.7%	2%	1.8%
1	3.5%	2%	6.1%
2	6.3%	10%	9.8%
3	2.8%	6%	9.2%
4	6.3%	12%	7.4%
5	14%	20%	13.5%
6	9.1%	22%	7.4%
7	12.6%	10%	12.3%
8	18.2%	12%	16%
9	10.5%	2%	6.1%
10 (much stress)	16.1%	2%	10.4%

CONCLUSION

The final two questions in the survey offered a chance for introverts and extroverts to share the struggles and successes they have experienced in relation to their personal self-identified temperament. Many of the comments featured the continued focus on the elements of acting that seem the most connected to each temperament: analysis and connecting to a partner for the introverts; spontaneous risk-taking and fearlessness for the extroverts. Refreshingly, a cross-section of these comments revealed not only an appreciation of the strengths of each temperament but also how both can be used to create even more successful work. Many of the extroverted comments highlighted an enjoyment of improvisation, an immediate commitment to the ensemble, and the boldness of their (extroverts') acting choices among their main successes while admitting an admiration for the quiet reflection often observed in their introverted peers. Extroverts noted their personal acting challenges in examples like always wanting to talk first in class and a lack of prolonged focus. Introverted actors found the most success in tablework, analysis, and becoming another, and often praised the energy and bravery of their more extroverted cast and classmates. Introverted respondents most often reflected on fear of judgment and failure, as well as pressure to be more energetic and social, among their biggest challenges. Comments provided by the introverted actors also revealed the importance and usefulness of stretching outside of a personal level of comfort, and the introverts admitted once this risk was taken, the reward was often invaluable to the acting work.

The overall results were clear. The through line of our book was created from this survey, where a majority of introverts gravitated to transformative acting, where they felt safe in playing someone unlike themselves. They preferred solo activities like script analysis, but could also thrive in more social situations. Introverts believed actor training, especially elements like improvisation and ensemble building, caused more stress than other solo activities. Other professional necessities like networking and auditioning were more stressful for introverts compared to extroverts and ambiverts. Quite clearly, being an introvert has an impact on being an actor.

Most importantly, our survey, filled out by hundreds of actors of all personality types, revealed a bias within actor training, where almost all respondents noted that extroverts are favored. This important pedagogical examination will be featured in the second part of this book related to actor training.

NOTES

1. "Are You an Introvert or Extrovert?" Quiet Revolution. Accessed November 22, 2019. https://www.quietrev.com/the-introvert-test/
2. "Extroversion Introversion Test." Psychology Today. Sussex Publishers. Accessed November 22, 2019. https://www.psychologytoday.com/us/tests/personality/extroversion-introversion-test
3. Anonymous respondents. "Introversion Survey." Qualtrics survey. Michigan State University, 2019

4. Anonymous respondents. Survey.
5. Anonymous respondents. Survey.
6. Anonymous respondents. Survey.
7. Anonymous respondents. Survey.
8. Anonymous respondents. Survey.

REFERENCES

"Are You an Introvert or Extrovert?" Quiet Revolution. Accessed November 22, 2019. https://www.quietrev.com/the-introvert-test/.

"Extroversion Introversion Test." Psychology Today. Sussex Publishers. Accessed November 22, 2019. https://www.psychologytoday.com/us/tests/personality/extroversion-introversion-test.

Anonymous respondents. "Introversion survey." Qualtrics survey. Michigan State University, 2019.

Training and the Introverted Actor

CHAPTER 5

Temperament-Inclusive Learning: Essential Strategies for Educators

A Brief History of the Quiet Schools Network

In the wake of the publication of Susan Cain's bestselling book in 2012, *Quiet: The Power of Introverts in a World that Can't Stop Talking* (Crown, 2013), she went on to co-found a "Quiet Revolution."[1] This mission-based company is designed to "unlock the power of introverts for the benefit of us all" and to "create a world where introverts are celebrated for their powerful contributions and, more importantly, for who they are." One of the co-authors of this book, Dr. Heidi Kasevich, co-founded the inaugural Quiet Schools Network, dedicated to the Quiet Revolution's mission for children: "Quiet kids can and must be raised to know their strengths."

The Quiet Schools Network Quiet Ambassador experience was designed to train educators in temperament diversity so they could work with their colleagues to: disrupt extrovert bias; enhance engagement, creativity, and kindness; foster the ability to communicate with presence and compassion; and tap into the power of quiet leadership.[2] The goal was to shift cultural norms in communities about what it means to be an introverted student and leader, and to foster inclusive cultures in which both introverts and extroverts can thrive.

A temperament-inclusive classroom is characterized by a balance between collaborative learning and independent work, group work, and solitude. It is one that prizes quality over quantity of speech, deep listening, reflective pauses, and writing as varied forms of classroom

© The Author(s) 2020
R. Roznowski et al., *The Introverted Actor*,
https://doi.org/10.1007/978-3-030-41607-2_5

engagement. By embracing a broader idea of classroom engagement, educators can begin to create opportunities for both silence and speech in the context of any lesson. The goal is to shift participation structures to value silence and not to assume that silence connotes compliance, insecurity, resistance, or boredom.

When shifting cultural norms around solitude in the classroom—in the form of short, reflective pauses, longer periods of independent work, or deep listening as a form of engagement—it is important for an educator to discern the energizing silence of the engaged participant from the silencing that may be the product of complex racial, gender, and/or cultural dynamics in the classroom. As we cultivate a culture of quiet in our schools, by balancing solitude with collaboration, we honor the learning styles of a third to a half of our students, who are likely to fall on the introverted side of the introvert-extrovert spectrum.

Promote Self-Awareness

Being true to our temperaments allows us to grow and expand, to explore our passions, and, ultimately, to serve those around us in ways that maximize our potential and impact. LA actor and writer Sean Patrick McGowan enlightens us on self-awareness: "The number one thing is to pay attention to how your body responds and how your psychology responds to all the different circumstances you are in. The more you pay attention to where your motivation comes from … then you can have a great respect and appreciation for who you are."[3]

Note that understanding of the self leads to more profound connections with others. If you do not fundamentally understand self through the lens of temperament, how can you, as an introvert, be empathic with an extrovert who craves social stimulation as a restorative activity, when you yearn for the solitary opposite? Or, how can you, as an extrovert, be empathic with an introvert who needs time to weigh options before making decisions?

Administer a Personality Preferences Indicator

Invite students to examine their sensitivity to stimulation and rewards by taking the following informal Personality Preferences Indicator:

Introversion and extroversion shape how we communicate, manage our energy, and make decisions. You can engage in a personal journey of self-discovery to understand how your neurobiology shapes your temperament by thinking about the following five preferences affiliated with your hardwiring as an introvert or extrovert. What are your preferences?

Introvert preferences—Check as many as apply to you:

- "I thrive on one-on-one conversations."
- "I need time to think. Please don't call on me."
- "I'm drained. I feel tired after a couple of hours at a party."
- "I am the first to claim a cubby in the library. I work best on my own."
- "I consider options before making decisions!"

Extrovert preferences—Check as many as apply to you:

- "I thrive on group work."
- "I process my ideas out loud. Please call on me."
- "I'm drained! What shall we do together after work/school?"
- "I need people nearby to get my work done. The open plan library is perfect for me."
- "Just do it!"

The importance here is to help your students explore who they are through an understanding of their preferences—which are connected to their inborn temperament—so they can feel empowered to be themselves. Don't hesitate to say: "Being true to our temperaments allows us to grow and expand, to explore our passions, and, ultimately, to serve those around us in ways that maximize our potential and impact." Further, emphasize that it is completely "normal" to feel more introverted in some areas and more extroverted in others.

Personal Responses: "Who Am I?"

We have interviewed scores of actors, and so many of them were eager to offer commentary about their own preferences, strengths, and challenges. We hope they will inspire you to ask yourself and your students: "Who am I?"

Here are some points to help your acting students consider their areas of success as related to the spectrum of introversion and extroversion:

- Introvert: I have good insight into characters. I can put myself inside the story easily and empathize with the characters and relationships in the play. My reflective, quiet side allows me to be the ultimate observer. Being introverted has helped me focus on layers, subtleties, and depth of feeling. Introversion helps me look for opportunities to share my feelings in structured ways.
- Ambivert: Script analysis, research, and privately developing a character come more easily at first. I take time to read and research. Once I'm in rehearsal, I feel free to make choices and try out new ideas. I've learned to harness my extroversion/introversion to collaborate and work with other actors to grow. Cultivating these habits takes conscious effort.
- Extrovert: I feel free and uninhibited in rehearsal and make lots of choices with no concern about what others think. I respond to my scene partner immediately and stay in the moment. I feed off the energy of the ensemble and look forward to group warm-ups. After the show, I need to go out with the cast or friends to wind down and relax in social energy.

Here are some points to help your students consider areas of challenge as an actor related to the spectrum of introversion and extroversion:

- Introvert: I feel lost being around people all the time or having to rely on others. I have difficulty initially meeting cast members and creating bonds with them. Sometimes it's hard for me to make choices when there's a lot of noise/movement going. I am uncomfortable in ensemble exercises early in the rehearsal process. These challenges tend to shut me down rather than awaken my creativity. I'm continuing to work at becoming more comfortable and open to processes like this.
- Ambivert: I experience some fear of being physically vulnerable. I can bare my emotions, but should I be asked to suddenly improv something, I get uncomfortable and anxious.
- Extrovert: I am so eager to jump in and make a suggestion that I don't always give others the chance to go first. I don't spend much time reviewing notes or analyzing choices, relying on those discoveries to come to me in rehearsal. I am not as productive working by myself and need the energy of others, so isolated research is a challenge.

With this range of comments, let's remember the fundamental intro-vert/extrovert concept of managing energy. You can begin the semester by simply asking your students: "What gives you energy? What saps your energy? How do you recharge your batteries?"

CELEBRATE INTROVERTED STRENGTHS IN ANECDOTAL COMMENTS

Experience with the Quiet Schools Network revealed that educators often overlooked—or neglected to celebrate—the strengths of their introverted students, even after they administered personality assessments.

Let's begin with a brief summary of such strengths. Introverts tend to think before they speak. They are likely to be contemplative, mild-mannered, and cautious decision-makers. Psychologist Adam Grant asserts that taking the time to carefully weigh options and not rush a decision can benefit all members of a team and lead to better, more creative outcomes.[4] Secondly, introverts tend to be excellent problem-solvers and deep think-ers. They have incredible abilities of focus and concentration, coupled with a desire to master complicated tasks. According to Jim Collins, such unassuming, humble individuals become great leaders precisely because they possess authentic conviction for a particular mission; they are not "in it" for personal fame or glory.[5] Finally, introverts tend to be good listeners, which builds trust and enables leaders to actualize the potential of team members. Deep listening is a valuable leadership skill that can produce remarkable outcomes with proactive team members.

The following are some examples of temperament-inclusive anecdotal comments that spotlight introverted strengths, promote introverted efforts to step outside their (introverts') comfort zones, and honor their need to recharge in solitude[6]:

- Strength—Emphasizing introverted leadership strengths:

River is deliberate in his thoughts and actions. When he says some-thing, everyone listens because they know he has chosen his words with care. Justine is an active listener: she captures ideas, ask questions, and restates issues to confirm understanding.

- Stretch—Promoting meaningful and manageable flex goals:

George has made a conscious effort to look at others while speaking instead of focusing on the passage from the text.

- Restore—Honoring the need to recharge during the school day:

Although Meadow is in high demand to join her friends during lunch, she often chooses to read by herself so that she can participate more fully in her afternoon classes. Ruben can often be found with books during recess, using time to recharge for the afternoon activities.

This "Strength-Stretch-Restore" approach to writing anecdotal comments empowers introverted students to take ownership of their learning and contribute to the classroom dynamic—on their own terms.[7]

MAKE TIME FOR DELIBERATE PRACTICE

In 1993 K. Anders Ericsson famously coined the term "deliberate practice" to describe the focused, solo practice that can lead to mastery of any subject or activity.[8] Ericsson's research found that the top athletes, musicians, chess players and academics don't excel because they are any smarter or more genetically gifted than their competitors (with the exception of genes for height and body size). Rather, gaining independent mastery involves careful reflection on what worked and what didn't work during practice time. Moreover, such practice is best conducted alone.

Think of a piano player focused on scales, a violinist untiringly running the same tricky musical passage, or a swimmer practicing the flip turn in the pool. Each one of these examples shows a dogged determination to master a concept or moment in order to become better through solo activity. And introverts thrive on doing much of their work alone.

You can support your introverted students by setting aside ample time for alone time, helping them identify a role that is not too easy, but not too challenging, and offering feedback at regular intervals.

Here is a simple "deliberate practice" checklist to share with your students:

- Set a clear goal for a challenge that is just hard enough, but not so hard as to lead to a sense of discouragement.
- Isolate, or "chunkify" skills and tasks. Break your long journey down into a series of manageable goals.[9]

- Develop mental representations of superior performance. These are mental tools that improve your ability to think about building your potential.[10]
- Practice just beyond your comfort zone. Limit the amount of time for intense concentration and practice to one hour per day. It is advisable to start with a maximum of 15–20 minutes.
- Obtain immediate and constant feedback so that modifications are continuous.[11]
- Constantly track your progress.

Provide Support for Calculated Stretch Goals

We need to intentionally teach our students about what it means to step outside their comfort zones, when it makes sense to do so, and the benefits and dangers of such personality-stretching. Educators, help your students set realistic goals, for a single class or a full semester, in whichever way seems manageable and achievable. Without such realistic goals, your students may shut down or burn out, and, in some extreme cases, even experience anxiety or depression. Begin by inviting them to create a *comfort meter* as a way to assess areas of their lives in which they can reasonably stretch without going too far outside their comfort zone. This *meter* can serve as a visual organizer and record of their efforts. It involves a simple table with three categories: "comfortable," "stretch," and "stressful."

Explain to students that they are going to think about things in different areas of their lives and categorize them according to their comfort level: activities in the "comfortable section" are things that are enjoyable and stress-free; activities in the "stretch" category are things they try to avoid when they can; activities in the "stressful" category cause the most anxiety and are often strenuously avoided. You can assign numbers to each category as well, to help students rate activities from 1 to 10: *comfortable* ranges from 1 to 3, *stretch* ranges from 4 to 6, and *stressful* ranges from 7 to 10. Have students individually brainstorm and record activities in each of the categories. Then, they can discuss with a partner, who becomes a "stretch buddy." The ultimate goal is to provide a safe place for students to gain the self-awareness and confidence needed to be able to comfortably stretch and even, over time, to be able to move their "stressful" goals into the "stretch" category.

Let's take the case of the introverted actor, who strives to engage in a highly social discipline without experiencing undue frustration, self-doubt, or anxiety. Broadway actor Matthew Marks reveals the critical role of "stretch buddies" in his life as he strove to navigate the demands of the business—while still feeling authentic and energized: "In my early twenties, I tried to be big and funny like everyone else. I ended up saying things I didn't mean just to get a laugh or feel included. In three years of therapy, I've been working on being myself, finding the few people that get me, and keeping them close."[12] It is important to emphasize here that compromising authenticity for the sake of social status is often a risk for our students, and the simple sharing of such stories can be an empowering part of the process of learning how to adapt with greater ease.

Overall, you can help your introverted and extroverted students to explore challenges in ways that honor their true selves by inviting them to continually engage in the process of setting stretch goals. Such goals can be set in class for engaging in an exercise, listening during a group discussion, or volunteering to share scene work. Further, in the rehearsal hall, leadership might also take the form of directing the cast in a vocal warmup, inviting others to speak first, holding questions until others have spoken, or making a bold new choice for a character. Knowing when your students are attempting to push themselves to explore behaviors outside their natural temperament sets the stage for the growth that comes with feelings of safety and constructive feedback.

Use the Long Runway Approach

Inspired by the acceleration time it takes for a plane to take off, and the gradual speed and momentum it requires to do so, the Long Runway approach provides preparation time for an introverted student to explore new roles and participate in the demands of the classroom.[13]

An important way of providing more introverted students with a Long Runway is to pair them with "bridge friends," or close intimates with whom they thrive. Discerning when the time is right for an introverted student to move outside his comfort zone to engage in a new activity with a different partner is a delicate and often difficult decision. When in doubt, keep the introverted student—especially if he seems stressed or anxious—with his bridge friend for support. The goal is to have students feel challenged, but not too scared or stressed: on an anxiety scale of 1–10, aim for 4–6. "Don't force, don't quit" is the temperament-inclusive educator's motto.

Educators can also fill the syllabus with details of what is happening each day so introverted actors in the class have more time to prepare. This offers the added bonus of keeping all students on track. Also, it is helpful to end each class with a clear explanation of what will happen in the next class, including examples of any exercises or elements that require immediacy in terms of participation. Inform your introverted students to use their processing time to prepare themselves for the work, anticipating how they might contribute to each exercise. Annotate your readings to know what questions you might ask, or prepare the points you'd like to contribute to the discussion.

SET FOUNDATION FOR GROUP WORK THAT WORKS

"Collaborative overload" is increasingly the norm in today's schools. How can we protect introverted kids and teachers from burnout?

In a typical Western classroom design, we are expected to do our best work in project-based groups, deploying brainstorming strategies from the 1950s, designed to spark creativity and productivity in a judgment-free zone of human interaction. Not only are typical "free for all" brainstorming groups dominated by fear of judgment and pressure to conform, but research shows that only three people in a group of six to eight tend to do 70% of the talking.

What we need is a paradigm shift in how we think about idea generation and evaluation—from brainstorming to brainwriting, flowing back and forth between solitude and collaboration. For instance, class work can start with a period of silent reflection, where team members generate solutions to a problem alone, using as many sticky notes as possible. Next, team members are invited to share their notes on the nearby wall, anonymously if possible. Once ideas are grouped together, a conversation about idea evaluation begins. Which idea(s) makes the most sense and why? Be sure that everyone gets the chance to speak. Build reflective pausing into the conversation, use a "Round Robin" participation technique, and offer those who are prone to speaking with just *three* participation "tokens." Once used up, they must make room for others to speak.

Further, when trying to accomplish tasks, it is critical to choreograph teams so that a balance of introverts and extroverts translates to real results. According to an article titled "Extraversion and Performance in the Perceptual Maze Test," researchers found that when working on tasks alone, extroversion is associated with faster, less accurate, and less reflective performance, while introversion is associated with slower performance, but far more accuracy.[14] When introverts and extroverts work together, the group performs better than when extroverts work exclusively with other extroverts.

OFFER SPACE AND TIME FOR QUIET

Our thresholds for stimulation from our environments define us as introverts and extroverts. Introverts need time alone, in quiet zones, to recharge their batteries. How can educators make sure this happens? A culture where headphones are routinely worn is a good beginning, but we can do better than that.

Experience from the Quiet Schools Network suggests that a "Quiet" zone in the cafeteria can serve as a space for recovery time for our introverted students, who often feel the pressure to socialize in hectic, crowded, noisy dining halls. Let's consider what two Quiet Schools Ambassadors accomplished for their introverted students—in the space of just a few months.[15] The first created a so-called Peaceful Lunch. During each lunch period, a group of approximately eighteen kids sat in a corner of the dining hall and enjoyed time alone to simply eat, doodle on the paper provided, or talk quietly to another child nearby. Out of 900 students, 400 signed up. Another Ambassador created "Quiet Zones" in their classroom. This educator had great success with "Cozy Corners," adorned with comfortable cushions and mindful coloring books, and "Zen Zones," designed to promote stretching to calming music and writing in gratitude journals.

The need is similar in university acting classes. Ensemble work and improvisation rehearsals are notoriously loud spaces. Michigan State University Assistant Professor of Acting and Improv Sarah Hendrickson admits, "[The noise] can be challenging, and it can cause sensory overload to be in a room where everyone is going and going. There have been times when I have shut down and physically cannot speak because I'm so overwhelmed. But I use coping strategies. Hopefully the ensemble is open to hearing what everybody needs."[16] The most effective improv is about creating an ensemble where quiet time is valued just as much as boisterous time.

Dr. Lisa Kaenzig has studied the noisy classroom and its effect on the introvert.[17] She notes, "All that noise, all the loudness of the teachers' voices, all those things can over-stimulate [students] because introverts' minds are already so active that all that additional external stimulation is total overload for them." She suggests offering another room where a group can go to work on their own or someplace where a person can leave. Space, time, and quiet all combine to help a director or teacher manage the ensemble and allow all voices to be heard and all learning styles to thrive.

Whether your students are more introverted or extroverted, try asking them to take this thirty-minute silent challenge. The goal is to better understand the power of solitude.

For fifteen minutes: Sit comfortably in a public place with the express purpose of observing human behavior. Notice the subtle differences in posture. The various body centers. The pace. Then begin to create stories about these people. Create a rich biography.

Begin to add another level of awareness about the way you are processing this information. Do your eyes and ideas hop from person to person? Do you stay on one person until they are out of view, creating a vivid "destination" for them? Are you storing these memories for use later or laughing at the way they remind you of a friend? Are you checking your watch or lost in thought? Are you creating their inner monologue, or are you excited to tell others what you observed?

For fifteen minutes: Sit and observe the same public space, but this time, imagine how your observations might be different as an introvert, or an extrovert, as the case may be. How is the experience different when you walk in the shoes of a complementary observer who has different personality strengths?

In order to expand your ability to connect with others, and to have a deeper awareness of the ways in which you interact with the world, do this as often as possible.

Benefits of Solitude for Us All

In our loud, distracted, and often noisy world, we cannot forget the benefits of solitude. In her article "Neuroscience Reveals the Nourishing Benefits That Science Has on Your Brain" (2016) Betsy Mikel[18] cites research by Duke University's Imke Kirste and others (2013)[19] which shows that two hours of silence per day prompts cell development in the hippocampus, the region of the brain associated with the formation of memory. During such still and solitary time, the brain rests quietly. During this time, we are able to deepen our understanding of ourselves by weaving our internal thoughts with outside input. In the process, we discover where and how we fit in.

In the next chapter we examine how these concepts can be directly applied to the acting studio. Here's to making time for quiet in our classrooms, in our rehearsal halls, and in our lives.

NOTES

1. Cain, Susan. "Unlocking the Power of Introverts." Quiet Revolution. Accessed November 22, 2019. https://www.quietrev.com/
2. "The Quiet Ambassador Network." Quiet Revolution. Accessed November 22, 2019. https://www.quietrev.com/the-quiet-ambassador-network/
3. McGowan, Sean Patrick. Personal Interview. 13 April 2019.
4. Whitbourne, Susan Kraus. "Why Introverts Can Be Great Leaders." Psychology Today. 8 Nov. 201
5. Collins, James C. *Good to Great*. London: Random House Business, 2001.
6. "Quiet-Friendly Comment Guide." Quiet Revolution. Accessed December 28, 2019. www.quietrev.com/wp-content/uploads/2018/11/RS-Quiet-Friendly-Comment-Guide.pdf
7. ChildCareExchange.com. Accessed November 22, 2019. https://www.childcareexchange.com/catalog/browse.php
8. Ericsson, K. Anders, Ralf T. Krampe, and Clemens Tesch-Römer. "The Role of Deliberate Practice in the Acquisition of Expert Performance." *Psychological Review* 100, no. 3 (1993): 363–406. https://doi.org/10.1037/0033-295x.100.3.363
9. "The Road to Extraordinary." Quiet Revolution, May 31, 2016. https://www.quietrev.com/the-road-to-extraordinary/
10. Visser, Coert. "Interview with Anders Ericsson." The Progress-Focused Approach. Accessed November 27, 2019. http://www.progressfocused.com/2016/05/interview-with-anders-ericsson.html
11. Anderson, Jenny. "How to Make Your Kid Good at Anything, According to a World Expert on Peak Performance." Quartz. Quartz, March 14, 2017. https://qz.com/915646/how-to-make-your-kid-good-at-anything-according-to-anders-ericsson-an-expert-on-peak-performance-and-originator-of-the-10000-hour-rule/
12. Marks, Matthew. Personal interview. 10 Jan. 2019.
13. Heinz, Amy. "Granting Kids the Time They Need to Socially Succeed." Quiet Revolution, June 20, 2017. https://www.quietrev.com/the-long-runway-granting-kids-the-time-they-need-to-socially-succeed/

14. "Extraversion and performance in the perceptual maze test." *Personality and Individual Differences* Volume 11, Issue 4 (1990) 391–96. https://doi.org/10.1016/0191-8869(90)90221-C.
15. "The Quiet Ambassador Network," Quiet Revolution.
16. Hendrickson, Sarah. Personal interview. 5 May 2019.
17. Kaenzig, Lisa. Personal interview. 15 Dec. 2018.
18. Mikel, Betsy. "Neuroscience Reveals the Nourishing Benefits That Silence Has on Your Brain." Inc.com. Inc., July 11, 2016. https://www.inc.com/betsy-mikel/your-brain-benefits-most-when-you-listen-to-absolutely-nothing-science-says.html
19. Kirste, Imke, Zeina Nicola, Golo Kronenberg, Tara L. Walker, Robert C. Liu, and Gerd Kempermann. "Is Silence Golden? Effects of Auditory Stimuli and Their Absence on Adult Hippocampal Neurogenesis." *Brain Structure and Function* 220, no. 2 (January 2013): 1221–28. https://doi.org/10.1007/s00429-013-0679-3

References

Anderson, Jenny. "How to Make Your Kid Good at Anything, According to a World Expert on Peak Performance." Quartz. Quartz, March 14, 2017. https://qz.com/915646/how-to-make-your-kid-good-at-anything-according-to-anders-ericsson-an-expert-on-peak-performance-and-originator-of-the-10000-hour-rule/.
Cain, Susan. "Unlocking the Power of Introverts." Quiet Revolution. Accessed November 22, 2019. https://www.quietrev.com/.
ChildCareExchange.com. Accessed November 22, 2019. https://www.childcare-exchange.com/catalog/browse.php.
Collins, James C. Good to Great. London: Random House Business, 2001.
Ericsson, K. Anders, Ralf T. Krampe, and Clemens Tesch-Römer. "The Role of Deliberate Practice in the Acquisition of Expert Performance." *Psychological Review* 100, no. 3 (1993): 363–406. https://doi.org/10.1037/0033-295x.100.3.363.
"Extraversion and performance in the perceptual maze test." *Personality and Individual Differences* Volume 11, Issue 4 (1990) 391–96. https://doi.org/10.1016/0191-8869(90)90221-C.
Heinz, Amy. "Granting Kids the Time They Need to Socially Succeed." Quiet Revolution, June 20, 2017. https://www.quietrev.com/the-long-runway-granting-kids-the-time-they-need-to-socially-succeed/.
Hendrickson, Sarah. Personal interview. 5 May 2019.
Kaenzig, Lisa. Personal interview. 15 Dec. 2018.
Kirste, Imke, Zeina Nicola, Golo Kronenberg, Tara L. Walker, Robert C. Liu, and Gerd Kempermann. "Is Silence Golden? Effects of Auditory Stimuli and

Their Absence on Adult Hippocampal Neurogenesis." *Brain Structure and Function* 220, no. 2 (January 2013): 1221–28. https://doi.org/10.1007/s00429-013-0679-3.

Marks, Matthew. Personal interview. 10 Jan. 2019.

McGowan, Sean Patrick. Personal Interview. 13 April 2019.

"Quiet-Friendly Comment Guide." Quiet Revolution. Accessed December 28, 2019. www.quietrev.com/wp-content/uploads/2018/11/RS-Quiet-Friendly-Comment-Guide.pdf.

Mikel, Betsy. "Neuroscience Reveals the Nourishing Benefits That Silence Has on Your Brain." Inc.com. Inc., July 11, 2016. https://www.inc.com/betsy-mikel/your-brain-benefits-most-when-you-listen-to-absolutely-nothing-science-says.html.

"The Quiet Ambassador Network." Quiet Revolution. Accessed November 22, 2019. https://www.quietrev.com/the-quiet-ambassador-network/.

Whitbourne, Susan Kraus. "Why Introverts Can be Great Leaders." Psychology Today. 8 Nov. 2011

"The Road to Extraordinary." Quiet Revolution, May 31, 2016. https://www.quietrev.com/the-road-to-extraordinary/.

Visser, Coert. "Interview with Anders Ericsson." The Progress-Focused Approach. Accessed November 27, 2019. http://www.progressfocused.com/2016/05/interview-with-anders-ericsson.html.

CHAPTER 6

Acting Classroom Design

Participation. Improvisation. Ensemble-building. Theatre games. Presentations. Performances. All are important elements of acting studio training. And all represent highly extroverted activities.

As evidenced in the survey, many actors overwhelmingly believe training methodologies in most current actor-training programs hold an implicit bias in favor of the extroverted actor. The traditional acting classroom features a reliance on improvisation, ensemble building, participation points, and theatrical games, all rewarding novelty and immediacy, putting introverts at a disadvantage, given their propensity for pre-planning and quiet reflection. How can actor educators approach such work in a way that respects all types of learners and still upholds the most basic and necessary elements of teaching the craft? What is the responsibility of the introverted actor to participate in such activities? How can the acting studio be restructured to respect both introverts and extroverts?

These questions and more are part of an ongoing effort to create an acting studio that offers parity so all types of actors can succeed. Current teaching methods used for creative work can be reexamined or modified to offer a level-playing field that allows actors to get the results educators and directors deem necessary. Think of it as the long-standing training debate of "process versus product." The process can be thought of as the introverted actor who thrives on processing time, and the product can be thought of as the extroverted actor who relishes a "just do it" approach. Both are normal, and both have their place in actor education.

© The Author(s) 2020
R. Roznowski et al., *The Introverted Actor*,
https://doi.org/10.1007/978-3-030-41607-2_6

To the Educator

The acting studio can be a noisy place, full of eager actors ready to share their work. It can also be a place for quiet, where students have time for reflection. Have you ever considered the percentage of time in your acting studio that is devoted to quiet? Have you ever discussed introversion in the acting studio or polled student actors to see how they might self-identify? Have you wondered whether traditional training methods value one personality type over another? Many of us teach the way we were taught. And for many of us in the theatre-based classroom, that means modeling behaviors that provide meager provisions for the introvert.

In the article "Positioning the Drama Teacher: Exploring the Power of Identity in Teaching Practices" (2009), author Prue Wales advocates for teachers to objectively examine their own teaching styles to see which types of students their classrooms might inadvertently marginalize and how they might reexamine and adapt their teaching to better empower those individuals.[1] But in order to do this, Wales admits that teachers must first embark on a serious journey of self-reflection, one that frees them from old discourses. As educators, we must consider how our own personality identifications influence how we choose exercises, create lesson plans, and even shape the day-to-day culture of our classrooms. And we could further realize that our own personality and learning styles might favor one type of student while undervaluing another. This marginalization is often done out of habit: the repetition of methods that have "worked" in the past and the inclusion of certain exercises and activities deemed "classic."

In writing this book, the authors met at Michigan State University to observe a week's worth of acting classes, from introductory to graduate-level courses, to examine the ways in which current acting training might benefit from a renovation, all with an eye toward creating a balanced classroom where introverted actors could be heard. Using concepts and methods from the Quiet Schools program, co-author Dr. Heidi Kasevich offered multiple interesting possibilities to achieve this goal.

Reconsidering Warm-ups

Let's begin with how the acting classroom is typically structured. Many acting classes get things started with warm-ups, and while some students will jump up right away to participate, the introverted students might feel uncomfortable from the very beginning of class. Most acting warm-ups involve a combination of physical, mental, and vocal exercises, often done as a group, standing in a circle or some other kind of shared space. These are standard techniques used to begin each acting class, and their purpose is clear and laudable: get students to focus their attention away from other distractions and on the needs of the work; begin thinking creatively and with intention; create an ensemble of shared purpose in the day's lesson. But if we take a step back and examine these techniques, we can also see what group warm-ups usually do not include: processing time (including writing), solo activity, and time for quiet. So, while extroverts gain energy from such large-group social stimulation, introverts find themselves easily drained. The results produced by many standard warm-up practices and activities can be anxiety-inducing, as the introvert is tasked with instant invention. One of the risks of the group warm-up is that it can quickly turn performative, putting pressure on students to "perform" their warm-up and turning the rest of the class into a de facto audience, observing and judging the work.

Consider any of the innumerable, spontaneous, energy-enhancing theatre games where students must create on the spot or quickly recreate or build on the work of another. These games often become more focused on who can come up with the wildest or most ridiculous contribution, make the group laugh the hardest, or stump their classmates and ultimately "win" the game. While shared laughter and play are valuable elements to building an ensemble at any level of actor training, they are not the overall purpose of the group warm-up as traditionally defined. Examine the warm-up exercises you regularly use in your acting classes to find ways where you might include important solo time or adapt a game to provide an introverted actor more time to warm-up. There is always room for a new warm-up, and new exercises need not follow standard participation criteria. Invite your students to consider what they need in order to feel safe, focused, and ready to engage in class. Both introverted and extroverted students can feel valued and empowered through creating their own warm-ups, while allowing for exercises that boost the ownership and creativity of all participants.

Like group warm-ups, ensemble-building exercises also heavily favor the extrovert, and many do not consider the introvert's learning style. Ensemble means a group working together as one, but introverts often do not fully invest in this level of group involvement unless they first feel fully comfortable in the social situation. The level of interactivity in a group setting can be augmented with solo thinking time before returning back to group work. In order to manage success in ensemble building, the teacher may wish to create protocols for check-ins with introverted actors to make sure their voices are heard.

RETHINKING PARTICIPATION

Another standard element of the acting classroom (and, truly, a common component to classes in every discipline) is that of participation. Participation is a graded and weighted contribution to the classroom, sometimes making up as much as 30–50% of the total points in the course, yet it is an almost completely subjective portion of the class. Rubrics for participation are often inconsistent and relative, as the act itself is hard to quantify, define, or evaluate. Some interviewees shared stories of positive tally marks being made for any student who spoke in class and final course grades being significantly reduced due to the negative final tally for lack of verbal responses. Participation points are mostly awarded to those who verbally contribute to class discussions, but these public contributions represent only one form of participation. Nevertheless, it tends to remain an integral part of the acting studio syllabus. How do we consider the important contributions of students who may be engaged in the material—actively listening, taking notes, giving support to their peers, getting ready for a verbal contribution—but who don't fit neatly into a narrow definition of "participation"?

As educators, change begins with one simple consideration: some students speak in order to think, while other students think in order to speak. Sometimes, educators feel nervous or concerned with silence and stillness in the classroom, so they tend to favor the extroverted student who shares ideas aloud as their means for processing the material. But these moments of quiet are actually the most valuable for the introverted students, as they find time to think about the question posed or the scene that was recently performed before being expected to share their ideas with the class. Acknowledging and observing student contributions, beyond talking or the initiation of dialogue, gives educators room to consider other forms of emotive engagement—laughing, smiling, looking at others, nodding, actively listening, taking notes—and these levels of engagement are vital to the classroom dynamic. A forced insistence that every student verbally participates in every exercise before moving on, for example, can keep introverted acting students in a perpetual state of apprehension and might even keep them from truly learning the material because they are more preoccupied with their inevitable turn in front of the class.

This is not to say that introverted students should be excused from these shared exercises. On the contrary, knowing they have the agency to choose when and how they participate might motivate them to find times when they are eager and willing to vocally engage with their more extroverted peers. The distinction seems to be not one of hesitation to perform or of stage fright that prevents the introvert from participating, but a need to prepare, reflect, or apply notes in a process of studied exploration. The question we pose is not "how do we adapt an acting classroom for a student who is scared to perform?" No. Rather, we ask, "How can we create a classroom where different kinds of engagement are equally valued?"

Confronting Anxiety

A temperament-inclusive teacher who understands there are different types of learners and actors can begin to analyze each situation and know when to guide forward or when to step back and move on. Educators can assist students in gaining ease with discomfort through awareness, recognition, and acknowledgment of the issue of anxiety. The word "anxiety" is loaded with layers of meaning as defined by mental health professionals today. Some, with an anxiety disorder, may experience panic attacks or the compulsion to engage in a specific behavior. Others, including many of our interviewees, may feel worry or dread, but do not experience a chronic state of nervousness; this allows them to ply their craft, but there is discomfort or apprehension related to some aspects of the work. It is interesting to note that according to a 2019 article in *Psychology Today*, Dr. Laurie Helgoe affirms that anxiety is more common among introverts, who tend to be more self-critical than extroverts.[2]

Obviously, there can be anxiety created by certain extrovert-based approaches in the acting studio: a personality-culture clash. How an educator deals with anxiety may be key to unlocking the potential of the introverted actor. A frank discussion about anxiety and its causes would be a welcome addition to any acting class, especially in the early days. This will invite an atmosphere of sharing and openness as well as acknowledge the different types of experiences that students will encounter. It will also offer some encouraging validation to introverted actors, who might feel an implied contradiction between their personality identification and their chosen field of study. There is also an opportunity to call out and discuss this contradiction as applicable to all acting students.

By definition, and regardless of whether they are introverts or extroverts, the work actors do is anxiety-inducing: actors present their souls, their private selves, for the world to see, and repeatedly open themselves up for scrutiny. LA actor and writer Sean Patrick McGowan reports on his relationship with anxiety and a teacher who allowed him to disarm his anxiety:

> I took a class where, when we were nervous, we were told to admit [to the class], "I'm nervous" ... We equated nervousness with caring deeply about doing well. I had never been in a space where we were encouraged to admit we were nervous about sharing something. It was incredible. I've been in acting classes since then where, when I get in front of the class to perform before I begin the piece, I say, "I'm very nervous because it's important that all of you think I'm good at this." Then I start the scene. This confession relieves so much anxiety in me, as I articulate the absurd fear that I have before I perform, and then hear that echo in the room.[3]

As McGowan suggests, it is often in the act of articulating these feelings that we are better equipped to work through them.

Another strategy is to be sure to offer students time to pause in order to lower the stakes when the actor's anxiety level is high and raw. This can be done through mindful deep breathing, telling a joke, taking a quick break, or providing a minor distraction—in order to get them to raise the character's stakes, you sometimes have to lower the stakes for the actor.

Consider this story from professional actor Andy Head while working in one of the co-authors' classrooms:

> We were in an acting class in grad school with Rob (co-author of this book), and another student and I were doing a scene-based improv where we were arguing. The goal of the exercise was to make me the aggressor in the scene, which I normally avoid. I couldn't do what was being asked of me. Rob was specifically saying "Try it this way." I kept reverting back to doing it the way that was safe and comfortable for me, which was not being the dominant person in the scene, but being the victim or the submissive character. If that hadn't been thrown at me as an improv exercise, if I could have had time to plan and prepare what I wanted to do...but in the moment, I was not able to do what was being asked because I felt anxious and nervous. That

[exercise] felt like a big failure. I think the qualities of being an introvert were some of the things working against me.[4]

Co-author Rob recalls, immediately after coaching this exercise, he asked Andy, "If I gave you the time to go home and process this tonight, could you bring it back tomorrow and do what was asked?" The student replied, "Yes." And that is what happened. Andy returned the next day, and the improvisation achieved what it was supposed to. Rob cites this as being a seminal moment in his teaching where he understood that introversion plays a unique part in an actor's learning.

EXAMINING ENSEMBLE WORK

One of the biggest challenges in our current classroom design, and one pivotal to the acting classroom, is that of nonstop partnered work or group projects. In the book *200 Best Jobs for Introverts* (2008), author Laurence Shatkin argues that "the team-oriented workplace is another environment that is not friendly to introverts.[5] A popular management theory says that workers are more productive and turn out work of higher quality when they are organized into teams. This may be true for extroverts, but introverts may feel that this environment prevents them from doing the kind of thoughtful problem solving that is their particular strength" (17). In considering that three people in a small group often do the majority of the talking, it is clear that when it comes to group work, learning how to pair temperaments and personalities in a productive manner is important to the entire group's success. Even more, when it comes to the acting classroom, group projects and team building require extra examination.

There are all kinds of criteria for forming pairs or choosing partners for a scene, and most educators consider a variety of strategies: pairing students with complementary strengths; pairing students who will challenge each other; pairing students with similar or contrasting working styles; drawing names from a hat; or using alphabetical assignments. Whatever your process for choosing such groups, it is important to then follow up the assigning of the partners with a discussion related to the variety of working styles these pairings will encounter. Ask scene partners to share their personality identifications and working preferences. Discuss the strengths of the extrovert's spontaneity and the introvert's strategic planning. By offering information about their individual ways of working, their strengths can combine to unlock creative potential. In the book *The Genius of Opposites: How Introverts and Extroverts Achieve*

Extraordinary Results Together (2016), author Jennifer Kahnweiler writes, "Magic happens when opposites tap into their strengths to play their natural roles. For instance, many opposites will use this style difference to their advantage by leveraging the easy-flowing conversation of the extrovert with certain customers, and not thrusting introverts into those awkward situations" (69).[6] Even though Kahnweiler is writing about business ventures, these concepts can easily be transferred to group acting activities.

Let students know they are all bringing a strength to the table. Acknowledge each of their learning contributions by encouraging them to assign roles that leverage their strengths. Individual group members can take notes, keep time, ask questions, or simply make other members feel more comfortable with pleasant small talk. All types can contribute valuably to the dynamic of the group and the success of their work.

MAKING TIME FOR REFLECTION

Many acting studios may wish to devote more time for processing and reflection. Such quiet time is another key element in creating an inclusive classroom. The added challenge to this charge is that theatre is a time-sensitive process (as it is for teachers in any classroom who are obliged to teach to a test). Whether it is the timeline of a syllabus or the looming opening night of a show, it may seem as though leaving time for incremental reflection is a costly or indulgent approach to rehearsal or classwork. The reality is that this timeline might just work to the advantage of the process as a whole. It is important to note that given extroverted students usually don't need as much processing time as introverts, educators need to be mindful of the ways in which they can help their extroverted students to stay engaged during moments of quiet by teaching about the benefits of solitary reflection for all learners. At times, extroverts may need to be given a more social task while the introverts are taking their time to think.

SELF-AWARENESS

As mentioned at the beginning of this section, self-awareness on the part of the instructor is a key factor in the success of these proposed classroom adjustments. An understanding, patient, compassionate director and/or teacher is pivotal to the success of the introverted actor. Instructors have a responsibility to understand their own personality style and how it might influence the class or be projected onto the expectations of how the class should function. Prue Wales argues we need to consider how we can move through and balance competing and shifting positions, or hold them simultaneously, to better gain an understanding of our (teacher's) own subjectivity and the ways in which our biases can affect our work in the classroom.[7] Wales believes we can gain a greater awareness of the way in which we work in the classroom and how that in turn can affect our future work as educators. Being open to new ways of delivering tested acting methodologies will require an awareness of our subjectivities and biases in relation to teaching methods that favor extroverts. We advocate for open communication about the impact of these personality types on the learning of each acting student. We envision an acting studio where open dialogue about introversion is part of the cultural landscape, where an acting classroom is a place where introverts can openly talk about the way they learn best, and where educators are open to adapting commonly used extrovert-based practices.

To the Introverted Student

While in the previous section we put many responsibilities on the educator to adapt their classroom practices, introverted students also have responsibilities to make sure they are doing their best work. You are studying acting, so to some extent, you understand the very public act of doing your job. As an introvert who prefers time alone, what is it that allows you to present your work for an audience? As we saw in the survey, there are numerous motivations for introverts going into acting, and when it comes to introverted actors, there are a lot of us! Simply knowing you are not alone can be an eye-opening revelation. Like your acting instructors, as a student, you also have a responsibility to evaluate and understand how your personality identification helps or hinders your own learning, and when and how you might be able to adapt these traits to help you succeed in your craft.

Creating Safety

Introversion is certainly ingrained within you, but this does not mean you can use introversion as a shield to avoid some of the basic duties of an actor. In other words, understanding what it means to be an introverted actor, and how this impacts your work in the acting studio, is your responsibility. For example, it has been observed that some young, introverted actors have difficulty making eye contact with their scene partners. In order to establish that essential connection with a scene partner, you must look them in the eye. This is a basic skill of acting, and it is you, the introverted actor, who must contribute to the process of feeling safe enough to make the required eye contact.

Psychology professor Brett Donnellan offers sage advice in relation to this potential challenge.[8] He encourages introverted actors to channel their attention and purpose into their partner, and thus find a sense of camaraderie with them in the moment. In focusing on the job of creating a character and telling a story, the introverted actor can avoid becoming overly concerned with their connection to their scene partner as a friend or peer. This idea allows for complete concentration on the relationship between the characters rather than between the actors. This approach is further enhanced with the comfort that comes with having a script. The script relieves the actor of any pressure to come up with something to say, as the playwright provides each exchange of the conversation. Further, as Donnellan suggests, the goal of the actor isn't necessarily to make connections with friends or peers but to play the role.

Taking Comfortable Risks

Another responsibility of introverted students is to take risks in their work. Some of your best work will happen there. It might be helpful to remind yourself that this expectation is not unique to you, but shared between you and your peers. Remember your best work takes place in the 4–6 range of the 10-degree anxiety scale; it is up to you to identify where and when your anxiety or fear becomes overwhelming. As you gain skills, trust, and experience, the scale will expand, allowing more and more freedom in your risk-taking. This is necessary in order to do the vulnerable work required of an actor.

Stretch goals can allow you to participate in the class in the ways being asked of you by your teacher, while helping you maintain a sense of agency in how you choose to participate. Setting daily thresholds or time limits for verbal participation in class is an important element to improving as an actor. Sometimes, these stretch goals are surprisingly simple. For example, go first! This approach helps avoid the negative self-talk you might "hear" in your head while waiting to perform: the damaging self-critique that usually gets worse with each subsequent scene performed by your classmates, making you progressively less likely to volunteer. Volunteering to go first also alleviates the anxiety that stems from waiting for your name to be called at random. Another perk of going first in an acting class is that, due to the nature of the discipline and the detailed coaching acting teachers often provide, the scene that is performed first is likely to get the most feedback. For an introverted actor who loves to process notes and take time to reflect, this extra time can enhance your work. Many introverted students report that the simple trick of volunteering to go first saves them countless hours of over-thinking in the classroom. It requires bravery, but it makes for an effective stretch goal.

Rethinking Group Work

Whether you are allowed to choose your own group partners or they are assigned to you, your approach is important. Help to create an atmosphere where you can all be successful. As with previous examples, sometimes this means taking the time to talk to one another and acknowledge your learning styles, personality identifications, and strengths. Opening up this dialogue is an invitation to the group to value each participant's styles and preferences. Create partnerships with actors who have temperaments different from your own and work to create a conducive atmosphere where you each can learn from one another.

Personal Advocacy

Each day, think about how much you can safely stretch yourself. Set yourself up for success. Look ahead on the syllabus or assignment calendar to anticipate when certain topics might be included in the daily lesson. Plan ahead for how you might contribute to these discussions or what questions you might ask to avoid feeling pressure in the moment to come up with a valuable contribution. If a concept or exercise seems to overlook your introverted temperament, consider some adaptations to the exercise that will make you feel more comfortable. Focus on why you are here. If ensemble-building exercises cause you apprehension, remember that, as an actor, you know the end goal to create a cohesive unit is an admirable one, and each individual member of the ensemble has a responsibility to the whole. If you aren't able to invest in the way that is asked, offer an alternative so both the spirit of the exercise and your contribution still hold value. Find ways to support your own way of working that is respect-ful of other learning styles.

Talk to your educators about how you best learn and how comfortable you are with certain exercises, while also acknowledging that your leader must consider a myriad of other learning styles. Setting participation stretch goals will help you find ways to modify and adapt your personal self to your professional one.

In one of the classes at Michigan State University observed by the authors, beginning acting students were asked why they took an acting course. Some of their answers included:

- Get me out of my comfort zone, which is always good.
- Find an outlet for my goofiness.
- Step out of introversion and start to kill the anxiety that I've always associated with performance.
- Get a new energy.
- Explore that which I am uncomfortable with.
- Find a safety zone where I can take risks and not take things personally.
- Just go for it and get over it.

In these comments, there is an undercurrent of dissatisfaction with the current professional self. Students want to change things about their rela-tionship to the work of acting and the public display it demands. And that is what classes are for—to challenge and expand our horizons. Knowing this as an introverted actor, strive to enter the classroom each day with the goal of finding ways to make your relationship to this craft into something you are fully proud of and invested in.

ACTING STUDIO ADAPTATIONS FOR EDUCATORS: FIVE STEPS

In this last section, we offer five simple ideas related to creating a temperament-inclusive acting studio.

Start a Discussion As evidenced in our survey results, there are many thriving introverted actors, and we want you to talk about it. Find and share role models of successful actors who are introverts. Interesting class-room discussions can be based on the stories of famous actors who have come forward as introverts. Examining the work of such celebrated actors reveals the diversity within the craft and the remarkable ability of so many professional introverted actors (such as Daniel Day-Lewis[9] or Meryl Streep[10]). This conversation also gives introverted student actors a sense of community, knowing they are not alone.

Don't Forget the Extroverts While the traditional structure of the acting classroom unequivocally favors the extroverted student, this does not mean the exercises and theories of these extrovert-based methodologies don't work. No matter the adaptations and considerations made for introverted actors, the acting classroom must be kept as a welcoming space for extroverts. It can, in fact, be harder for an extrovert to learn how to listen than it is for an introvert to learn how to speak.

Plan Ahead Educators include detailed syllabi, calendars, and discussions, and give as much notice as possible about what is happening in upcoming classes. This advanced notice and preparation time is enforced by the pedagogical concept of the Long Runway covered in Chap. 5.

Change It Up When you design your class, work in as much variety as possible and make it different daily. Mix up exercises that value introverted and extroverted learners. A classroom that remains stylistically diverse can provide every student with an education that is unexpected and exciting and can educate all participants in the ways people learn differently. Sometimes, ask for an immediate post-performance response, and at other times, encourage students to record their performance and watch at home first, and then offer an assessment in writing at the next class.

Model Vulnerability There is no doubt that accessing authentic vulnerability is a chief goal in every acting class, regardless of the pedagogical approach. This human experience isn't limited to acting exercises and character development. There is vulnerability from an educator who is working to implement new ways to reach all students and showing a willingness to be flexible. There is also great respect—and power—offered to the student in asking questions such as, "Did this exercise align with your personality type or learning style?" or "How did this warm-up impact you as in introvert?" Students can share their own experiences with classmates and instructors, and the group may be able to offer assistance with overcoming any roadblocks. Showing and sharing vulnerability can create a place of trust where all feel heard and can do their best work.

Through mutual and honest communication about strengths and challenges, actors are nurtured to thrive. And while these adaptations can create a more balanced classroom, there still remains one major element of theatrical training that many readers might say cannot be adjusted to allow for introverts to do their best work. We write, of course, about the immediacy and inventiveness of improvisation. Can improvisation, which literally means spontaneity or lack of premeditation—traits identified with extroverts—offer a place in the studio for introverts? Yes, and …

NOTES

1. Wales, Prue. "Positioning the Drama Teacher: Exploring the Power of Identity in Teaching Practices." Research in Drama Education. Routledge. http://www.tandf.co.uk/journals, April 30, 2009. https://eric.ed. gov/?id=EJ856893
2. Helgoe, Amy. "Revenge of the Introvert." Psychology Today. Sussex Publishers. Accessed November 22, 2019. https://www.psychologytoday. com/us/articles/201009/revenge-the-introvert
3. McGowan, Sean Patrick. Personal interview. 13 April 2019.
4. Head, Andy. Personal interview. 15 Aug. 2018.
5. Shatkin, Laurence. *200 Best Jobs for Introverts.* Indianapolis, IN: JIST Pub., 2008.
6. Kahnweiler, Jennifer B. *The Genius of Opposites: How Introverts and Extroverts Achieve Extraordinary Results Together.* Oakland, CA: Berrett-Koehler Publishers, 2016
7. Wales, Prue. "Positioning the Drama Teacher…"
8. Donnellan, Brent. Personal interview. 1 Dec. 2018.
9. Tran, Christine, Dancy Mason, Christine Tran, Mathew Burke, Matthew Burke, and Factinate. "43 Intense Facts About Daniel Day-Lewis." Factinate, September 25, 2019. https://www.factinate.com/people/43-intense-facts-daniel-day-lewis/
10. Miller, Julie. "Here's Where Meryl Streep Found the Confidence to Become an Actress." Vanity Fair. Vanity Fair, June 19, 2015. https://www.vanityfair.com/hollywood/2015/06/meryl-streep-confidence

REFERENCES

Donnellan, Brent. Personal Interview. 1 Dec. 2018.

Head, Andy. Personal interview. 15 Aug. 2018.

Helgoe, Amy. "Revenge of the Introvert." Psychology Today. Sussex Publishers. Accessed November 22, 2019. https://www.psychologytoday.com/us/articles/201009/revenge-the-introvert.

Kahnweiler, Jennifer B. *The Genius of Opposites: How Introverts and Extroverts Achieve Extraordinary Results Together.* Oakland, CA: Berrett-Koehler Publishers, 2016.

McGowan, Sean Patrick. Personal Interview. 13 April 2019.

Miller, Julie. "Here's Where Meryl Streep Found the Confidence to Become an Actress." Vanity Fair. Vanity Fair, June 19, 2015. https://www.vanityfair.com/hollywood/2015/06/meryl-streep-confidence.

Shatkin, Laurence. *200 Best Jobs for Introverts.* Indianapolis, IN: JIST Pub., 2008.

Tran, Christine, Dancy Mason, Christine Tran, Mathew Burke, Matthew Burke, and Factinate. "43 Intense Facts About Daniel Day-Lewis." Factinate, September 25, 2019. https://www.factinate.com/people/43-intense-facts-daniel-day-lewis/.

Wales, Prue. "Positioning the Drama Teacher: Exploring the Power of Identity in Teaching Practices." Research in Drama Education. Routledge. http://www.tandf.co.uk/journals, April 30, 2009. https://eric.ed.gov/?id=EJ856893.

CHAPTER 7

Improvisation and the Introvert

Improvisation and introversion might feel like oil and water. They don't mix. Few other elements of traditional actor training strike fear in introverts more than this on-your-feet, immediate-response, processing-free form of gameplay. The survey and our interviews both bear witness to this reaction. But read on, some things may surprise you.

This chapter relies heavily on two improvisation experts, and most of their ideas and interviews are included in detail, as they both so eloquently describe how introversion and improvisation can co-exist and how introverts can actually thrive in the form. Both have extensive improv training and teaching experience. And both are introverts.

Sarah Hendrickson is Assistant Professor of Acting and Improvisation at Michigan State University and finds a surprising fallacy about improvisation. Sarah notes:

> There's a misconception that improvisers are extroverts, and they're the ones that jump out with all the big ideas, want all the attention, and attack the stage. The best improvisers are the ones who listen and know where they need to fill in the blanks. As an introvert, I'm comfortable hanging back until I know exactly what the scene or my scene partners need, and then I can come in and take care of them. My desire is not to be the biggest and the loudest on the stage; it's to make sure the scene is the best it can be.[1]

Andy Sloey is an adjunct professor at Webster University in St. Louis, MO, and the Artistic Director of The Improv Shop's Harold Program. He

© The Author(s) 2020
R. Roznowski et al., *The Introverted Actor*,
https://doi.org/10.1007/978-3-030-41607-2_7

notices introverts gravitate toward improv in surprising numbers: more than half of his improv classes are composed of introverts. He also acknowledges introverted and extroverted improvisers need to be cultivated in different ways, especially at the start. Andy reports:

> One of the early tells with improv is when people first get started. [Extroverts] go for the joke really hard; they play over-the-top characters right out of the gate, even in an introductory level class, because they have a lot of confidence, and they feed off the energy of the people in the room. This boosts their confidence level, but they usually don't have the skills to back up the confidence level yet. Introverts are more likely to make subtler choices at first, choices that aren't as big, so they need to be lifted while they are improvising.[2]

With so many introverted actors gravitating toward improv classes, why does the stereotype of the predominantly extroverted improv artist continue to persist? Additionally, why do so many introverted actors who benefit from this training admit to feeling most apprehensive when honing in on this skill? The simplest answer is that, for introverts, there is true fear when approaching this sort of work, even while they are drawn to it. Psychology professor Dr. Brent Donnellan understands the fear of working in this way for introverts.[3] He notes improv might be particularly hard or even terrifying for introverts because this style of performance works against their personalities. But there is hope: with determination and mindful practice, one of an introvert's greatest strengths, an introverted actor can succeed and thrive in improvisational and ensemble work. Donnellan continues, "If you're motivated to be outstanding in your career, you can force yourself to do things, but it's going to be demanding, and it's going to feel trying. Whereas for some people, it's going to come naturally, and they're going to find it easy, [for introverts], it will be work." The introverted actors who take the risk and dare at improv may find great reward and satisfaction by working in unexpected ways. In fact, improvisation can become a welcome respite from constant, thoughtful analysis and other ingrained introverted personality characteristics.

Several members from Capitol City Improv in Springfield, IL, convened for a roundtable interview for this book, and a few improv artists shared their ideas about how introversion and extroversion can affect improvisation:

Improviser 1: I like doing a scene with someone outgoing because they can start it. I can sit back and observe to see where they are going, then I can follow and mirror that.

Improviser 2: If you're extremely extroverted and too over-the-top, it can confuse the scene. Introverts might hesitate more, which is tricky because you don't hesitate in improv, you just go. So, it's finding a balance. Both can be dangerous if you're not honed in on what you're doing.

Improviser 3: An introvert might rely on doing the same thing too much because it's comfortable. And an extrovert might do too much or lack focus, like being big in a scene but not with any clear purpose that moves it forward.

Improviser 4: Or too many people jumping in all at the same time; if you've got nothing but a group of extroverts who all come out with high energy, where's that scene going to go? If you're starting at ten, you can't get anywhere higher than that; it's not going to be as successful as if you start somewhere lower.[4]

In nearly all of their commentary, these improv artists recognize the need for both introverts and extroverts to strike a balance or complement each other for improvisation to work. Their ideas of what an introvert or extrovert might bring to the form offer some generalizations about the two temperaments in action, but this doesn't address the larger question of why introverts are drawn to this art form. For many actors, like Andy Sloey, it is the foundational "yes, and …" requirement of improvisation that provides the inspiration necessary to attract introverted actors. This pivotal mantra taught in every style of improv invites a continuously positive nature of the training that inspires introverted actors, who are often powerfully critical of their own work. Sloey also notes improv training is incremental, where concepts and rules are shared prior to the work and followed meticulously—another boon for the introvert. Improv training is a safe place for spontaneity within structures, where every contribution is heard and supported, and where mistakes are valued and lauded. While it might seem contradictory that an acting style so tied to spontaneity and a lack of preparation could be rooted in rules and structure, it is the presence and implementation of this clear structure that draws many introverts to the style. Sloey praises the unique nature of improv as an art form that offers the introvert "a relatively simple entry point … where I can speak my truth, or be vulnerable and supportive and honest." Improvisation allows for public vulnerability to be bolstered by private structures.

MISCONCEPTIONS

Hendrickson and Sloey have similar points of view when asked about the misconception that improvisation favors and entices only extroverts. Hendrickson notes, "There's a misconception that to be a successful improviser is to be the funniest one. Yes, this is important if it's a comedic show, but the funniest things are the things the people in the audience relate to, the things that are real, truthful, honest reactions." Sloey concurs, noting that being the loudest and funniest is not what improv is about. He continues, "The stereotypes of the players are that we are always loud, going for a joke, wanting to be funny, and the same of improv: that it's stupid, it's low humor, it's blue humor." But these generalizations often prove false when we consider not just the training and structure involved in improvisation, but also the great skill and honesty that shape the work. These are the same foundations we find in any acting style—the goal to achieve honesty, vulnerability, and truth for the actors and the audience.

At first, extroverts may be drawn to improv because of the high energy and fast-paced turnaround, and through careful training, those elements remain, but as the skill of the improviser grows, they are also refined. Hendrickson hypothesizes that many extroverts might initially gravitate toward improv because of the freedom of the style, thinking anything goes and there are no rules. "I can do anything," "I can really shine," and "everybody has to go along with what I do." When they enter a training program or find themselves in an ensemble that knows how to do things correctly, that behavior is honed and polished in support of the ensemble over the desires of the individual.

The enthusiastic freedom of improvisation still exists, but it can also pose a challenge. On the one hand, it might be where the more extroverted actors feel they can stand out, take risks, and explore big, wild, or bizarre choices with the full support of the ensemble. On the other hand, it might make more introverted actors feel trapped or obligated to play and support no matter what. Does "yes, and ..." mean an actor can never say no? Sloey agrees training is necessary in order to correct incoming students' perceptions of improvisation. Sloey continues, "There are a lot of preconceived notions that improvisation is the Wild West, where [actors] can do whatever they want, and there are no rules. If [students] see a fast-paced improv show done by professionals, it looks intimidating. It looks like the improvisers are very witty, funny, smart people to begin with." Through training and a deeper understanding of the art form, that stigma quickly goes away. Sloey reveals the real skill is in the work underneath, the agreements, pushing forward, and heightening the specifics; it's these mechanical skills that, when practiced, make it appear as though improvisers are the life of every party, when in actuality, it's practice and time spent with a team. Thriving through mindful practice, reflection, and training, introverts can thrive in some improv situations.

Like any other form of actor training, both introverts and extroverts contribute to the success of improv in important ways, and debunking these common misconceptions about the style does not imply that improv is not for extroverts. Extroverts are a necessary component to a team's success, and their energy can be contagious for others in the group. Hendrickson works toward a balance, knowing extroverts tend to introduce great ideas and jump up with their innate bravery to take risks. This is then balanced with the traits of the introvert, who is able to listen, observe, follow, and set aside a desire to be the biggest and the loudest, and who uses these traits to uphold the "yes, and …." mantra. Sloey agrees the partnership between introverted and extroverted improvisers is crucial to the success of both the team and the performance. According to Sloey, the team creates a "group mind" that is greater than the sum of its parts. Introverts and extroverts work in concert with each other to create the most successful teamwork. This approach takes the pressure off any one individual to set and sustain the tone for the team and underscores the importance of the ensemble.

IMPROVISATION WITHIN ACTING CLASSES

Improv and acting are inextricably linked. The skills learned in improv help form the basic foundation of many acting classes. In this section, we will examine how improvisation is used to augment a standard acting course as a tool for character study, where the tenets of improvisation are often used to enhance several facets of actor training. Improv teaches actors much more than simply saying "yes, and …." Sloey values the numerous benefits of improvisation to training the actor when he notes, "[Improv is] a constant practice in using emotions because scenes always start there. It works every skill actors use: stage presence, relaxation, observation, listening, remembering, retaining, ensemble work. It's a playground for acting skills." Sloey's enthusiasm highlights the residual benefits of improv that offer profound connections to the acting studio. But the influences don't end there. Sloey also notes the real power is that improv is also a playground for real-life skills. The more you are surrounded by agreement, the more you are surrounded by people being positive, then the more ideas you have and the more confidence you have in yourself and those ideas. This all naturally translates to real life, in any sphere. The benefits of improv extend far beyond the acting studio to create a more positive way of approaching life.

Many acting teachers use improv as a tool to pull introverted students "out of their shells." That coded language is sometimes another way of saying, "You should be less introverted." The misconception that introversion is something to break free from or to overcome subverts the beliefs of this book and introversion/extroversion personality research. We know from the biological essence of introversion that these "shells" are often where many actors were born to remain. So why then do educators repeatedly tell more introverted students to take an improv class as an easy solution to push them to make bolder choices, gain confidence, build more stage presence, and loosen up? These encouraging outcomes are all further forms of coded language that inadvertently undercut the creative contributions of the introverted actor. Certainly, there are times when those phrases do point to issues other than introversion that must be addressed in the actor's education, but more often than not, these popular suggestions are directed at introverted student actors.

Hendrickson hears many teachers make suggestions about taking an improv class to their introverted students, and she understands the reasoning. But improv is not designed to make an introvert become an extrovert, and this should never be the goal. Hendrickson notes, "If teachers are asking the introverts to get improv training, usually the instructor wants them to have more confidence … What they're really asking is for introverts to make bolder, quicker choices. That might happen for them eventually, but improv is not a quick fix." The idea that introversion can be overcome through improv dismisses introverts' contributions to acting. Hendrickson laments that the oversimplification by many acting educators implies improv is an easy fix for the "undesirable" behavior of the introverted actor. Hendrickson notes that improv is not a band-aid. These elements of confidence and making bolder choices may be a residual effect of the improv class, but it should not be designed with that end goal as the main focus.

When used by untrained educators, improv can sometimes backfire, causing students to be forever fearful of any idea of improvisation in the future. Employing improv in the acting classroom to fill time or boost the energy of the ensemble can actually cause unwanted stress for the introvert. Hendrickson warns this approach can even be dangerous. A lackadaisical approach that implies improv is easy and actors should just "jump in" is reckless. Like any other form of acting, the training of improvisers must be handled with care. Approaching improvisation exercises without training or guidance can damage some people and, according to Hendrickson, can do more harm than good, having an adverse effect on introverted actors. Hendrickson warns that unless an acting instructor is also well-trained in how to facilitate and troubleshoot improvisational exercises, they should not use them. Hendrickson's assertion about causing harm is an important warning about understanding the purpose and function of each exercise.

If you do use improv in the acting classroom, allow students to choose whether or not they actively participate and offer them other ways to still remain engaged. Use the concepts of the Long Runway by letting them know one class in advance that improv exercises will be used, what games you will be playing, and the rules that surround those exercises. This kind of notice and discussion will help the introverted students learn to love and not fear the art form. Hendrickson recalls one moment in class when an introverted student "was not stepping out, and I privately and quickly asked 'are you okay?' She's responded, 'I'm on sensory overload today.' I said 'Don't worry about it.' Eventually, she stepped in when she was ready." Quick and respectful check-ins like the one Hendrickson modeled can assist in divining the student's comfort level on a given day. When asked for her strategies with working with introverts who don't want to participate, Hendrickson shared that, of course, every student is encouraged to participate, but she also acknowledges that the lesson of an exercise can be learned, appreciated, and applied, even if some of the class chooses to sit out on occasion. In the acting classroom, the use of improv and the connection of the ensemble can be enhanced by giving students the agency to establish their own levels of contribution, rather than basing it on the teacher's belief of exactly how a student should be participating.

All of the improvisers we interviewed admitted that while there is a clear stereotype that improvisation is a comedic practice, the acting concepts garnered in improv serve acting far beyond simple comedic games. An instructor at the Dubai roundtable talked about his relationship to improv in the acting classroom using the ComedySportz model of improvisation that uses competitive improv for comedic purposes, balanced with script and character-based improvisation as another of the canon of acting exercises useful in an acting class. Similar to the risk described for group warm-ups, there is a danger this end goal of comedy or entertainment actually cheapens the goal and skill of improv by reducing it to novel parlor games. Rather, improv can be used as a means to fuel the actor's impulses and keep them from getting stuck in those cerebral moments of doubt and self-censorship. In considering ways to make introverted actors more comfortable with the style, he encourages improvisation targeted to the needs of the student actors rather than stereotypical, game-based exercises. Contrary to most popular experiences with improvisation, the end goal is not to be funny and make classmates laugh, but to build on ideas with cohesion and creativity, free from judgment and self-doubt, all while contributing to the connection of the ensemble.

Even though many actors recognize the importance and benefits of improv to their craft, this knowledge does not alleviate the pressure they feel when these exercises are implemented in class. Professional actor and educator Patrick Midgely recalls the pressure of improvisational work based on scripted characters, an exercise often used in the acting classroom.[5] Midgely recollects, "Explorative work with very high stakes and highly emotional improvisation can be a profound experience. But I put more judgment and weight on those moments than more extroverted actors did. I noticed [extroverts] were able to shake off those improvisations, whereas I was more shaken after something like that. I felt my extroverted colleagues had an advantage." Midgely is talking about the lack of processing and reflection time so necessary for introverts. In comparison, Midgely notes when working with a provided text, the experience was quite different than performing in a purely improvisational sense. With a scripted performance, he felt more comfortable and motivated to work. In moments of character-based improv shaped by a script, this actor experienced most of their breakthroughs as a performer. For Midgely, "sometimes things that are the most terrible and frightening are also the best things for you." This idea of working beyond an introvert's perceived limitations refers back to the idea of the stretch goal. The anxiety can lead to a breakthrough.

Despite the anxiety it may produce, we cannot discount what an actor gains from an improv class. The residual benefits for both the introvert and the extrovert are clear, benefits Hendrickson summarizes with, "Every actor should take an improv class because people often come out of those experiences getting something from it … if they come out of [the class] with more confidence, it's amazing. If they feel their ideas have value, that's awesome. They're a better actor now because they're able to listen and react organically. We want actors listening and reacting." With key principles of improv at the forefront, extroverts can gain skills in listening, and introverts can gain skills in responding—without self-doubt.

THE IMPROV COURSE

Beyond a featured exercise or strategy in acting classes, improvisation is often taught as an entirely separate course on its own. These courses can have the same residual positive effects on the actor of listening and responding and confidence boosting mentioned earlier, but they are devoted solely to the art form of improvisation. An entire class devoted to improv can be something an introvert might fear, but Sarah Hendrickson and Andy Sloey have some excellent advice to allay those anxieties.

Sloey suggests introverts look at improv through a different lens. Rather than thinking about the jokes and the laughs, the introverted actor can think about the work as a process—something that introverts thrive on. He notes, "Improv does not have a delineation between the creative process and the final product like a lot of other art forms. The whole thing is a creative process. In improv, we are showing off the process as the final product." With this distinction, we return to the product-versus-process analogy. The introvert can take more ownership of the process by shifting the goal from garnering laughter to mastering the techniques at the root of the games. Similarly, Hendrickson suggests looking at the process. She understands the fears introverts may have but also knows the benefits of going through the experience of taking the course. She admits if you've gone through this process and you've experienced any amount of success, you know the process is necessary to get where you need to be. You've got to trust you're going to come out richer on the other side.

Improvisation can require you to act foolishly through bizarre characterizations in strange situations. While extroverts may latch on to these concepts immediately, the introvert might take a bit longer to embolden themselves to such work. Improv artists from the Springfield Capital City Improv Roundtable offered some advice:

Improviser 1:   In a recent class, a student opted not to participate. I decided to show them it was okay for a grown-up to be silly. And we're all going to do it. If I can be silly, you can let go a little too. As the teacher, I'm going to be goofier than anybody else, so they all feel comfortable bringing their level of goofiness up. I don't say that, but I try to model it by example.

Improviser 2:   Sometimes when you're doing a game with non-improv people, they feel silly, or wonder what we are doing. So you have to be the person willing to show them it's okay.

Improviser 3:   No look it's fun! I swear! In a classroom, you want people to succeed, and they're not going to succeed if they're completely uncomfortable. So you're silly, but if they're not silly, you don't call them out. You let them be silly at their level. If they feel unsuccessful, they gain no confidence and get nothing out of it.

Improviser 4:   Find something that works for them. Some people are better at certain [improv games] because they have a certain dynamic. Some are good at the physical ones, when you're falling over and doing silly stuff, but others are better at one-liners, the clever ones where they can find a way to end the scene. If there's an uncomfortable student in a group setting, you have to reassure them. If they aren't a fan of the silly noises game, then try one where they are a specific character. Some people are good at guessing games; they aren't a character, but they are involved in the scene ... as yourself but still engaged.[6]

These suggestions all seem to examine the participants' comfort with outlandish choices. Each artist has a unique suggestion related to engaging with reticent students. Whether it is through modeling the behavior or switching up the type of game being played, the goal remains to find a way for the introvert to engage while still maintaining the integrity of the art form.

The structure of the class is of utmost importance for an introvert, as entering into an unknown situation is sometimes met with caution about rules and structure. This is further exacerbated by the idea of improvisation, which seems at first glance to be based only on immediacy and invention. As we have learned, that is not the case. If you are an introverted actor entering the improv class, you can help to prepare yourself for the unknown of the situation by doing some reading on the rules of the various games and exercises beforehand. Hendrickson notes she likes to introduce a framework immediately, believing any actor expected to improvise is going to need rules. Improvisers must learn the structure, so they can do it "correctly," and you only get better by doing it. Having the foundational base of the rules for each game can be a point of comfort for the introverts should things go awry. They will be able to recognize the levels of the game, watch them play out in the first few rounds, and anticipate how they might contribute. This structure offers a kind of safety net for introverted actors because, when exercises go off the rails, they can rely on the parts of the scene they do understand—essential and common acting elements like relationship, objective, and tactics—and realign the focus of the scene. This approach gives the introverted actor a benchmark for moving forward. These acting fundamentals are points the introverted actor already knows, so they can rely on the basics of the acting study to help guide the improvised scene.

Hendrickson describes her approach to developing an improv classroom that values the introverted student:

> I explain everything ahead of time. I never make actors jump up on stage and do whatever they want. It's more about explaining the structure of the exercise, the objectives of it, and then saying, "Jump up when you're ready." The confident extroverts often feel ready and go right in to do it. I let them, and I never force anyone to go. I encourage them. I also reinforce the idea that there are no mistakes. We look at mistakes as gifts. This helps because some students are fearful of saying something wrong or making a mistake and embarrassing themselves. Or they have an idea, but it isn't quite formulated, so they hesitate. But there could be something exciting in that accident, in that mistake, that can be celebrated and explored and heightened. It's important to not force people to do something that might paralyze them; that's the antithesis of what improv is trying to accomplish.

Allowing the participation to occur in its own way and the celebration of "mistakes" are all ways of coaching designed to create a more temperament-inclusive space for introverts and extroverts alike, and may have extra benefits for those who are predisposed toward perfectionism.

One of the biggest issues related to introversion and improv is the lack of processing time. It appears skilled improv artists can easily create hilarious lines out of thin air. How can they do that without reflection time?

There are some ways around it. Intimately knowing the structure of the games relieves some anxiety, even as you receive new suggestions from the audience. In collecting suggestions from the audience, improv artists have a short window of processing time before putting those suggestions into performance. This is a prime opportunity for the introvert to ponder possible scenarios or ideas. Another strategy, says Hendrickson, is letting the extrovert do the initiation because they may have an idea right away. Then the introvert's job is to say "yes" to whatever that idea is and add to it. This strategy gives the introverted actor a way to process and even to reflect on what the suggestion is before they feel pressured to contribute to it. It also supports the extrovert's strength of creative spontaneity by allowing them the space to begin the scene.

Another commonly held fear in improvisation is the immediacy of performance related to the audience. The audience appears to be an important feature of improvisation, from invited suggestions to raucous laughter. When asked if improvisers are playing to the audience all the time, Hendrickson responds with vigor that catering to the audience can be detrimental to the art form. In fact, she argues that taking down the fourth wall in the context of the scene and acknowledging the audience can make an improvised scene "crash and burn … It doesn't work." Because the actor and their fellow improvisers are in the scene together, the scene is more about the relationship between them; the audience isn't there. Hendrickson does admit applause and laughter (or a lack thereof) can affect the performer, but that happens in every form of live theatre where the audience is there to watch. An improviser's motivation to connect with the audience is the same as any actor's, and so is the goal: to stay focused on your scene partner, tell the story, and do the work. Again, we rely on the basics of acting, which the introverted actor has hopefully already mastered.

In improvisation classes, there are usually two forms of improvisation to explore, and either can offer unique benefits to the introverted actor. The first category, usually referred to as "short-form," consists of fast-paced games. These games have a variety of rules and structures, but they are usually more comedy-based than long-form improv. Short-form, with its quick pace and rapid-fire jokes, might seem at times to favor the extrovert. But introverts can still find comfort in knowing the show will have a line-up of games, all of which have been rehearsed. When asked if any style of improv games actually favors the introvert, Sloey responds affirmatively. He notes that introverts often connect to long-form improv, which takes its time and is not necessarily as comedic as short-form. Introverts' powers of observation also serve them well in long-form improv. Specifically, Sloey lauds the strength of a long-form improv style called the Armando, which is based on improvised monologues. Sloey goes on: "the audience gives a suggestion, and [the improviser] looks back through their life for thoughts, opinions, or stories, and does a monologue based on that. They usually cap it with some kind of emotional moment, revealing how it made them feel, how it changed them, or the lesson or moral they learned." That sort of emotional connection to the form requires knowledge of an interior life, and many introverted artists state this is something they can access with ease. Sloey offers another possibility, in an improvised form that starts with a conversation between improvisers and then explodes out into scenes based on that conversation. Sloey describes these scenes as being relatively deep and thoughtful, adding that, in his experience, "[i]ntroverts might be more drawn to that kind of emotion-based, internal content, and making the internal content external by talking about it and putting it out into space." In forms like these, where several different scenes all stem from one initial idea, an introvert's power of observation becomes an advantage to the ensemble. Sloey admits keen observational skills and the ability to notice and remember the subtle moments can electrify a performance. Sloey notes he has seen introverts often pay close attention to the people around them, moving through social settings with care. These details can inspire great moments of improvisation less observant artists might not notice or remember. Because of this, introverts are often great at calling back to previous jokes from earlier games in the sequence of one show. Extroverts may certainly possess those skills as well, but Sloey has seen it more prevalent with introverts.

In demystifying the stigma and misconceptions of the improv class, and identifying some of the strengths that an introverted actor can bring to the form, there are definite possibilities for the introverted actor to succeed. But as Hendrickson notes, improvisation is not for everyone (extrovert or introvert), and understanding this can allay some of the doubts. While it is an important tool in most actor training, it is only one portion and won't be required of every professional job. For introverts like Hendrickson, the work of improv requires bravery, and she reassures, "it doesn't have to be for everybody. I was terrified of it, but I kept getting asked to do it in commercial auditions. The part of me that wanted to work was greater than my fear, so I knew I needed to learn how to do it correctly. I started taking classes. That's where the bravery comes in. I know I have the training to tap into if I feel like I'm drowning." Understanding that improvisation is sometimes a necessary component to professional life forced Hendrickson to overcome her obstacles.

Sloey offers some final, compassionate advice for introverted actors about to enter an improv class:

> Trust yourself. You're probably already better at this than you think you are. You don't have to try. You don't have to push. You are valuable, you're useful, you are what's going to make this art form work. Bringing yourself to it has already made it better because you're now a voice that can lend itself to creativity. So trust yourself, listen to yourself, and take notes in class. The battle that we introverts are always fighting is one of self-doubt and worry. But I see [introverted] actors go from starting classes to graduating and doing one-person improvised shows…They can take a suggestion and keep an audience going for twenty-five minutes by themselves because they've built up enough confidence to first say "yes" to the idea. It's awesome.

These heartfelt observations about overcoming self-doubt and gaining confidence can be your journey as an introverted improv actor. For Sloey and others, it's about those first brave steps into the improv class.

Ensemble

One of the enduring effects of studying improvisation is the idea of creating an ensemble that supports each other and promotes everyone's ideas. Sloey often refers to this focused ensemble as "group mind." The dynamic of an ensemble has to be carefully cultivated. Of course, the idea of ensemble and ensemble-building exercises is not entirely the domain of the improvisation-based classroom, so many of the concepts shared within this section are transferable to rehearsal processes for standard productions.

Ensemble work and improvisation rehearsals are notoriously loud spaces. How can introverts navigate them? It is here that the leadership of the director of the team or the production must advocate for some quiet time. The most effective improv is about creating an ensemble where the reflection is valued just as much as the boisterous time.

Introvert expert Dr. Lisa Kaenzig has studied the noisy classroom and its effect on the introvert.[7] She notes, "All that noise, all the projection of the teachers' voices, all those things can over-stimulate [students] because introverts' minds are already so active that all the additional external stimulation is total overload for them." How then can the raucous acts of improvisation honor the quiet classroom? Kaenzig suggests making sure there are calm environments and calm classrooms. She does not mean there can't be moments in improvisation where obviously there's a lot of action and things going on, but instead, making sure all students have space to move around. She suggests offering another room where a group can go to work on their own or someplace where a person can leave. Space, time, and quiet all combine to help a director or teacher manage the ensemble and allow all voices to be heard and all learning styles to thrive.

Sloey has a suggestion for that sort of work as well, reminding improv artists they are working to build a group mind; he calls it dynamic leadership. It's following the follower. No one is leading and everyone is leading, but all are keeping equality in conversational turn-taking between all of the groups. He notes such leadership recognizes when introverted members are more silent, and the attention is then carefully thrown to them to see if they wish to contribute. This group mind approach is egalitarian, in that "everyone is lifted up."

Both instructors highlight the importance of compassionate leadership in the success of the ensemble. Hendrickson advises that, in coaching an ensemble, the best directors emphasize the idea of give and take. Extroverts have to also remember they are part of a team, and even if they constantly have great ideas and are more inclined to jump in, it's important to take a beat. If the introverts are taking a step out to participate, let them do it. That sort of respect certainly contributes to an ensemble. It also has a residual effect that empowers introverts to realize their ideas have merit and the rest of the ensemble wants to hear what they have to say. While respect takes time and fostering this environment can be very challenging, such practice allows the introvert—and the extrovert—to gain confidence and bravery. Hendrickson notes introverted actors take comfort in working within a true ensemble mentality, where everyone is there to help one another and there will always be others there to listen and help no matter what.

Hendrickson recently directed a cadre of freshman theatre majors in an improvisation show in their first semester where she put many of these ideas into practice. At first, the group dynamic was timid and the members' approach to the work was fear-based. When asked about strategies to create an ensemble that valued both introverts and extroverts, Hendrickson noted her approach was very carefully structured and did not have the students start any scene work until they were about a month into rehearsals. Everything prior was ensemble and group games constantly. She spent the time discussing the theory and structure of the art form and the games. No one was asked to do anything that put them on the spot in a scene until she thought they were truly ready. Hendrickson chose games that were task-based rather than individual or partner work. Students slowly became more confident in their work and, unbeknownst to them, the ensemble was created. Hendrickson valued the introverts' aversion to group work by allowing them to contribute as they saw fit and investing the time necessary to allow for discussion and reflection. Slowly, their place and role in the ensemble were self-created.

Once this sense of ensemble was clear and shared, only then did she introduce more partner and scene work into the class. Only when the students functioned as a group were they ready for the focus to become more individualized. This individual focus became an important part of the improv training as well. In this, the partnered work was not for others to see, but for student actors to rehearse on their own. Improv takes a lot of time and ensemble building. The actors must feel they can trust everyone in the group and know that, if they make a mistake, it's going to be celebrated. It is a process that cannot be rushed. This approach allowed the introverted students to gain trust with themselves, with their partners, and with the group as a whole.

Psychology professor Brent Donnellan understands the extrovert often has an advantage in group work.[8] He admits, "Extroverts have a leg up. The people who are not so extroverted have to cope with that. But if they're motivated for other reasons, I think they can find a way around that." The anxiety some actors feel about group improvisational work is real and needs special attention. Sloey offers a reminder and solace to introverts that because the art form itself is built on protection, you can't make a mistake. So, introverts, don't fear improv or let the volunteering extrovert intimidate you. Your contribution will be just as valued and celebrated.

ADVICE

If you are an introverted actor still hesitant about improvisation, Hendrickson and Sloey have some final words to offer. Hendrickson encourages the introverted actor to lean on the structure of the improvised exercises. The set rules to how a game or exercise is structured will always allow the more introverted actors to go back to the original framework to find support. Hendrickson also invites the introverted actor to "redefine your relationship with failure, and embrace what could potentially be a mistake, to explore and heighten those moments." Sloey understands the trepidation, but assures improv is an art form introverts can enter into freely. And while it may be intimidating at first, "once you feel comfortable, it can be empowering. It starts to bleed out from the training and from the classes into real life."

Are you convinced? Yes, and …

Introverted actor Carol Schultz has always loved improvisation and ensemble-building work, celebrating that, even as an introvert, she thrived in improvisation, a skill that has stuck with her throughout her professional career.[9] But in examining this specific and valuable element of actor training, Schultz raises one important point: "I don't know about other countries … but it is true in this country, the loudest voice or first to raise their hand does seem to win." Schultz's question about other countries will be explored in our next chapter, where we examine cultural differences in actor training in relation to introversion.

NOTES

1. Hendrickson, Sarah. Personal interview. 5 May 2019.
2. Sloey, Andy. Interview.
3. Donnellan, Brent. Personal interview. 1 Dec. 2018.
4. "Improvisation Roundtable" *Capital City Improv*. 11 March 2019.
5. Midgely, Patrick. Personal interview. 23 Mar. 2019.
6. "Improvisation Roundtable."
7. Kaenzig, Lisa. Personal interview. 15 Dec. 2018.
8. Donnellan, Brent. Interview.
9. Schultz, Carol. Personal interview. 20 Jan. 2019.

REFERENCES

Donnellan, Brent. Personal interview. 1 Dec. 2018.
Hendrickson, Sarah. Personal interview. 5 May 2019.
"Improvisation Roundtable" *Capital City Improv*. 11 March 2019.
Kaenzig, Lisa. Personal interview. 15 Dec. 2018.
Midgely, Patrick. Personal interview. 23 Mar. 2019.
Schultz, Carol. Personal interview. 20 Jan. 2019.
Sloey, Andy. Interview.

CHAPTER 8

Cultural Comparisons

So far, this book has concentrated on the assumption of the very Americanized extrovert ideal. And surely it has been well-chronicled by Susan Cain and others that America's zeitgeist is that of an extrovert.[1] Does introversion affect the acting studios and actor training across the globe? Do introverted actors in seemingly introverted cultures have similar issues as their American counterparts? Do other cultures that may be stereotyped as introverted differ in their approaches to acting? We decided to examine three cultures with a rich theatrical background: India, Greece, and England. These three cultures seemed varied enough to offer a unique cross-section of theatrical styles, as well as represent centuries-long theatrical traditions.

A caveat to this section: we acknowledge that, for this chapter, we are operating within cultural generalizations and social tropes. We also understand we are asking a few representatives to speak for an entire culture, and as with discussing any cultural or artistic perspective, there will always be outliers, differences, and disagreements. There are numerous and diverse approaches to actor training in each of these countries. What we are examining are the experiences, ideas, and opinions of a few students, teachers, and professionals from each of these countries so we might extrapolate a broader overview of how introversion is valued internationally. So, please, no angry emails.

© The Author(s) 2020
R. Roznowski et al., *The Introverted Actor*,
https://doi.org/10.1007/978-3-030-41607-2_8

THE UNITED STATES

Before we can examine a different culture, it is wise to first examine our own, to better understand how the United States and its society have become so closely linked to extroversion. It is also prudent to understand and label your own national, local, and academic cultures to see how those communities affect the introverted actor. And finally, generalization starts at home; if we can't generalize about our own culture, how can we do it about another?

There is no denying that, on the whole, the United States values extroversion. This point was made in the discussion of the American extrovert ideal in Chap. 1. From its frontier and pioneering days, America has created a legend that rewards speaking up, finding your own voice, and making your opinion heard. Psychology professor Dr. Brent Donnellan explains, "There is something to the new world idea of pushing frontiers that's part of our national character, and the stories we tell about ourselves pull for the lone wolf prioritizing of the individual. It's a bit of a stereotype, but the American story does push for extroversion."[2] The stories of our culture feature a bounty of extroverted characters: the hero who stands up to injustice and shouts down tyranny; the self-made entrepreneur who sells their newly invented product; the go-getter who keeps pushing in the face of failure and opposition.

All these American tropes display an air of extroversion. This extroverted attitude permeates our language and is reflected in a host of idioms we've probably all heard (and used) in order to encourage others to take a risk or speak up: "Think outside the box!" "Break out of your shell!" "Get out of your comfort zone!" "The squeaky wheel gets the grease!" or others that have an even more performative nature, like "He loves the spotlight," "They are always the center of attention," "She was the life of the party," "It's his time to shine," or "She stole the show." This American point of view seems to value the gregarious extrovert who isn't afraid to act out, speak up, be loud, and demand attention. Of course, introverts are also capable of all those things, but these American fables contain a level of gumption that skews toward extroversion. Donnellan continues, "The stories we tell ourselves play out in the quintessential American text [where] you might see elements of fake extroversion. You can be anything you want. Try hard. Keep going. Be positive. For whatever reason, that seems to resonate in the United States, or has historically."[3] These verbal and behavioral patterns represent and resonate within the United States and become ingrained in the culture and in society. The more we hear and witness them, the more we start believing we must also embody those ideals, until slowly, we see them as the cultural norm. Donnellan explains, "Extroverts probably have an easier time navigating life because there aren't so many clearly defined paths. They can make it up as they go ... extroversion helps in making connections with people and having the energy and positivity to pursue your own path, even if it's unclear." So, Americans continue to pioneer and forge their own path, while upholding and promoting the extrovert ideal.

Dr. Richard Lucas, who specializes in the study of personality traits and extroversion, sees a different relationship with extroversion across cultures.[4] He notes that mistakenly, "[i]n Western cultures, extraversion correlates with happiness. There are some reasons why, within different cultures, the social desirability of extroversion might also be different ... so that in more collectivist cultures, there are weaker correlations [to extroversion]." In his work, Lucas found that despite extroversion's mistaken correlation to happiness, extroversion did not affect the culture in other countries as deeply as it did in America. He does maintain, though, that even in other cultures, extroversion does have a more "positive" definition. He continues, "We also find being positive and energetic is, by definition, a part of extroversion, too. You might expect it to be similar across different cultures. So, the [attributes] of extroversion correlate to wellbeing or attention from other people." Lucas does admit there is a generalization of extroversion here that links it solely with positive attributes. He concedes, "Of course the relationship to extroversion varies across cultures." The intersection of extroversion and well-being is not as predominantly a part of the cultural landscape in many cultures outside the United States that place a higher cultural value on introversion.

Examples of this might include Eastern countries such as India or China, where introversion seems the cultural norm. Despite their bustling crowded streets, these are countries where quiet is honored and often expected. Dr. Lisa Kaenzig agrees, noting from her personal experience, "Asia is a very different kind of culture, much more valuing of introverted skills. Students who come to our campus from China, for example, can sometimes take longer to get used to the fact that the professor wants to hear their voice in the class; we want them to participate."[5] But the introversion of the culture goes beyond quiet politeness in the classroom. Kaenzig continues, "It's also true in the work environment, when folks come from different cultures where listening is a very valued skill." A quiet work environment stands in stark contrast to the extroverted American corporate world so vividly described in Susan Cain's *Quiet: The Power of Introverts in a World That Can't Stop Talking*. Kaenzig explains the difference. She notes, "There is an urgency in the U.S. that everybody needs to participate in class exactly the same way, and everybody should be talking in a meeting, or they're not engaged or paying attention. And it is deeply problematic." Even while Americans have become more aware of extroverts monopolizing the conversation and leading with their energy, very little systemic change has actually taken place to offer a more equitable work or learning environment for the introvert. Kaenzig concludes, "It's very specific to our American culture. We have a lot to learn from other cultures, where the values of listening help to synthesize information at a much higher level than [the American] quick response." Learning about other cultures and their relationships to introversion offers a new and helpful perspective in the larger residual cultural impact, and also in how different approaches to valuing introversion might be adopted in the American acting classroom.

Well-known Indian actor and teacher Soumyabrata Choudhury deduced, "I find America to be an extremely extroverted culture. Surely that's a myth. Nevertheless, let's work by the myth. To the extent they're extroverted, [American] actors come out [in interviews] and talk about whatever is on their minds."[6] Choudhury sees American actors as gregarious creatures whose entire lives are open books. He continues, "The thing I love about America is the actors are the most open and exposed. No other actor from any other culture displays that sort of unreservedness. That creates behavior that affects other actors." Choudhury is referring to the extrovert ideal where actors present themselves in a demonstrative fashion. He says the "theatrical" behavior of the American extrovert then becomes normalized to fellow actors in that culture. But is this influence necessarily a good thing? Choudhury cautions, "Nevertheless, if they were to do the opposite, and try to get back to an acting flow ... sometimes it doesn't work. Suddenly those parts that suit an extroverted personality don't fit their character." Choudhury offers a glimpse of how Indians may perceive the American actor, but how does training differ in his home country?

INDIA

From its ancient backgrounds in religious ritual to its contemporary political street theatre scene, India has a rich theatrical tradition. In the book *Indian Method in Acting* (2013), Anuradha Kapur, Director of the National School of Drama, writes in the foreword that Indian actors have a sweeping variety of acting methods to work with.[7] From the ancient Sanskrit text on performance which includes many notes on acting, the *Natyashastra*,[8] dating as far back as 200 BCE, through colonization and the introduction of Western acting methods brought to the region mostly by English colonists and missionaries, to the current thriving Bollywood cinema scene, Indian actors have a variety of styles from which to base their work and root their training.

For centuries, theatre in India retained the ritualistic aspect as its acting base. Epic theatre, or traditional theatre in India, requires largely expressive, physically specific, holistic actors portraying powerful gods and goddesses in high-stakes, extravagant situations. When asked if this style of acting might also seem highly extroverted, actor, director, and scholar Benil Biswas replied, "I think the epic theatre or traditional model is very extroverted. Let out your emotion, be happy, and get back."[9] But importantly, the structure behind these classic stories features a plot that always ends with a restoration to life as usual. It is interesting that even these centuries-old epic adventures return to a calm stasis, a lasting moment of quiet reflection that mirrors the introvert's need to decompress. Biswas notes, "The traditional theatre is where you see all these activities done by our epic heroes, like Rahman, or there's a war ... and if there's chaos, that gets restored when you're back in society." In a way, these experiences could be thought of as a glimpse into extroversion before returning to introversion. Biswas notes, "It's a safe way to vent out emotion, like to cry with their loss, and then get back and think about the great loss." This post-celebration reflection offers another correlation between extroversion and introversion, allowing distance and quiet following emotionally demanding exchanges. Also, of note, these theatrical performances are most often presented at festivals and carnivals, a public environment where people tend to let loose and embody their more extroverted selves. Biswas concludes, "In a traditional model, every major ritual would also have a performance attached to it, so the performance then becomes a part of that particular training process." Traditional Indian actors are trained to perform at loud and animated celebrations, requiring an acting style to complement the crowd's energy and the exaggerated size of the characters.

The next major change in Indian acting, says Biswas, appears in the late eighteenth century, when for the first time, the British theatre arrived, with colonial theatre houses established in Mumbai. The presence of British theatre and acting styles also influenced some Indian producers, who created proscenium-style theatres around India and opened Parsi theatres. This style of theatre blended folk theatre with English overtones. Parsi theatres started presenting Shakespearean plays in a folk theatre style. Biswas explains that Parsi theatre companies performed using the format of the British playhouses, mostly because since the British companies were there, it seemed like an easy combination. Indian performers who were doing traditional folk performances also benefited from a steady supply of money. These resources allowed them to have their own theatre houses and produce works in several Indian languages like Hindi and Urdu, essentially merging British acting styles and texts with Indian folk theatre and local languages. This hybrid of acting styles is also prevalent in contemporary India with the proliferation of street theatre.

Street theatre in India is often used for political messaging or propaganda and many shows pop up in the most unlikely of places, similar to the American flash mob-style of performance. Street theatre in India is fast-paced, as audiences are caught unaware a show is about to commence. Biswas describes street theatre as a blend of the traditional Indian style and the Western proscenium mode of acting. The blend of ancient traditions in acting and the realism introduced by the British make for a unique brand of acting in street theatre. Biswas continues, "The traditional sphere is an epic mode of stylization. It's very out of the box. In a realistic model, it would be [considered] melodramatic. So, traditional theatre in India is completely melodramatic, from a Western perspective. But the melodrama is real; it's a mode of realism for India." In describing Indian street theatre, we see another merging of styles that demand a wide range of training from the Indian actor, where the style requires high energy and specific physical demands of India's traditional theatre style and the modern proscenium training associated with the classics of Western realism. Street theatre falls somewhere in between. This hybrid brand of theatre specific to India requires a versatile actor able to make bold physical choices balanced with the subtleties required of realism.

The majority of major acting schools in India have co-opted the Westernized approach to acting founded during the English colonization, and that model remains today. Biswas notes, "When [Western] theatre came to India, it brought with it training into being an extrovert. And as a whole, theatre training needs that workshop model of training and improvisation." Western-style training in India is unique because the extroverted model of training is now being modeled in a society that is generally introverted.

Besides the historical background, one must also understand the cultural landscape in order to examine the Indian actor. The Indian culture may be thought of as stereotypically introverted based simply on its connection to the meditative qualities of Hinduism, which might favor the introvert. Several Indian actors interviewed for the book supported this claim. However, they offered similar testimony to their American counterparts. Introverted Indian actor Kavya Misra states, "My mind is too clouded with the stories and lies that I have made about my entry into acting. I did not explore acting to do away with my introversion, but because I thought, 'I can do this.' My introversion has helped me remain calm in a state of chaos. To have peace within my thoughts. To become a great listener."[10] Another Indian actor, Shafali Jarial, a self-described introvert, was asked why the profession of acting was appealing.[11] Jarial shared, "I did it for the love of it. Even though I am scared, I have this tiny faith in myself that I am bigger than my fears. Besides, I live in my fantasies, and acting helps me to do it better. While acting, I can be anything, and I want to live as many lives as I can without restricting myself." It seems the allure of acting for the introvert knows no cultural boundaries.

Well-respected Indian actor and educator Soumyabrata Choudhury examines the Indian culture as well.[12] He understands (as we mentioned in the introduction to this chapter) that we are speaking about the stereotypes of a culture, which is always challenging to do. Choudhury warns, "It's very difficult to generalize. Yes, you have associations, for instance, that India is a more introverted culture, and America is extroverted. These can be refuted by individual cases. You may have an extremely extroverted Indian, so contextually, people are extroverts or not. In India, if you were to be present at some of our festivals, I doubt any culture is more extroverted than that!" His observations that Indians can embrace extroversion in individual cases or within some social contexts are sound, but he does concede that "[i]n other contexts, you're right. For instance, in the family context, the nature of the Indian family is still extremely patriarchal. In the presence of the patriarchal figure, yes, people are introverted, but that's not psychological introversion. That's a social binding of behaviors."

There is an interesting distinction between biological and psychological introversion as we've defined it and the performance of introversion as a social construct described here. Perhaps the social norms of the patriarchal structure actually enforce an introverted veneer, but beneath that structure live many extroverts.

The website CulturalIndia.net describes the rich diversities of the country, highlighting specifically the array of religious practices throughout India, which include Hinduism, Islam, Sikhism, Christianity, and Buddhism, among others.[13] These deep religious traditions most certainly affect the culture and, therefore, acting. Benil Biswas thinks the role of religion and its related customs plays an important part in defining the culture's introversion. He states, "There is religious diversity in India, and I think all of these religious communities have embraced introversion in their practices."[14] He notes the clothing worn or the use of the body in some of these religions act as a metaphor for the introversion they promote. Biswas continues, "In Islam, we think about Hijab, and in Hinduism, the way they dress, they need to have their bodies covered. It is also part of the Buddhist teaching, for Irham, that you need to be calm and quiet, and don't need to be expressive, no matter body movement, your body has to be very restricted." In these examples, the clothing associated with different religious beliefs might be tied to piety, modesty, or humility, all characteristics that could be correlated with a culturally specific definition of introversion. The idea of religious clothing restrictions as a metaphor for an introverted society is continued when Biswas notes, "Given this outward formation, we can see these manifestations in the body of the people. Such thought processes, if we have carried it, will come into the rehearsal space. It becomes a little difficult for us to bring in [acting] exercises from a very different context." Biswas reported, in many cases, Indian actors bring a physical and sometimes emotional restriction to the rehearsal room. Working in highly physical ways requires them to shed metaphoric trappings in order to gain a more physical connection to their work. Biswas concludes, "Trust building exercises or theatre games are a problem. This continues even after the ice-breaking sessions. It's deep-seated in the bodies." The physical demands of the work of acting might be further complicated by the social and religious constructs dictated by an actor's everyday social expectations.

Diversity of a different kind might also account for other possible challenges for the Indian actor. Biswas mentions the ideas of language diversity, caste and class tensions, and gender dynamics, all molding an Indian actor, who might be a bit more reserved than an extroverted American actor. Biswas notes, "Because India is so diverse, when actors deal with others, there is an immediate understanding of the auto-othering that happens, where there's a clear distinction between self and the other." This cultural divide within the rehearsal hall no doubt impacts the ability of the actors to interact openly and honestly and to establish a sense of ensemble with fellow actors from a different sect. This might feel like an insurmountable task because, in order to act with openness, actors would have to overcome centuries of cultural tensions. Biswas notes, "I think their own culture influences the way they interact with others. And that would be a universal idea of introversion." Biswas describes cultural influences on social interactions that offer an important difference unique to the Indian actor.

In his work as a director, Biswas finds Indian actors to be very introverted and has some interesting suggestions for educators wishing to allow them to explore playing alternate temperaments. Biswas suggests, "Any facilitator should be aware of the culture and context of individuals no matter where they teach." He suggests studying characters from famous, traditional stories might allow the actor to explore extroverted personalities and "help the students be at ease with this large method of performing because they already have concepts of this folklore. It becomes easier for them to overcome [their] inhibition [by using] an example they are familiar with." Rather than traditionally Western characters, like those that come from the plays of Shakespeare, Indian actors might find it easier to play the characters from their country's epic tales. These stock characters and situations have been played in extroverted fashion by other actors, which many in the Indian acting classroom will have seen. Actors will have a framework for their choices that offers a blueprint for the large physical and vocal choices they are asked to make in this sort of work. Rooting the acting in the folkloric tradition of storytelling demands they create more extroverted characters. Every culture contains its own common lore and characters, and these characters and storylines can easily be recalled with little preparation and might even offer a bridge between cultural or caste differences. As Biswas describes, "These are stories everybody knows. They know every character and bit of subtext or inner monologue. And it's not restricted to one particular community. It's a national epic. Everybody will draw some references." Biswas contends that because student actors are so intimately acquainted with these characters, they can more fully embody them. This approach might be particularly useful with introverted actors, who are apprehensive to work with others. They are able to transfer their focus onto the character relationships they are already familiar with and "get in the skin of the character first, and then deal with the other person." If cultural inhibitions create barriers related to working closely with other actors, Biswas believes this commonly shared source material and the epic mode of storytelling might help them "quickly forget who they are … it might be a very comical stock stereotypical representation, but for a moment, they are taken away from their own selves." Using intimately understood characters can offer a liberation into an alternate temperament, and this idea has merit in any classroom, where Biswas hopes student actors might be provided with a "space of ease" due to their shared familiarity.

It should be noted that, in these examples, "inhibition" is used almost synonymously with "introversion." Biswas hopes by transforming an actor's introverted temperament, even for a moment, they may be able to create multifaceted characters. Biswas concludes:

> When they [take on the character] and then come back to themselves, we [as educators] can say, "See what happened when you were trying to become that [character]?" You know the larger story. If that can happen with these characters, why can't we think of it in a very different sense of newer characters, newer narratives, and build the relationships therein so you are comfortable acting less inhibited?

Biswas' has thoughtfully created a road map for exploring alternate temperaments that upholds the cultural values of the students while also leaving room to explore the stylistic demands of an ancient and valued acting tradition. Biswas concludes, "Maybe theatre has to become an egalitarian space."

Educator and theatre director Soumyabrata Choudhury spoke about the idea of directing an introverted actor who may not be fulfilling the extroverted demands of the character, which he admits often represents "a general imperative for acting because you must remember, acting is also utilitarian. You have to get the actor to do something and produce something in a limited period of time."[15] Choudhury also shared some of the techniques he has used over the years to assist actors in finding ways to play another. He continues, "When I was directing and working with an actor, I'd do all these things to push and cajole them, shout at them, do tricks to get them to do something. Even sometimes do it myself. Why?

Because we're all working against time. The curtains are going to rise after fifteen days." So, while there may be ways in which the culture of introversion affects the type of actor and actor training provided in India, it seems the frustration some directors feel toward what they perceive as inhibition might actually represent a lack of understanding in how best to reach introverted actors.

GREECE

In the book *Indian Method in Acting*, the author Prasanna draws direct comparisons between Indian epic theatre and the Greek theatre, particularly how they were both founded in ritual and created highly theatrical forms of acting.[16] The Greek cultural perspective might be described as a more ambiverted society, as opposed to India's more introverted culture. Greece has a rich background in Philosophy—a discipline more stereotypically linked to introversion—while also combined with an extremely extroverted and social way of living. Think of the boisterous fishing villages or the busy town squares. Some may argue the stereotypical Greek is entirely extroverted, with loud voices and extremely animated body language. In fact, theatre director and educator Maria Frangi says of her Greek people, "They make much theatre. I believe they make theatre in their everyday life. Not only on stage."[17] No matter your ideas of the people of Greece, there is a difference in the way they approach theatre, as opposed to the American model.

Ancient Greek theatre acting styles are well documented, including the importance of large, sweeping gestures and loud, booming voices as integral parts of the actor's toolkit. But Frangi sees a thread from Ancient Greek theatre in contemporary Greek theatre. Frangi compares Greek theatre to theatre she has seen in America or England, saying, "For Greeks, it is more important, the text. They want to hear something interesting, and they want to talk about something interesting. In Greece, there is no way to make theatre without text." Dating back to the most famous Greek playwrights, the reliance on text contains hints about the kind of actors necessary for such acting work on the Greek stage. Frangi continues, "That is why we don't have pantomime in Greece. Instead, we have many kinds of theatre that are only speech, only language. For example, Karaghiozi, the Greek shadow theatre, is based only on dialogue." Even in alternate forms of theatre, Greek actors have a great reliance on the text. Frangi devotes much of her rehearsals to text-based, intellectual work, admitting, "It is a little bit messy because tragedy and comedy are both based on speech. Even the newer, more modern kinds of theatre are based on speech." The idea of script analysis, with its patterns of annotation, research, and table work, falls squarely in the domain of the introvert. Many introverted actors from across the globe highlight these aspects of actor training as some of their most meaningful. It seems in the Greek actor training model, this textual focus takes priority over other approaches. So then, as in India, we must also ask, is the Greek actor also affected by expectations and patterns in Greek culture?

Frangi believes so. Much of current theatre in Greece is driven by issue-based work, using text to debate issues pressing society. This could be seen as a connection to their philosophical forefathers. Frangi says Greek audiences use theatre as a means to examine political issues, noting, "[Actors] prefer to participate in a community's interests. That's why I have an idea about theatre that it is more political than a cultural or artistic event. The Greeks, my generation and before me, want to participate, to be in something very important in the decisions and the future of our community or our country." Frangi describes theatre as a political event that engenders vociferous discussion and a community commitment that has endured for generations. Frangi illuminates the theatrical mood in Greece as one of great passion: "They play in the street. They express everything. They express their hunger; they express their love. They like theatre." In taking on passionate and timely topics and subject matter, Greek theatre and acting styles do not shy away from large emotions or difficult questions. Particularly, as Frangi notes, there is a Greek tradition of using theatre to expose "problems or themes or sadness from everyday life. It's more than history. It is political. Because, from actual political problems, they can make theatre." Engaging in this dialogue through theatre requires an actor who must first understand how to process and facilitate public discourse. This charge provides a shared opportunity between each temperament; the processing skill is where an introvert can excel, while the public facilitation can feature the skills of the extrovert.

Frangi is aware of both types of actors in the rehearsal hall, and when asked if she prefers to direct an introverted or extroverted actor, she notes, "If I have good actors, of course, it is easier for me to have somebody who is extroverted. The extrovert is easier to finish quickly and to have a result." Frangi highlights one of the many strengths of an extrovert—getting to a quick outcome. However, she continues, "It is more interesting to work with somebody who is introverted because by the end, maybe it is not a success, because you don't know if he can finally arrive, but it is an interesting procedure." Here Frangi refers to the more measured approach of the introvert. She surmises the extrovert may get to the result quicker, but the introvert may offer more interesting choices within the rehearsal process. Her conclusion, though, strikes a balance: "But I cannot say I prefer that or this because I like working, so for me, it is very interesting to work with both." That quick summation (and generalization) of the ways in which introverted and extroverted actors work seems to know no international boundaries.

In the rehearsal hall and the classroom, Frangi also notices a disturbing trend with young students. Frangi laments, "The new generations are very different. My students don't like to show anything. They keep everything inside." She notices a trend among the younger generation away from the overtly gregarious members of some Greek society, toward a more introspective vibe. She suggests perhaps this new generation's growing reliance on screen time, a fundamentally private and introverted activity, has affected the work in the classroom. (It should be noted too that screen time can also be considered an over-stimulating and extroverted activity, depending on the numbers of people you are interacting with.) But Frangi has addressed what she believes these actors need. She notes, "Through my courses and direction in the theatre, I like to take everything from inside to outside. It is a way of reversing things." In her example, Frangi advocates for releasing the introverted temperament in order to find more passion and willingness in the student's work.

Frangi has ways of working to facilitate this release. True to the Greek theatrical style, she approaches the work first from a place of text, but rather than using the written text, she uses the actors' own words. She lets them share what is important to them. Frangi notes, "[In] working with the dialogue first, I don't push things to my idea. When I enter the class, I prefer to hear them. I want them to talk about themselves, as people, not as actors. They are studying theatre, but they need to express themselves, so they need to participate [as themselves]." Frangi believes this inspires trust in the classroom, as well as autonomy for the artist, that will allow either introverted or extroverted actors to acquire the skills necessary to create the political theatre of the past.

Next in Frangi's quest to create more passionate actors is another pedagogical tactic, one in which she works physically first, and then works vocally. She sees a generation of actors disconnected from their physical selves and wants to create a more holistically engaged actor. Frangi sees this physical-first as a way to "play with the body to make the dialogue of the body. I believe that both sides, the material body and voice – and the other part that it is not material, the thoughts – everything can be in a kind of workshop together." What Frangi advocates for here is the ideal synergy of body and voice that also allows the thoughts of the introvert to be present as an equal contributor to success within the craft.

ENGLAND

In looking at England's relationship with introversion, Dr. Brent Donnellan noted some interesting distinctions.[18] Rather than introversion versus extroversion, he said the dichotomy is more of "collectivist versus individualist cultures, with the United States as more individualistic than England in the context of extroversion, agency, and being outgoing and demonstrative, whereas the stereotype of British folks is that they're more buttoned up." Again, we understand we are stereotyping for the purposes of the book, and not all British people are buttoned up and not all Americans are rowdy cowboys. Donnellan understands this as well, noting, "The stereotype of being buttoned up and having a stiff upper lip is not an American value. We wear our hearts on our sleeves and are super outgoing and emotive, and that's not a British stereotype." He returns to the idea of collectivism versus individualism in relation to other cultures by pointing out that "even in Asian cultures, we might think of collectivism, where individualistic traits like extroversion are not as highly valued or conditioned, and parents tell their extroverted kids they have to fit in. In the United States, we don't have that press." Donnellan's point that in another culture, an extroverted student might be told to conform to a more introverted demeanor is certainly an interesting one and is supported by the anecdotal cultural evidence shared by other interviewees. John Baxter, the Head of Movement Training at the London Academy of Music and Dramatic Art (LAMDA), agrees that culture and society play a great role in training the actor. He notes, "good actors always reflect the society from which they spring – in all its myriad and various ways. In shape, in temper, in class, in gender, in culture, in sexual orientation and in mood – extrovert or introvert."[19] A connection to a culture rich with theatrical tradition may create a unique way of training actors.

England's theatrical history has been enhanced by the excellent training programs offered there for ages. Rather than offering an American perspective on the differences within UK actor training here, we look to a

2016 article from the UK publication *The Stage* titled "UK vs US: How Is Drama Training Different?" by Nouska Hanley.[20] Hanley makes this assessment of UK training programs: "UK drama training is predominantly structured toward preparing students for the stage, for sustained performances, achieved through consistent solid technique, vocal discipline, and physical and mental stamina." This assertion makes sense, based on England's brilliant theatrical history on the stage. Hanley compares, "In the US, the focus is largely on screen acting. The two require different approaches, and the pedagogy reflects that. If you're going to achieve brilliant performances eight times a week on stage, classical technique is your friend. Film is an entirely different landscape, requiring a subtler, more life-like realism." Now, before tempers flare, we should note this quote was used to articulate a UK perspective on how actor training in America is taught. The assertion that American drama programs are more geared toward film might irk many American readers, but the international perspective is, at the very least, interesting and necessary to acknowledge. If we take the American film training assertion as true, it seems that, at least in the way Hanley describes, US training would favor the introvert and England the extrovert, with the American style being more singular and subtler, and the British style with more traditionally theatrical public presentations. We know from our research that the opposite is true. Another generalization in training is that England works from the "outside in" (starting with an external choice and letting that affect the psychology of the character) and America from the "inside out" (starting with the psychology to affect the externals). We know, of course, both countries use a variety of methods to achieve the work of the actor, but if that generalization were true, the American way of working would also favor the introvert and the British version the extrovert. These questionable generalizations are simply ways of looking more closely at the cultural differences related to acting and uncovering the contradictions that might result in this examination.

LAMDA's John Baxter also notices differences between the American and British students, as cultural difference manifests through approaches to the work in training:

> American actors in training often overthink initially – they have to be released in a trusting environment and given the freedom to fail and to fall. This can sometimes be seen as a fragile state. It isn't. On the other hand, they can seem bolder and quicker than their UK peers once they give in to

actually *feeling* the lesson ... British actors in training are initially less inward-looking and seem less cluttered with self-appraisal, but often need encouragement to sustain things discovered en route. They are also slower to free up the emotional response.[21]

These differences seem to belie some of the perceived American-only ideas of the extrovert ideal approach to education. If American actors overthink, is that introverted behavior? If British actors are less inward-looking, does that make them more extroverted? Does the idea of one's perception and understanding of introversion and extroversion lead to unique generalizations? Is such labeling reductive? Clearly when asked about the differences, the cultural perception might be different than what Baxter initially identifies.

Professor Baxter has another keen observation. He notes that in the UK there is certainly still a similar stereotype of the professional actor as a gregarious extrovert, but believes this opinion to be held mostly by people outside of the industry. He says, "From the inside, this is not always the case, and this perception is frequently seen as a cover, a coping mechanism for anxiety and insecurity by an artist in a profession where they are confronted daily by criticism and rejection on a personal level." One can note in Baxter's appraisal of the extrovert that bravado in the studio could be perceived as a way to manage the constant stressful situation the actor must navigate daily.

Such nurturing is already taking place in the training at LAMDA, where introverts and extroverts are both valued for their vastly different work. Baxter actively encourages a diverse dynamic in the studio because he believes so completely in the ensemble. Baxter recalls, "[Ensemble] reaches all the way back the first actors in the cradle of civilization: the Greek tragic chorus. The strength of the extroverted artist is the bold leap, the initial response before thought or analysis. The strength of the introverted artist is the relish of the abstract and a natural rebellion against cliché or push. The strength of the ensemble is the embracing of both of these dynamics." Such inclusivity is the goal of this book.

Baxter shared how he places value on the introvert in the classroom. He notes: "I have actively encouraged my students to preserve their individual instinctive responses and to prize them over applied cliché for the simple reason that this will give them the edge once they get their foot in the door." Identifying and celebrating unexpected differences in the base instinct work for an actor relies on an educator savvy enough to understand the differences between extroverts and introverts when acting.

However, nurturing an individual artistic response needs to be combined with a rigorous dynamic. Baxter calls this a fragile process, taking determination and rigor from the first moment of training, and as an educator, he admits he must tread a fine line to achieve this balance when dealing with the introverted acting student. Empathetic and equitable actor training poses the challenge of supporting the introverted instinct while also cultivating the necessary commitment to enter the audition space in the first place.

This "fine line" brings us to another important question: are audition experiences similar in both the US and the UK? Baxter has noticed a more balanced atmosphere in the waiting room situation, where auditions are often places of high nervous energy, which of course can involve competitive behavior, showboating, and overt display. However, he notes there is "usually some sort of space for an introspective actor to sit quietly and prepare. Sometimes the corridor outside the waiting room will reveal one or more of these artists approaching the situation in their own way. There is often a healthy mix of both approaches – depending on the nature of the work in the audition." Prior to an audition, most American waiting rooms lean toward a much more social event. Private space and time are scarce, a fact which may affect many introverted actors. Several actors offer commentary about the challenges of an extroverted waiting room, and the anxiety that comes with it, in the upcoming chapter on auditions.

Baxter surmises that "the introvert and the extrovert actor exist in both US and UK training, despite cultural and educational differences. I am glad that they do." His understanding that both personality types make for a richer experience for the ensemble and the audience drives his approach to training. As revealed from the survey covered in Chap. 4, the inclusivity of actor training Baxter describes was not experienced by a majority of our respondents. Perhaps inclusive actor training rests with the educator and is based on individual pedagogical approaches that cross cultural structures.

We are not leaving England just yet. In the next chapter, one of the book's authors interviews Rodney Cottier, Head of Drama at the London Academy of Musical and Dramatic Art. In that interview, Mr. Cottier examines the British versus American aesthetics of the introverted actor. He discusses how a predisposition to introversion for the actor may yield a more exceptional portrayal of some of Shakespeare's more introverted characters. He also examines the concept of extroversion in the British Academy and shares his observations over his decades-long career educating in both the British and American actor training systems.

NOTES

1. Cain, Susan. *Quiet: The Power of Introverts in a World That Can't Stop Talking.* London: Viking, 2013.
2. Donnellan, Brent. Personal interview. 1 Dec. 2018.
3. Donnellan, Brent. Interview.
4. Lucas, Richard. Personal interview. 15 Jan. 2019.
5. Kaenzig, Lisa. Personal interview. 15 Dec. 2018.
6. Choudhury, Soumyabrata. Personal interview. 14 Feb. 2019.
7. Prasanna. *Indian Method in Acting.* New Delhi: National School of Drama, 2013.
8. The Editors of Encyclopaedia Britannica. "Natyashastra." Encyclopædia Britannica. Encyclopædia Britannica, Inc., April 12, 2011. https://www.britannica.com/topic/Natyashastra
9. Biswas, Benil. Personal interview. 14 Feb. 2019.
10. Misya, Kavra. Personal interview. 12 Feb. 2019.
11. Jarial, Shafali. Interview.
12. Choudhury, Soumyabrata. Interview.
13. "Information on Indian Culture, Tradition & Heritage." Cultural India. Accessed November 22, 2019. https://www.culturalindia.net/
14. Biswas, Benil. Interview.
15. Choudhury, Soumyabrata. Interview.
16. Prasanna, *Indian Method in Acting.*
17. Frangi, Maria. Personal interview. 22 Feb. 2019.
18. Donnellan, Brent. Interview.
19. Baxter, John. Personal interview. 3 Sept. 2019.
20. Hanley, Nouska. "UK vs US: How Is Drama Training Different?" Accessed November 22, 2019. https://www.thestage.co.uk/features/2016/uk-vs-us-drama-training-different/
21. Baxter, John. Interview.

REFERENCES

Baxter, John. Personal interview. 3 Sept. 2019.

Biswas, Benil. Personal interview. 14 Feb. 2019.

Cain, Susan. *Quiet: The Power of Introverts in a World That Can't Stop Talking.* London: Viking, 2013.

Choudhury, Soumyabrata. Personal Interview. 14 Feb. 2019.

Donnellan, Brent. Personal interview. 1 Dec. 2018.

"Information on Indian Culture, Tradition & Heritage." Cultural India. Accessed November 22, 2019. https://www.culturalindia.net/.

Frangi, Maria. Personal interview. 22 Feb. 2019.

Hanley, Nouska. "UK vs US: How Is Drama Training Different?" Accessed November 22, 2019. https://www.thestage.co.uk/features/2016/uk-vs-us-drama-training-different/.

Jarial, Shafali. Interview.

Kaenzig, Lisa. Personal interview. 15 Dec. 2018.

Lucas, Richard. Personal interview. 15 Jan. 2019.

Misya, Kavra. Personal interview. 12 Feb. 2019.

Prasanna. *Indian Method in Acting*. New Delhi: National School of Drama, 2013.

The Editors of Encyclopaedia Britannica. "Natyashastra." Encyclopædia Britannica. Encyclopædia Britannica, inc., April 12, 2011. https://www.britannica.com/topic/Natyashastra.

CHAPTER 9

Interview with Rodney Cottier

The London Academy of Music and Dramatic Arts (LAMDA) is the oldest drama school in the United Kingdom. Founded in 1861 as the London Academy of Music, LAMDA remains a pioneering theatrical training program that has graduated numerous well-known actors for decades. Among those who have studied at LAMDA include Chiwetel Ejiofor, Benedict Cumberbatch, David Oyelowo and many more.[1] A note on their approach to training on their website shares:

> Conservatoire training is, by its nature, selective, as we train only the best – limiting our course numbers and teaching in small groups. The ensemble is at the heart of our work; drama is a collaborative art form, and our training stresses the importance of collaboration to achieve excellence. The training is vocational because drama is a vocation, and we are training students for a profession. The training is practical because drama is about doing and being. We offer an inventive environment for artistic development; our commissioning and creative programme gives artists and practitioners time to reflect, examine their own practice, and contribute to an ever-evolving industry.[2]

What follows are excerpts from an interview with Rodney Cottier, the Head of Drama at LAMDA.[3] The discussion reveals several of the key points in the program, from the make-up of the classes and courses to the trajectory of the actor training. Throughout the discussion, points are

© The Author(s) 2020
R. Roznowski et al., *The Introverted Actor*,
https://doi.org/10.1007/978-3-030-41607-2_9

drawn for how this classic and well-respected training program might consider and impact introverted actors:

Rob: How many students are in a class?
Cottier: We tend to take in a cohort of thirty. So there'd be thirty, or maybe twenty-eight, in our MA and MFA [programs]. Most of our classes are in half groups. In other words, groups of fourteen or fifteen. We've found that this is the best number to work with, which is actually quite interesting. I always argued Shakespeare's company was fourteen actors.
Rob: Why do you think that number works?
Cottier: It definitely seems to be a number that works. In Shakespeare's plays, it's extraordinary how many times you find there are seven major characters and seven in the background. I suppose it does give rise to thinking this was the size of his company, fourteen or fifteen. The evidence points that way … If you have an ensemble of that many actors, you start to share and explore together. Obviously, with two groups, we're mixing all the time. You don't go through with the same people.

Right away, we see how the number of students in a class might impact the temperaments of the actors. Limiting the number of students in a cohort and allowing them to change groups makes good pedagogical sense. A smaller class size is a value to the introverted actor, while the changing of groups and acting partners is a boon for the extroverts:

Cottier: We change groups. There is a difference in the way we do things inasmuch as, in American universities, I hear, "I auditioned for this." Here, they don't audition. We cast. We choose the plays, we cast, we decide what we think is right for that student at a particular point. There's absolutely no audition because students will develop at their own rate, and the group will encourage each other. The point of any drama training is that [students] feel they are able to fall flat on their faces, and dare, explore, and try things.
           I remember when I trained, I thought, "I'm going to be the class valedictorian and join the Royal Shakespeare Company. I'll do Arden and Pinter." And "Why aren't we doing tryouts? Why are we doing this? Why are we doing that?"

And of course, in year two, you realize you learned so much in training, but it wouldn't actually fully drop until after you left.

Removing the pressure of auditioning allows introverted actors to focus entirely on their training and trust their efforts in the classroom without worry for whether or not they will be cast. This offers another interesting pedagogical idea allowing introverts to thrive in the rehearsal and exploratory process without the public scrutiny and competition of the audition:

Rob: Do you find, in the creation of ensemble, there are some people who are left behind, or some people who are overshadowed? How do you make sure all people are heard?

Cottier: If you look at our timetable, we are very different to many other drama schools. That is largely to do with course content. We are the most physical of any drama school. A lot of our training has come to us through people who have trained most particularly with Jacques Lecoq. We're looking at animal lessons, clowning, masks, all of these areas where actors are, as an ensemble, creating, whether it's anarchy or whatever it may be…a lot of our physical training is because we want the actors to sense and intuit; the verb you use for rhythm is feel. You cannot think the rhythm.
You can intellectualize rhythm … Shakespeare writes in rhythm. If you get the rhythm right, suddenly you realize, "I can do it. This makes sense." Waves are an image I use as well because, if you fight the wave when you're surfing, you fall off. Whereas, if you go with the wave, if you go with the rhythm and start to explore, whether you're doing it as a group or a two-hat or whatever, you're surfing.

The reliance on physical work might be a surprising one, as it works against the concept of the head-centered approach some might have expected to come from British actor training. As we know, the focus on specific and stylized physical work can be a source of anxiety or fear for many introverted actors, but guided exploration can also offer great rewards:

Rob: What do you do when an actor is trapped inside his or her head?

Cottier: This is why you need physical training. Don't get me wrong; I'm not saying voice work isn't physical. It is very physical. Everything we do is physical...So people come to us for the MFA who have been to a university where they've been in a drama society, and they arrive doing the "Shakespeare voice." But eventually they let go of old habits and suddenly they're in there together.

There are encouraging words here of the idea that even the most ingrained physical or vocal acting habits can be overcome with advanced training and a supportive ensemble. Additionally, the concept of actors creating their own content is a great boon for introverts who excel at solo activities like writing and analysis:

Rob: What happens when you get an actor who might be reticent about something physical? When you're trying to help them find the rhythm, and they are tentative. How do you approach getting them out of it?
Cottier: There are many exercises you can do. There's a support system as well. Obviously, you don't want to make somebody jump the highest fence in the field the first time around because they'll refuse. But gradually ... the support mechanism of the group makes people want to try. If you feel you are being supported by one another, then you are willing to take risks.

As we have already pointed out, risk-taking is a major expectation in most actor training programs. The idea of safety and risk-taking is a partnership introverts crave, and it can be fostered by a close-knit and compassionate ensemble. It appears the approach to education at LAMDA truly and explicitly considers this as a priority in the actors' training:

Cottier: If an actor feels they are exposed and everybody's looking at them and judging, they will disappear into a little, shallow, human ball. That's one of the reasons we're very careful. To give you an example, there is a three-year course. In the first year, [students] do scenes and work on style. They do Jacobean scenes, and finish the year very deliberately doing a Greek play where there are Greek choruses. It is all about voice and body.

Then they go away and reflect. The only people who see their work during this entire year will be themselves and the faculty. In the second year, we start doing two-hour versions of Shakespeare, Restoration comedy, Russian naturalism, and possibly some musical theatre. At that point in the training, we allow other students, selected groups, to come in and observe the work so [actors] in the space get used to the idea of an audience. But it's an audience of people who've been down the path before and are there to support. So [the student actors] feel supported, but they are also getting a response.

Then, in the third year they go public, and that's when we allow direct transit.

Rob: Do you notice a difference? Do you notice students revert or regress?

Cottier: It's very good you said that. It's why we've got to be so careful in the extraordinarily delicate work in the second year. The minute the public arrives, we've got to be careful the support will carry [the students] forward. Otherwise, they all suddenly think, "Oh, God, the lights, the agent, the casting director, and, worst of all, the parents." And they withdraw. That's why it takes two years to get them to that point. I think it's very important. You don't want to expose them too early. Of course, casting directors would love to get to a couple of our first or second years.

This gradual approach to public viewing shows a tremendous respect for the introvert and also places value on the process of learning over the product of performance. After years of safety and privacy in training, some of the anxiety that often accompanies the addition of an audience might be somewhat alleviated. This extended training, with a profound focus on ensemble and a delayed inclusion of the audience, seems to exemplify the idea of the Long Runway pedagogical approach as it might be applied to actor training:

Rob: Do you find it difficult to have a great actor, someone who is free and alive on stage, but when it comes to the professional side, the networking, talking with agents and casting directors, they clam up? How would you work with an actor in that way?

Cottier: We have a very good support system in our final year where
             actors work with an industry liaison. She is a professional cast-
             ing director who works alongside the students, preparing them
             through the final year. Not only that, we have another system
             in place. I don't know if you do this in the United States, but
             it's called mentoring?
Rob: Yes, we do.
Cottier: For the last six months of training as an actor, and the first six
             months a student is out in the business, they are with some-
             body who's already trod that path.
Rob: Is this an alumnus from your program, normally?
Cottier: Absolutely. So, those who work in Los Angeles or New York
             from our three-year program are paired up, sometimes with
             more than one person, if they do east and west coasts. Obviously,
             it relies on the good will of our alums, but so far, it seems
             to work.

The realm of professionalization and the extensive networking so often
required of this business can be overwhelming, for introverts and extroverts alike. Assigning a mentor who has received the same training, and
has already navigated the professional forays of the industry is a gift:

Rob: If we talk in the most generic and general terms, would you
             consider a typical British actor to be a more introverted type or
             would you consider them ambiverts or extroverts? What would
             you consider to be the norm?
Cottier: I don't know that there is a typical [type] to be quite honest. If
             you're talking about somebody who is introverted, but then
             when they're on stage, magic happens. I was very lucky. I
             worked with Paul Scofield. In rehearsal, he'd be very quiet,
             working things out. And you'd think "Hang on, all he's doing
             is mumbling." But he was gradually piecing things together.
             Then suddenly at the run-through, you'd see what had been
             going on. His process was so detailed ... And people who say
             "Do you work from the inside out or the outside in?" Ideally,
             you should do both. Obviously, you can explore the world or
             what you were wearing, or whatever it may be. And at the same
             time, there's everything Stanislavsky has been teaching us all,
             not only the character in the play, but the backstory, the life of

the character, the life of relationships, everything before the play began.

Rob: Which, in some ways, an introvert might be more prone to do because they're often more comfortable with analysis.

Cottier: Yes. Being able to sense the [character's] backstory … There are certain people who do emotional sense memory incorrectly. And then you wonder why the actor is having a mental break-down. Well, if you put yourself through that sort of process, that's not good. If you're playing Richard III and trying to access a personal sense memory of how you were a serial killer, I don't think I'd like to be in the room with you, to be quite honest.

But nevertheless, [Richard III] has an extraordinary moment where he has to say to this woman "I've never cried in my life. And you have made me cry." And how does he access that, especially as he's faking it? It's brilliant.

If introverted actors are more in tune with a range of human emotions and have an extensive interior life from which to pull their experiences, they can likely access these personal elements for the use of developing and expanding the believability of a character. Doing this safely, in a process of support, is a valuable actor skill:

Rob: Have you ever found an issue with an extroverted actor having to portray an introverted character, or vice versa, an introvert playing somebody who is completely free on stage, and either struggling to get there?

Cottier: I can talk about myself; a part I struggled with, and I never got there, was Hjalmar Ekdal in *The Wild Duck*. I tried every way. I could not find it because there is an extroverted side to the char-acter. He is introverted and extroverted at the same time. I found him hugely difficult. And he's incredibly repetitive as well. Polly Thully directed it recently with our MFA students, and it was absolutely brilliant. I thought "Oh God, I made such a mess of that forty years ago. [I had] no idea whatsoever." It is difficult. I directed *Hamlet* a few years ago. I have five different Hamlets. And that's a brutal department. You try the ending different ways with different images, and suddenly you think, "It worked!" It's how you unlock it.

ob: So, related to that, let's say we're doing soliloquy, and an actor who is more introspective is unable to get to that place of really asking questions internally. How would you approach your Hamlet?

Cottier: Okay … but I won't give *Hamlet* as an example. Let's try Emilia. She's getting Desdemona ready for bed. She's got that speech about husbands. That can come out as a bitter speech, with absolute bile. And then you put the actress through the process:

Who are you with?

"I'm with Desdemona."

What emotional state is Desdemona in?

"She's crying."

What are you trying to do to her?

"Stop her from crying."

So if you are bitterly vicious, do you think you're going to stop her from crying or make her slit her wrists?

"Ah, right."

So, let's look at it a different way. Try cracking jokes.

"Okay."

Alright, now try it again. This time, imagine you are wearing thick makeup to hide the bruises.

Then you apply that to it. You're trying to cheer her up, but at the same time, you're hiding the bruises because you don't want to tell her Iago bashed you the night before. So you start to build up the layers. And by building up those layers, you start to find the details of the character. That will suddenly open things up.

Cottier is suggesting a way in which to deepen the introspection within the scene through a variety of questions. In this way, an extrovert could appear to have the introvert's connection to reflective thought:

Cottier: I get the same thing in North America. Paulina in *A Winter's Tale* is popular at auditions.

[Leontes] is already there. He's just found out his son is dead. You come in, and you've brought another bit of information. He's weeping. So very gently, take him by the hand. Stroke his hand, and ask him some questions. "What do you want to do to me? Do you want to boil me in oil? Fry me with shallots and balsamic vinegar? Do you want to do this? Yes?" Try to put more wit and humor into the situation, which is only going to make it worse for him.

Then, at the end, suddenly we get the turn. "Oh, well, yes, alright. But here's the information I actually came in to tell you. She's dead." Twist the knife. Then the audience listens to you. And we don't go to a generalized shoutfest.

The work is trying different things, which may be completely opposite of the way it's going to end up.

In Cottier's approach, he is offering a variety of opposite or unexpected choices to present actors with a variety of ways to approach the character. In this way of working, Cottier allows actors to think beyond what their personal temperament and approach might be in order to find new and unexpected ways of acting the role. These choices can be introverted or extroverted:

Cottier: With improvisation, you could be improvising the script. Improvisation doesn't mean you have to change the words. Use those words, but change the scenario.

Rob: So the actor can feel safe rather than creating his or her own words, but they have the basis of the scene and character in which to improvise?

Cottier: You improvise the situation whilst using the text, rather than doing it in your own words.

Here we are presented with a kind of improvisation that offers introverted students the structure of the text while asking them to improv around a new scenario for the characters. This balance of structure and improvisation allows more introspective actors to frame their work around a text they already know and understand, and simply experiment with new possible scenarios for the characters. This approach might be less threatening for introverted actors who are apprehensive about improv:

Rob: I would imagine you see actors come at their training from two different places: some who want fame and attention and the life of the public, and others who want to approach acting to create or to become someone else. Do you find them to be different in the classroom?

Cottier: No. There's a reason for that. It's a problem in certain areas, with certain schools and what they are training. I can get a number of people, and in their delivery of the speeches, you realize they're actually rather good, but they have been doing these [monologues] for a drama festival competition. There are a lot of these awful presentations. There was one man who'd just graduated. It took me an hour at the audition. I knew there was something there, but I had to try every single way possible to stop him from performing. Seals perform. Actors don't. They act. I'm not interested in a performer.

There are certain actors, where, I come out [of the theatre] and feel I have just seen the actor. I never saw the character because the actor gave me camel spins, double lutz, triple salchow, all the rest of it, and I don't buy it...It's not acting. That's performing ... It's a zoo.

Rob: What do you notice is the biggest difference between your approach to training and the American approach, in general terms?

Cottier: I've been doing these lecture tours ... I do a 300-level Master Class on Shakespeare and the Globe ... One of my treats is going to the North Carolina School of the Arts. The ethos of that school and the discipline in the rehearsal is breathtaking. If you were to ask about the difference between the North Carolina School of the Arts and LAMDA, I would struggle to find a difference. It depends entirely on the school and the interviewers.

What is clear, though, is there is a strong influence, and you can look on the resumes, as to what young actors have been doing before they apply. Far more [actors] in North America have been doing musical theatre, whereas in [England], we don't do musical theatre nearly as much, if at all. I know because every time we do a musical here, the Americans wipe the board with us. It's part of the culture.

One of the dangers in auditioning is of the presentational approach. For example, [actors] come in and they say "Well, for my tragic monologue, I'm doing this and for my comedic, I'm doing that." And I always think, "What are you doing for your acting?"

And tragic [piece] very often is license to shout for three minutes, and comedic means license to pull faces for three minutes. And that [habit] comes from musical theatre. Nevertheless, underneath all that is a very talented, young, sensitive individual…Or they wouldn't be doing it in the first place. Unless they really are, it's just saying, "Look at me." [One American celebrity] came to speak to our students years ago, and the last piece of advice he gave the whole school was "Leave your ego at the door." Bang on the money. If you come in, and you're part of the ensemble, your ego stays out there.

Rob: I would imagine that also means leave your issues. So that might mean the characteristics of your personality in terms of being either extroverted or introverted. Leave that stuff and get focused on the work.

Cottier: Absolutely.

Rob: Are there any last words you want to say about the strengths or barriers an introverted actor might have?

Cottier: An introverted actor is inevitably a sensitive person, and [an actor] brings those senses to Hamlet or any other sensitive character. They're going to find somebody who senses and intuits, and that's going to be exciting. So it can enrich the work, so long as you're not putting yourself through unnecessary psychological torture. Because at the end of the day, you're going to leave the stage, go home, and cook dinner. When you chop the onion, you're going to do it with pleasure, not take half your hand off.

So, Cottier, in his wide-ranging interview, offers a real glimpse into the LAMDA way of actor training. While this physical approach to acting may not be required at other British schools, LAMDA's philosophy does seem to value the introvert in the acting studio in various constructs. From small class sizes to slowly allowing public performances, LAMDA has a unique approach to actor training that can be mimicked in American programs.

In our next chapter, some simple adaptations to an American acting studio were piloted in an undergraduate acting class. These changes allowed for a classroom similar to the LAMDA approach that equally values introversion. The changes in the classroom made for a parity in learning for both introverts and extroverts.

Notes

1. "Alumni." London academy of music & dramatic art. Accessed November 22, 2019. https://ww2.lamda.ac.uk/students-alumni/alumni
2. "Homepage: London Academy of Music & Dramatic Art." Homepage | London academy of music & dramatic art. Accessed November 22, 2019. https://ww2.lamda.ac.uk/
3. Cottier, Rodney. Personal interview. 24 July 2018.

References

"Alumni." London academy of music & dramatic art. Accessed November 22, 2019. https://ww2.lamda.ac.uk/students-alumni/alumni.
Cottier, Rodney. Personal interview. 24 July 2018.
"Homepage: London Academy of Music & Dramatic Art." Homepage | London academy of music & dramatic art. Accessed November 22, 2019. https://ww2.lamda.ac.uk/.

CHAPTER 10

Case Study: Comedy Class

To put some of these temperament-inclusive pedagogical suggestions into practice, one of the authors experimented with an upper-level acting course devoted to scene study within various styles of comedy. The pedagogical suggestions contained within this chapter added little extra time to the course, but did allow for a semester-long awareness of introversion in the classroom. The course was divided into five sections, each representing a different style of comedic performance: commedia dell'arte, sketch comedy, sitcoms, comedy of manners/farce, and standup. Each of these sections contained a strategy for presenting the course materials that uniquely considered actor temperaments, either in the make-up of actor partnering or the way in which the material was rehearsed. Although not overt throughout the course, the class was designed with a through line that respected and valued each student's temperament. Student reflections regarding these course features were collected after the end of the semester and in no way impacted final grades, with the goal of encouraging self-evaluation and candor. Student contributions to this publication were anonymous and completely voluntary. The course design, syllabus, and several student responses all serve as the basis for this chapter. Many of these valuable reflections have been included in detail so as to provide as much first-person insight as possible.

© The Author(s) 2020
R. Roznowski et al., *The Introverted Actor*,
https://doi.org/10.1007/978-3-030-41607-2_10

Syllabus

The first day of the course began with a discussion of introversion in both the acting studio and the profession. In this first class, students were asked how they self-identified and what they thought of as the perceived strengths of introverts, extroverts, or ambiverts. The class also examined work and interviews from famous actors to see if there were ways to identify whether or not they were introverts. We then reviewed the syllabus, which contained the following language.

Introverted/Extroverted Learners

All types of learners will be respected in this course. Where most educational models reward extroverted personalities (especially in theatre), this class hopes to honor all types of learning. If immediate group dynamics, rapid results, or other extrovert-based imperatives impact your best work, please inform the instructor in order to adjust the experience for optimal learning for all. The course design is intentional in its inclusion and recognition of introverted and extroverted pairings. The subject of the introvert-extrovert spectrum will be explained at the start of the course and reflected upon by you at the end of the course, and throughout, you are asked to notice the ways in which you work together, respect and listen to each other, and collaborate with both your introverted and extroverted peers. We may not return to the subject daily or even monthly, but the design of the course should allow you to determine how your temperament affects your work and affects others.[1]

For many extroverts in the class, this was the first time they understood how their behavior might impact their fellow classmates. For introverts, this was the first time they felt valued and supported in class rather than penalized for being quiet or reserved. For many, the simple addition of this temperament-specific language engendered a deeper understanding of the way different personalities and learning styles work, create, and learn together.

By its design, the acting course featured a heavy reliance on students creating their own content, many times in partnerships or groups. Incorporating temperament awareness into self-monitored group work was, admittedly, a lofty goal, and some of the reflection papers still revealed dissatisfaction with group work because, when not under supervision, it was perceived that the extroverted students continued to dominate the conversation. While there did appear to be some change in student group dynamics, this awareness was not as drastic or as consistent as was hoped. As mentioned earlier, group projects can be overwhelming for the introvert, so the syllabus addressed this challenge:

> *Group and Partner Projects: Group projects can sometimes be overwhelming and unfair. Consider this: in a typical group of 6–8 people, three people usually do 70% of the talking. Let's work to change that. There are several group projects in this course, and your work with partners and groups must maintain a respectful, collaborative nature that allows any type of learner or actor to succeed. If you feel un-heard (by people not listening to your contribution) or unsupported (by partners not wanting to rehearse when necessary), your first line of action is to talk with your partner or group. If you are dissatisfied with the answer or the results, you should then come to the instructor for a facilitated discussion.[2]*

The syllabus also followed an earlier suggestion from this book related to participation in class with the following language:

> *As you may note, there is no participation grade for this class, as participation is often considered only as part of an extroverted ideal. In this class, there are both introverted and extroverted ways to participate. You can participate by being quiet and engaged, taking notes, and listening, as well as by talking, volunteering, giving feedback, and asking questions. It is expected that all students complete all varieties of work and activities, including creating an inclusive and welcoming atmosphere for various types of participation beyond being the loudest and first to answer.[3]*

It might be assumed that the inclusion of such language or policies risks alienating or excluding the extroverted students. The responses collected from many extroverts in the class confirmed that not only did they not feel alienated, but even more, they expressed gratitude for the discussion about personality.

Following the first day of class, students were asked to take two online personality tests that dealt with introversion and extroversion. The results would not be reported but would be used by each individual to help them self-identify for upcoming projects. Students were also assigned to read a chapter by the instructor about introversion and acting called, "Reforming Theatrical Education from Its Extrovert-Based Model."[4] In the next class meeting, there was a brief discussion about the chapter and the tests. These two days were the only days of class time devoted to the discussion

of self-awareness. In the rest of the course, changes were related to pedagogical practice and issues of classroom management. The authors invite
educators to adopt and adapt such strategies and policies to encourage
parity in the classroom.

GENERAL COMMENTS FROM STUDENTS

Prior to diving into the projects, we wanted to share some overview commentary from the students who took it. For obvious reasons, these comments do not use the students' names, but a wide cross-section of
introverts, extroverts, and ambiverts was represented in the course. The
course comments below highlight the importance of this kind of valuable
work in the classroom. For most student actors, this course was the first
time temperament was explored in any theatrical setting. Having a better
understanding of personality types helped students to work more effec-
tively with others in class, and many noted such self-awareness would be
useful in other educational and professional settings:

Student 1:   Starting the class with a discussion and a reading on intro-
              verted and extroverted temperaments helped me have more
              patience when working with a group. I used to find myself
              irritated because I did not always feel I had a voice during
              group discussions, especially since I like to consider my
              thoughts before voicing them in a full class, [but I] felt
              forced to speak up because of my participation grade ... I am
              so thankful this is the future of education because I have
              never felt more comfortable in a class.[5]

Student 2:   I'm glad [this class] acknowledged that introverts have a
              place in acting and there are valid, non-contradictory reasons
              for an introvert to want to act ... perhaps in the future there
              will be more consideration in acting classes for different
              comfort levels, and experimentation with ways to empower
              introverts while continuing to let extroverts express
              themselves.

Student 3:   When I decided to get a theatre degree, people told me I
              could never become an actor because of my shy, quiet per-
              sonality. This is simply not the case. I am not alone as an
              introverted actor. In fact, there are lots of us! I've learned ...
              to be okay with needing extra time to collect my thoughts

and prepare and plan for a scene. Understanding and accepting myself and others through the lens of introversion and extroversion created a safe, inclusive space in the classroom. I found I get along well with all temperaments, and everyone seemed to be accepting of my introverted ways.

Student 4: I enjoyed incorporating this kind of awareness into our classwork. As actors, we are consistently tasked with understanding a character's perspective. We try to fully comprehend what it's like to walk in a character's shoes, to think like a character, and to see the world through a character's eyes, but we don't always do that with the people around us. It was beneficial to think about my peer's perspectives on a regular basis, rather than primarily focus on my own experiences. [Theatre] can sometimes promote a culture of competition and disregard for other people ... when we tried to consider the perspectives of our peers in the same way we attempt to understand the characters we portray, we promote a more positive, ensemble-based environment.

Student 5: I often feel excluded or undervalued in acting classes, though I never before was able to put my finger on the reason why. Now it makes sense. Extroverts are rewarded in drama training for their willingness to jump up and participate with fervent enthusiasm, while we introverts are more likely to wait on the sidelines until we feel prepared and ready to share. While this is especially true in improvisational activities ... I feel similarly about scene work; I prefer to perform after several other people have shared, rather than go first. Seeing others be vulnerable in their work first makes me feel more comfortable in front of them. However, as the semester carried on, I felt more comfortable around the group of my peers in my section, so I was more willing to volunteer to go first. The structure of the different personality types working together in class helped me accomplish that.

These expressions of frustration and isolation are moving and brave. The students' feelings of finally being heard are powerful. We hope that in sharing the students' feelings of isolation and a lack of representation, educators will rethink some approaches in the traditional acting studio.

How many more students can we reach if the conversation about temperament diversity is regularly facilitated in our classrooms?

INTROVERTS

After just the first discussion, the introverts in the course felt validated and included—a key objective in these pedagogical adjustments. Their reflections often revealed a keen awareness of how their personality style impacted them in the past, and many expressed gratitude for the opportunity to share these experiences with their more extroverted peers:

Introvert 1:   The class asked us to work with others and act with more awareness of different personality types. This is something I already do. As an introvert, I feel much more aware of other's personalities and who might be an extrovert or an introvert. For me, this is because [introverts] sit back and notice more, while extroverts stand out more. It seems to me as though extroverts don't understand the idea of introversion because it never crosses their minds. I've met many extroverts who are confused at the idea of needing to be alone and recharge because this is something they rarely feel. So, when asked to pay more attention in class … the extroverts are suddenly aware of the introverts. It is nice for them to be more understanding—or at least try to be.[6]

Introvert 2:   This class was a good starting point for raising awareness that people have different comfort levels and approaches to creativity. Of course, in acting, being outside the comfort zone is often necessary, but going forward, I hope we remember that there is such a thing as being made to go too far outside one's comfort zone. There likely won't be much dedicated about the introvert and extrovert discussion in the classes, shows, and collaborations I do in the future, but in the end, it's still important that, despite our differences in temperament, we all lift each other up so we may all succeed.

This hopeful tone of working with different temperaments in a truly ensemble-driven manner was echoed numerous times in student responses.

So, too, was the willingness to engage in honest self-reflection and share that self-knowledge with others in open dialogue.

AMBIVERTS

Most experts agree there are more ambiverts than extroverts or introverts in the world, so it made sense that the course was made up of a large section of self-identified ambiverts. Many ambivert assessments also supported our foundational hypothesis: by including an open discussion about personality types and the ways they learn in our classes, students will feel empowered to be their truest and best selves—and gain interpersonal skills. Our first respondent in this section is an international student from a culture not traditionally favoring of extroversion, offering a different cultural perspective on the topic:

Ambivert 1:   The result [of the quiz] makes sense to me. I love to be extroverted. I love to express myself to others. Most of the time, I work with my impulse. Meanwhile, because of my background, I come from a culture that encourages introversion. I used to live in an environment that hated individuality. Theatre encourages people to show their specialty, but my subconscious keeps asking for a safe environment to learn acting.[7]

Ambivert 2:   I am an ambivert, but I found this [classification] to be a copout until I processed more. I am more than capable of behaving in an extroverted manner. It varies from environment and mood. I take a while to warm up to others. Being open and vulnerable is a struggle of mine, so I tend to keep that introverted.

Ambivert 3:   In a sense, [my ambiversion] is like a psychological outfit that I choose to wear. In public, I dress up one way so people perceive me in that way, but with my close friends, I can wear relaxing clothes that are the most comfortable.

Ambivert 4:   If someone is more extroverted, I steer away from working with them because I have a hard time speaking up for myself and what I need as a collaborator. In these partnerships, there is a sense of fear I won't be able to have a say, and if I do get to speak, fear that I will say the wrong thing. If someone is more introverted, I get the sense that they have a negative opinion about me. I assume I will have to do most of the work, come up with all the ideas, or be the spokesperson for the group. Finding other ambiverts like me gives me the initial feeling it will be a relatively even partnership.

Ambivert 5:   While I find myself latching on to other ambiverts, I look for guidance from extroverts to help me come out of my shell, especially in acting ... It was helpful to look for those people to help me out and play my ideas off of, even though that idea itself scared me too.

Ambivert 6:   Being more aware of the different personality styles gave me a new perspective. I'm fueled by the energy of others, and I enjoy large games with lots of interaction. This class usually consisted of working in smaller groups to create and perform the material. Working in this setting pushed me because I was held accountable for everything expected of me. When I work with teams, my work is better because I don't want to disappoint my group members. Working closely with different actors in the class made me more empathetic ... most of my classmates, myself included, did their best writing when they were alone. I liked hearing other people's ideas and contributing to them, and when there was more structure to the assignment. Having a better understanding of personality types helped me work with others in the class and will continue helping me in other educational and professional settings.

This last quotation reveals a keen understanding of personality types and their connections to varying modalities of learning. Our deep dive into temperament enabled these learners to gain a glimpse into the artist's psyche; some of these comments reveal a keen understanding of how they, as actors, best engage in the creative process. It makes sense these ambiverted students also clearly recognized the switching they often undergo between their personal and professional selves.

EXTROVERTS

The extroverts in the course waxed philosophically about the inclusion of this focus in the acting studio. In the first response, the extrovert has gained an appreciation of the power of solitude as a prelude to collaboration:

Extrovert 1:   It is sometimes difficult to come to terms with these personality traits, as social circles in groups of actors almost always favor and cater to those who speak the loudest and say the most. Yet throughout this journey in class, as we were introduced to more research and teaching models willing to embrace introversion and observe it not as a negative aspect but a unique and undervalued one, I found myself more eager to let those tendencies take over and catalog how my creative mind changed while embracing an approach from a place of solitude.[8]

In this second comment, the extrovert is engaging in an honest process of self-examination to better understand and articulate how they lead:

Extrovert 2:   The way we worked recognized the personality differences and character traits of everyone in the group and was helpful in crafting a safe working environment where everyone's ideas could be heard without fear of judgment or failure. It was as different as it was eye-opening, often due to my natural "take charge" attitude. I find myself being the point person in group projects, the one compiling and assisting in the development of everyone's ideas. This class made me ask why I am always the person doing this in a group setting. Is it because I am skilled and efficient at leading groups to a successful final product? Or do I subconsciously place myself at the forefront of the group because I fear I am inefficient as a follower? I believe it's a blend of both.

The thoughtful tone of these responses is exactly what the inclusion of this type of dialogue in the acting studio hopes to promote. Ultimately, our goal is to provoke reflection about the ways in which actors work on their own and with others.

No Labels

It is important to emphasize that an understanding of yourself through the lens of temperament is meant to set you free—to be your most creative self. There is always a danger that a student will feel "boxed in," confined rather than liberated by what may seem to be "fixed labels." Note this one student response:

> I was not a fan of the useless division between "extroverted and introverted" actors, and I don't believe this model is beneficial for actors ... just treat each artist as an individual who has different learning and creative needs. If this means including more "individual" development opportunities, then I am for it, but I'm not sure these benefits need to only be applied to help introverted students. An extrovert can also greatly appreciate their own work and need to learn to function outside of a group. There are certain styles of comedy that work better with some types over others, and I'm not sure all the introverted preparation in the world can change that.[9]

Such a response is one that we need to take into account as we embark on this important work of creating more temperament-inclusive environments. The goal is never to marginalize any particular type, but rather to better understand one another so we can work stronger together and support each other to be our best selves. This message may need to be reiterated through the course of a semester, and we need to constantly check in with our students to be certain we are truly honoring all types of learners.

Commedia

The first section of the course was devoted to the study of stock characters in commedia dell'arte. Students were asked to learn the qualities of the stock characters and create bits of business, or lazzis, intermingled into a ten-minute original presentation. The groups were assigned by the instructor and were purposely created with members of varying temperaments. The groups were then given time over several classes to create a commedia presentation that embraced the highly physical and cartoonish style of storytelling. The syllabus included the following language:

> *In discussion and group work, allow both loud and quiet ways for working together – group ideas, solo reflection back to group sharing.*[10]

One pedagogical adjustment: for every forty minutes of group work, there was a mandated ten-minute solo time where students took time alone to process or create new scenarios. The syllabus also reminded them daily:

> *Rehearsal will include both group and individual processing time announced by instructor. When returning to groups, allow all voices to be heard.*[11]

For the most part, students were positive about the adjustment, though one introverted actor thought ten minutes was not enough time and actually made the creative process feel more hurried and stressful. The student went on to explain they would prefer to work "in a small group, bouncing ideas off someone else. Working alone is great for me, but I need lots of time and no distractions. I'm constantly judging my own ideas in a short amount of time. Talking with other people or listening to their ideas could spur ideas in me."[12] Perhaps another adjustment could be explored to offer equal amounts of group and solo time. The sheer fact this student took ownership of the way they learn is remarkable and will serve them well in future collaborations.

However, the student did not feel successful overall in this section of the course. They summarize, "The whole section of commedia was difficult for me. It didn't matter that I had a mask on or I was in a safe place. I can't get myself to make big choices, which is what commedia needs."[13] This was a similar issue related to the section on bold choices in Indian epic theatre mentioned in Chap. 8. The student was confused by the lack of success and questioned whether the frustrating results were due to their introversion or their social anxiety, or a combination of both. For many introverts, this style of comedy was, in fact, the most difficult. Large physical and vocal choices demanded by this material could not be summoned in a short time. A longer gestation period is necessary for effective commedia work. Allowing the students time to reflect in class also assisted in deeper. The syllabus noted:

> *After your presentation and notes from the instructor, take some solo time to reflect on how you would make your future work better. Share that with the group if you feel comfortable.*[14]

After reflecting, some students reported working in the same way they had in the past, perhaps out of habit or out of an aversion to group work.

One student reported, "I found myself in the same position I generally take in group work. Without a defined director, I take a passive role. I shut down with extroverts and introverts. I never feel comfortable running with my own work."[15] Despite the focus on new ways to collaborate, this student reports no change in the process. One extroverted student trying to adjust hung back in certain decisions, fighting the will to speak first or react quickly. The student reported that they found themselves overcompensating in quietly taking care of their group members. In this example, we see an extrovert monitoring their usual inclination to verbally command the situation by considering the needs and styles of the group.

The mix of temperaments offered unique challenges for each commedia group. The composition of one group, composed of one extrovert, one ambivert, and three introverts, was particularly challenging. From the observation of the instructor, the group did not work as well as they could have together, resulting in high tensions and frustration. This dissonance was largely due to the fear amongst all types of learners of this demanding style of work, leading to low morale and an unsuccessful presentation. The extroverted student in the group later admitted they felt pressured to motivate the others in the group, and due to the challenging group dynamic, all temperaments found more success in the solo work more traditionally preferred by introverted students. The extroverted student went on to concede that a detriment to the process was their constant pressure for results, admitting, "I may have pushed too hard and too fast and ultimately sparked some of the low group morale I was so frustrated with later."[16] It is heartening this student recognizes that their tendency to push for immediate results and work quickly may have contributed to the tensions within the group, even as their group mates resisted that impulse. The reflective tone offers hope for group members that future collaborations with mixed temperaments might be more seamlessly collaborative.

SKETCH COMEDY

Students were grouped by the instructor with varying temperaments and tasked to come up with five ideas to pitch or present to their group. The pitches would be done in five different presentational styles, highlighting the preferences of both introverted and extroverted students. Below are the guidelines for the sketch comedy unit as outlined in the syllabus. The instructor offered pedagogical adjustments to offer parity to introverts and extroverts throughout the entire section of the course:

> Based on our discussion of the sketch writing rules, begin to think about five different types of sketches. They may be used as possible entrances to improv, comedy, or reel material. These sketches should be funny to a mass market and to people in your future locations.[17]
>
> Sketch comedy writing in particular rewards the first to respond. How can we offer a new model? The goal of this section is to create the best sketch comedy through a re-evaluation of the standard process of creative group work that rewards the extroverted voices in the room. There are a few options for collaborating in order to examine the best practices for ALL learners. This section will examine possible alternatives.
>
> In each section below, you will note that there are five strategies for sharing ideas – use each one to examine the best possible process for creative collaboration. You also can try each and discard or adapt if it is not working for you as long as you make sure all feel all have been heard.

1. *Pitching Ideas: When pitching your five ideas, you must pitch each idea with one of the following styles:*
   a. *Pitch one sketch in written form. Let your partners read your idea.*
   b. *Pitch one sketch by simply talking about it.*
   c. *Record a video version of you speaking/reading about your sketch.*
   d. *Use a PowerPoint or outline to speak from.*
   e. *Use a way to pitch your sketch that is not suggested above. (Perhaps social media?)*

2. *Choosing the Sketch: As a group, you must decide which five sketches from the many presented will be used. Because this could evolve into a process were the loudest voices win, the decision-making process will also be tested in a new way. If forced to respond immediately, introverts can feel forced into the spotlight in these moments. So, how can you allow all to be heard? Options to consider are:*
   a. *Vote on the Top Sketches. Each member gets five votes. Each sketch will be ranked from 1–5. This will be done without discussion. Votes will choose the sketches.*
   b. *A free-flowing discussion that still allows introverts to speak.*
   c. *Silent ballot where you vote on the best sketches.*
   d. *A timed discussion where each person is given three minutes to offer their opinion.*
   e. *Find your own process that allows all to be heard.*

3. *The Writing Process: In this process, there are several ways to go! Look at the following examples and choose the one that works best for your group. You may try various ways to create and then examine which process worked best.*
   a. *Get on your feet immediately and try out various scenarios.*
   b. *Improv and edit.*
   c. *A riff on an idea and then separate, so each actor can consider options and brainstorm alone. Come back and share notes.*
   d. *Write the scene away from class and come back in and try it out.*
   e. *Create a new way of working that allows all to be heard.*

4. *The Rehearsal Process: In rehearsal, the louder voices or bigger choices can sometimes overshadow quieter creative work or interrupt the revision process. To avoid this, here are the ways in which you must rehearse. Each scene should be rehearsed in a different manner:*
   a. *Assign a director for an individual scene.*
   b. *Observe the scene and give feedback as a group.*
   c. *Do not offer feedback until you leave rehearsal and write feedback to the group. Email the feedback to the group for each member to process on their own.*
   d. *Work as an ensemble. Offer no notes but shape the scene from within.*
   e. *Create a different way of working that plays to the group's strength.*

As a group, you will decide which scenes will either be filmed (at least two) or performed live (at least two). As you choose, examine the decision-making process and the assignments of duties within the group. Did your group use any of the earlier methods for decision-making? Throughout this process, your work as a member of a team should be apparent in your contribution and to your teammates. Am I leading or taking over? Am I supporting or not contributing? Am I allowing another to take a leadership role out of laziness, fear, or respect? Is my voice getting lost or am I the loudest on the team?

These pedagogical adjustments in the above layout offered unique ways to work as a group. Some students found these suggestions offered new and exciting ways to collaborate by offering so many options. One student wrote:

I appreciated that we were able to use five different ways to present our ideas. That experiment allowed me to see which ideas worked best. My favorite sketch comedy pitch was writing down my ideas for my partners to read ... Whenever I get in front of people, I get anxious and convince myself my ideas are stupid and no one will like them, so writing my ideas out helps take care of this problem.[18]

The student found a way to better present ideas for group work, which was the ultimate goal of the variety of options related to presentations. The result was less anxiety and negative self-talk. A definite step forward.

Others too discovered their preferred way of working, often finding a balance between their usual approach and a new one. One student discussed an equal affinity for their preferred method—speaking aloud and sharing ideas with an immediate opportunity for conversation and feedback—and a new valued skill—writing down ideas and allowing people to read them on their own. By offering new possibilities, some students test and reinforce their preferred method of communicating, and some find success in more than one new style.

Other actors had a more mixed reaction to the work, as they enjoyed having new tools for developing content, but felt hindered and sometimes overwhelmed by the variety of details and changing of pitching styles. One student, who described the process as both restrictive and freeing, confessed, "It was restrictive because I found myself focusing less on the actual ideas and more on how to present them. [The process was] freeing, because in thinking less on my ideas, I also worried less about the judgment of my peers."[19] For this student, the experience of the process also helped to alleviate some of the negative self-talk. One student understood the benefit of such work, but offered a few suggestions on how to adapt it for the future that addressed the overwhelming feeling of variety. Some suggestions included either picking one presentation style to present all five ideas or assigning each member of the group a different presentation style. These are great options to consider if you decide to include such work in an acting class. Overall, even the frustrated students were able to recognize the reasoning for the options and the value in encouraging each temperament to work outside of their usual style. You may find similar adaptations in your courses or create even more ways to approach the material, but the benefit of offering a variety of styles in which to work seems clear.

As this section of the course continued, the way in which students collaborated shifted. They became more responsible for each other. They spoke about the ways in which they could highlight each other's strengths and the intricacies of their personalities in the process. Their differences created dynamic teams of writers that appreciated each other's strengths and compensated for each other's challenges. One student shared a story of how their group worked with an introvert who was fearful to contribute and chronicled the adaptations the group made to value everyone's voice:

We had a mixture of ambiverts and a single introvert. During group meetings, the introvert was very quiet and did not offer contributions without being prompted. Knowing he was an introvert allowed us to take brief moments to him if he wanted to add to discussions and make sure his voice was heard. Also, as ambiverts, we found an easy balance of [shared] conversation. We also purposefully structured private work time into our group meetings. This setup allowed those with introverted tendencies the time they needed to craft their work alone. At the same time, being around the same table while doing our solo work allowed us to bounce ideas off of group members to help with moments of creative block, as well as get a second opinion on difficult areas of the sketches. When it came to practicing and performing the scenes, we again found ease with establishing roles and "directing" scenes. In the interest of introverted tendencies, we allowed each group member to cast their sketches outside of the classroom, instead of in front of the group. Much of the prep work was also done outside of class and then discussed and confirmed within the group setting. Overall, it was one of the most effective groups.[20]

Clearly, the adaptations the group made to appreciate and respect a variety of modes of learning are beyond the norms for group projects in an acting class. In understanding and embracing the strengths and challenges of the other, and offering room to appreciate each student's unique contribution, this group was able to achieve exactly what the course guidelines were created to do. The benefit of such work, and offering new possibilities of collaboration, created a positive experience for all.

Sitcom and Comedy of Manners/Farce

In the next two sections of the course, students were allowed to choose their own partners within certain parameters. For the comedy of manners/farce, they were asked to select a partner of a different temperament. For each of the two required sitcom scenes, they were asked to work with two different partners, someone of a different temperament and someone with the same temperament. The goal was to create a mixed temperament team that leverages the strengths of the individuals. The syllabus reminded them:

As you rehearse your scenes, notice how your differently classified partner (introvert, extrovert, ambivert) works. What can you learn from the other temperaments?[21]

By requiring them to work with a variety of learners, there was a forced responsibility to find ways to successfully collaborate. By this point in the course, students had begun to develop ways to work together in larger groups, but the pairings were designed to challenge preconceived notions, as well as find ways to complement the variety of modalities with which they worked. Students also had an understanding and appreciation for complementary temperaments and embraced these requirements with success. Some students embraced this variety as an opportunity to interact with people similar to themselves, as well as actors who have completely opposite personalities. Many were excited to see they worked well with diverse groups of people. Such successes were reported throughout the reflection papers. Even small challenges were overcome, as one student revealed, "It was a roller coaster of process changes as I went from an incredibly extroverted partner to an incredibly introverted one, and then to an introvert with some extroverted tendencies. Switching approaches to each partner was 'stop and go' at first, but became easier with time and repetition."[22] This compassion and consideration for working with another is a clear benefit of bringing such work to the forefront of the classroom.

Some students began to experiment and test boundaries with their scene partners. One ambiverted student chose to work with one introvert and one extrovert in the sitcom section, saying they wanted to experience working with an extrovert while focusing on their own introverted qualities. They also wanted to work with an introvert with a focus on their own extroverted qualities. In this, they were able to see the beneficial contributions of all learning styles, and what they can bring to the creative process. The student praises, "The extrovert is able to throw out original ideas right off the cuff, and the introvert is able to take those ideas and edit them into something that really works. I wish I would have implemented that ideology [earlier] in my life."[23] This ambiverted actor obviously recognizes the value of working with different temperaments as well as understands the power of collaboration with those of differing personality types. So, for this actor, the experiment was a resounding success.

STANDUP

The last section of this course strikes fear in almost every student—introvert or extrovert—standup comedy. The "final exam" for this course was a performance at a local comedy club, so there was a very public showing of the work with no place to hide. From the first moments of the course, students shared their fears regarding this project, and by using a Long Runway approach throughout the semester, they felt ready to perform: they had been working on material for months with assigned check-ins and monthly drafts, continuously honing their standup sets to feature their individual styles and create their own unique brand of comedy.

This unit's placement as the final in the course contributed to its overall success because, by this point in the semester, students fully understood each other's learning styles, making it easier to help others through trouble spots in their sets. Their classmates were already familiar with their senses of humor and specific acting skills. But even with this awareness and appreciation, the assignment still struck fear in many student actors, especially the introverts. One introverted student commented that the work didn't feel like acting because there was no character to play, or as she put it, "a mask to hide behind."[24] This perspective reinforces our ongoing hypothesis that introverted actors largely prefer to become another through their acting. We have heard this same sentiment borne out in the survey and from several introverted actors interviewed throughout the book. The very nature of standup comedy removes the safety of the mask so many introverted actors feel they need.

To offer support, the professor made one other pedagogical adjustment. The students were offered the safety net of first performing half of their set for just the instructor and one other student. Then, slowly, more students were added to watch the set in later classes, and then a few more over the next few classes. The size of these groups was limited to the same six students. This was done so that, on the night of the presentation, the introverted student's set would still be fresh to the majority of the class. The six students in each group who had already seen the material could also offer deeper feedback about what was being edited and written. Note that extroverted actors provided extensive feedback on this aspect of the process. Some enjoyed trying standup comedy in a small group because it provided the comfort of knowing that, if something went wrong or a set didn't land, they had the safety of only failing in front of a few people. Then, with the time and freedom to revise on their own, they could showcase their polished work to a large crowd. Another extroverted actor, who admitted they loved to feed on the energy from the crowd, shared that the more intimate setting of the small group encouraged honest and helpful feedback.

While this approach worked for some students, it did not work for all, as the intimacy of showing their work to a smaller group left no place to hide. An ambivert student admitted the smaller group was more intimidating than they thought it would be as seeing the faces in the audience up close was harder than "blurring them out" from the stage. This intimate way of working has both benefits and drawbacks for some students, as the process certainly does favor the introvert, who benefits from the repetition of work and a sense of preparation.

Through the use of the Long Runway technique and the intimate rehearsal process, this once terrifying final public performance was an opportunity for success. Each student developed ownership of their style of working and appeared supremely confident on the stage. The class's supportive attitude extended to the comedy club, and their excitement at hearing a majority of their classmates' sets for the first time was contagious. One student wrote in the final reflection, "Each student, no matter the personality type, arrived at the club with a prepared set and rose to the occasion. It was wonderful to see the final outcome. This final performance proves it isn't necessary to be an extrovert to be an actor. Students are able to move at various speeds and still achieve the goal set at the beginning of the course."[25] The experimentation and focus of the class seemed the best way to achieve what we were ultimately seeking: the introvert's comfort to create. But even more importantly, the success of the course was not limited to the introverted actors alone. All personality temperaments seemed to benefit from more focused and thoughtful course design, an open invitation to consider their own personality types in their learning, and a variety of combinations of partners and learning styles throughout the work. This inclusivity is indeed the best possible outcome.

CONCLUSION

Overall, the focus in the class on leveraging one's strengths along the introvert-extrovert spectrum was a success that resulted in an acting studio respectful all types of learners. In these final commentaries, we ask educators to notice the students' consistent pleas for continuing this work in all acting classes. We reiterate: these course additions require just two classes and some pedagogical adjustments. This student feedback can help shape new approaches.

Below are some student responses on the course revealing the potential of this sort of revision of the classroom:

Student 1:   I have hope in the idea of providing the same amount of access to those with differing temperaments by making the classroom equally accessible to introverts, extroverts, and ambiverts. Feeling silent, unheard, and alone are some of the worst things in the world. I tend to feel the cons of being an introvert more often in the classroom setting because of my public introverted self. It is so important to recognize there isn't one right process to approach different work. It is not fair to exclude someone because they are biologically-wired a different way. We learn and grow from all different types of people and all different types of learners.[26]

Student 2:   The introverts, extroverts, and [ambiverts] were all rigorously challenged in the class, but they were also greatly rewarded for the dedication and effort made possible by the structure of the course. Any class that involves performance with introverts and/or extroverts should employ the same tactics used in this acting class.

Student 3:   The safety and security of the class, and the expulsion of the pressure to be the center of attention in order to succeed…set the tone for the whole semester. With these reassurances in place, the class became even more stress-free. Furthermore, it allowed the sharing of ideas from all parties, not just those who talk the most. We witnessed performances and emerging strengths from people I had never expected before the beginning of this course.

Student 4:   I am not afraid to take the time to slow down and process my choices and feelings, but I'm also excited to show off what I've created and enjoyed being the center of attention. This class has taught me to appreciate both equally and to further recognize not everyone learns and acts the way I do. I need to exercise patience when I am tasked with working with others who contrast my process. We all desire the same thing, and the awareness we gained this semester made us more sensitive and collaborative actors.

Student 5:   This class made me more aware of what it is like to work with people who fall all over the introvert/extrovert spectrum. There is serious value in understanding why people work differently within a group. This is different than the way I have worked with groups in the past, especially because I have never thought about the differences between introverts and extroverts related to academics. Thinking more about how these two personality types work in a class setting helped me to be more understanding and calm when it came to working within a group. Every group member was able to feel comfortable voicing their ideas without fear of being spoken over or laughed at.

The compassion and empathy that runs throughout these responses is quite heartening and the responses all lay the groundwork for future work to be done in other classrooms. With the goal that our students feel respected, heard, and safe, educators have a chance to reflect on current practices for similar results.

It is our hope that acting educators will be willing to experiment with some of the ideas shared here and create even better approaches for equally considering the learning styles of both introverted and extroverted actors. In any regard, the important conversation has begun. So, let's listen to these students and extend the conversation into more acting studios.

In the next part of the book, we move from the training aspect of acting and focus solely on the professional actor. And the conversation continues …

Notes

1. Hendrickson, Sarah, and Rob Roznowski. "THR Comedy Syllabus." *Robroznowski.com*, 16 Jan. 2020, 1d594aef-d38f-4245-9fff-d7446cbeab2d. filesusr.com/ugd/ed5f7f_c62ad451cc1248f08f9b3b130bcf8843.pdf
2. Hendrickson and Roznowski. "Comedy Syllabus."
3. Hendrickson and Roznowski. "Comedy Syllabus."
4. Roznowski, Rob. "Reforming Theatrical Education from Its Extrovert-Based Model." In *Creativity in Theatre: Theory and Action in Theatre/Drama Education*, 105–20. Cham, Switzerland: Springer, 2018.
5. Anonymous student responses from the Michigan State University comedy class.
6. Anonymous student responses from the Michigan State University comedy class.
7. Anonymous student responses from the Michigan State University comedy class.

8. Anonymous student responses from the Michigan State University comedy class.
9. Anonymous student responses from the Michigan State University comedy class.
10. Hendrickson and Roznowski. "Comedy Syllabus."
11. Hendrickson and Roznowski. "Comedy Syllabus."
12. Anonymous student responses from the Michigan State University comedy class.
13. Anonymous student responses from the Michigan State University comedy class.
14. Hendrickson and Roznowski. "Comedy Syllabus."
15. Anonymous student responses from the Michigan State University comedy class.
16. Anonymous student responses from the Michigan State University comedy class.
17. Hendrickson and Roznowski. "Comedy Syllabus."
18. Anonymous student responses from the Michigan State University comedy class.
19. Anonymous student responses from the Michigan State University comedy class.
20. Anonymous student responses from the Michigan State University comedy class.
21. Hendrickson and Roznowski. "Comedy Syllabus."
22. Anonymous student responses from the Michigan State University comedy class.
23. Anonymous student responses from the Michigan State University comedy class.
24. Anonymous student responses from the Michigan State University comedy class.
25. Anonymous student responses from the Michigan State University comedy class.
26. Anonymous student responses from the Michigan State University comedy class.

REFERENCES

Anonymous student responses from the Michigan State University comedy course.
Hendrickson, Sarah, and Rob Roznowski. "THR Comedy Syllabus." *Robroznowski.com*, 16 Jan. 2020, 1d594aef-d38f-4245-9fff-d7446cbeab2d.filesusr.com/ugd/ed5f7f_c62ad451cc1248f08f9b3b130bcf8843.pdf.
Roznowski, Rob. "Reforming Theatrical Education from Its Extrovert-Based Model." In *Creativity in Theatre: Theory and Action in Theatre/Drama Education*, 105–20. Cham, Switzerland: Springer, 2018.

PART III

The Professional Actor and Introversion

CHAPTER 11

Interview with Jennifer Simard

Ms. Simard is a well-respected Broadway veteran who appeared in the original Broadway casts of *Hello, Dolly!* (revival with Bette Midler), *Company* (revival, female Bobbie version, with Patti LuPone), *Shrek The Musical*, and *Sister Act*. Simard was nominated for a Tony Award for her inspired comedic performance in the musical *Disaster!*. She is also a four-time Drama Desk Award nominee, a two-time Drama League nominee, and a Lucille Lortel Award nominee. She is also an introvert. Her work as a character actor has brought her great attention, but with it comes the personal and professional trade-offs this self-identified introvert must make in order to thrive in extroverted situations. Ms. Simard shares her personal coping strategies, navigating everything from auditions to closing nights, and offering advice to other introverted actors so they might succeed in this demanding business[1]:

Rob: Why and how did you first begin to classify yourself as an introvert?

Simard: It was a gradual thing. As a child, I would have classified myself as an extrovert … I certainly knew through theatre … While I enjoyed going out with everyone, I started to notice I craved my alone time. Like a classic introvert, I derived energy from recharging my batteries in my own space. I was depleted by the things most people found fun. While I found them fun, I definitely had to recover.

© The Author(s) 2020   189
R. Roznowski et al., *The Introverted Actor*,
https://doi.org/10.1007/978-3-030-41607-2_11

Rob: Why did you go into acting, which is seemingly such an extro-
          verted field?

Simard: It was a calling, really. I knew from a very young age it was
          something I was pulled to do on visceral level. It wasn't an
          intellectual choice for me. It was an emotional choice. There
          have been times in my adult life where I thought about doing
          other things ... [but] it didn't feed me the same way. I stuck
          with [acting] because I needed it for different reasons. I real-
          ized my skill set was improving, and you never stop learning. It
          was the area in my life where I was most expert, having had
          years and years of experience.

Rob: How do you respond when others classify or assume you're an
          extrovert based on your work as an actor?

Simard: I respond with humor and a little bit of wryness. I tell them I'm
          an introvert. If they don't know me, they generally perceive me
          as being extroverted. Years ago, when doing *Shrek*, I said [to a
          friend], "No, I'm an introvert. I'm actually quite shy." And she
          said, "You're not shy!" She was laughing while saying it. It was
          very *Laverne & Shirley*. And I remember saying, "I'm really shy.
          I really am." I think over the years when people have gotten to
          know me…when they become intimate with me, they see that.

Rob: In which aspect of your acting do you see this trait has the
          greatest impact?

Simard: There are different ways of acting. There's outside in or inside
          out. I tend to work inside out. Even in a broad scene, comedy
          or drama, it has to be based in truth inside of me first. That's
          the best way I can explain it.

Rob: When you were training as an actor, did you ever struggle with
          your introversion in the classroom? Or in the lab or rehearsal
          hall? And if so, in what way?

Simard: I don't know if this is so much introversion as much as, I think
          it could get convoluted with my depression or anxiety. There
          were times where I felt like a fish out of water. I definitely some-
          times felt disassociated from the classroom. Like outside the
          fishbowl, looking in. That's a little bit hard for me to answer
          because having sometimes suffered among those obstacles, they
          can overlap. I do think there have been distinctions before
          where I definitely know I deal better in smaller groups. So a

large classroom, I would work through it, but internally, I would feel a little anxious.

Rob: How has introversion impacted your auditions, including preparation and risk-taking?

Simard: I'm an introvert, but I'm also House Gryffindor, which is very strange. So, I believe in taking big risks. I'm able to take bigger risks when I'm more prepared. I have tried to prepare as much as possible with memorization and getting off book, even if I'm holding the page. If you're not prepared, I don't think you're as confident. To help my introversion, I also sometimes rent the audition room my audition will be in. It's not a secret anymore. I've started telling people, and I've noticed friends of mine have started to do it. Then, even if they switch rooms, it's usually that venue. I'll try to go there and practice my sides or my scene or my song in the room so I can eliminate as many variables as possible that day, and any nerves that may come up. It gives me a boost of confidence to know I've done everything I possibly can with the variables I can control. That said, I always leave room on the day of [the audition] to be in the moment because it's also silly to plan everything out and be anesthetized to what is happening and to the energy in the room. If I can get in there and hear the sounds, see the lights, look at myself in a mirror, see what I actually look like and what colors might look good…really basic stuff, it helps me in the actual audition.

Rob: In the waiting room, how does your introversion impact your process?

Simard: I love a hood, and I love sunglasses. I will usually make a bee-line for the restroom. And if I have a hood and glasses, I can kind of case the joint first … it sounds pretty mercenary, but it is my time, and I want to stay in the zone. I might run into someone that … whether I like them or not, I might have to engage with them. That happened to me recently where I ducked in, and I saw at least three people I knew, but I was okay. I had my headphones … which is the international signal for "don't talk to me." If someone does talk to you, you have to be polite, of course…sunglasses are great because that helps people not recognize you. You can see them, but they can't see you. You can't control everything, but you can at least give yourself an advantage. It can be anxiety-producing for anyone, but especially someone who is a bit introverted, having to socially interact can be nerve-racking. If you can give yourself time and a breath, that's a good thing.

Rob: Have you ever lost a role or failed an audition due specifically to your introversion?

Simard: I think so … I've befriended enough directors who've told me overlapping information who, in general, don't ever say anything negative about auditions. I don't know if every director would ascribe to that, but two directors I really respect have said that to me. I know, in my introversion, I've apologized for things. I think I'm being casual, but I'll say something like, "Oh, I'm sorry, I forgot that line." Or "I flubbed that. I'm sorry." I've thought about it later, that I think my shyness sometimes has affected it.

And I've definitely made a conscious effort to be inwardly still, even if I'm outwardly excited, to try to inwardly be still and calm. Actually, by my standards, I failed recently at a big audition for an upcoming Broadway show because I didn't feel still inside. It was evident to me and probably to the room. I chalk it up to "not meant to be." I definitely learned from it because I was a little rusty. I hadn't auditioned in a while. That is part of the reason I was a bit uncentered inside.

Rob: Are you drawn to introverts in rehearsal?

Simard: Oh, yes! It takes one to know one. When I was doing *Hello, Dolly!* there was an actor in the ensemble who I saw on breaks with me…We were at 890 Broadway, and there was a back room with this little corner near a brick wall with different kinds of chairs. I would go back there and I see him with headphones and his laptop. And I was doing the same things. It's amazing how many corners you can find…it's very cat-like, where you feel comforted if you can have a vantage point but have some cover. It's soothing. It's literally, physically soothing. I brought it up to him one day. And he said, "Yes. I can't give to other people if I don't tend to myself first."

Rob: Are you jealous of extroverts in rehearsal?

Simard: Oh, God yes! Again, in this show I just did, one of the actors who I think is one of the greatest leaders of our company … is absolutely, unabashedly an extrovert. And I definitely play along. I helped him organize. The difference is, I see him truly loving it from a visceral place. I love it in a sense that I have fun, but it was more from a place of being proud of myself for doing what I knew was right and would make other people happy. But it was really exhausting for me, and I knew it wasn't exhausting for him.

Rob: What is the best part of rehearsal for you?

Simard: It's the character. Finding stuff that works, finding where the acting meets the text and seeing it come alive. Knowing it's resonating. Not necessarily for the room, but knowing it's going to resonate for the audience. I'm a big believer in being confident with your introverted self in a rehearsal room, and trying not to succumb to rehearsal lax ... often what happens in the rehearsal room is not going to translate on stage. I'm always compartmentalizing. There are times I know if I play it one way, it's going to make the room laugh. And very often, if you're rehearsing long enough, the room is going to laugh if you make different choices because they get bored seeing the same old choice. So sometimes you have to save those things for later. Sometimes you can keep trying things, but you always have to keep an eye out for what's going to serve the text, and what's going to serve the show for someone who's never seen it before.

Rob: You play so many characters. That's one of the amazing things about you is your ability to play so many people. Do you find a pattern of introversion or extroversion in these characters? Your character from *Disaster!*, for example, is a pure introvert who's released into extroversion.

Simard: I'm glad you brought up *Disaster!* I think whether it's introversion or extroversion, there's something that can apply to both. My co-star and now friend, Faith Prince, and I were on the same page about this. She saw me, and I saw her. And her character, Shirley, was extremely extroverted. And she had quite a bond [with my character], as opposites attract. But as actresses, Faith and I are very similar. We shared such camaraderie and passion and belief that humor and pathos go hand in hand, no matter how broad it is ... there's one scene where we're fighting back and forth on this precipice, where I'm thinking of throwing myself over the edge. I'm on my knees, and she's yelling at me to stop. I specifically remember Faith talking about the push-pull of that scene … a push-pull of how low her voice gets and then how high. And that push-pull was not only in the physicality of it, the thing you're hearing from the outside, but pushing and pulling internally too. I would do the same thing. We would throw the ball back and forth.

So, I think both can exist. And they exist better when you acknowledge the truth about who you are and bring yourself to that on stage every night. Faith also reiterated something to me I believe in, and I think I've never seen anyone do it better than her. She said wherever you are in your day, bring that to your show that night, instead of trying to hide from it. It's probably imperceptible to the audience. So if you're having a day where you're feeling … very internal, for example, use it. Don't shy away from it. Because it's only going to get in your way.

Rob: Do you see a through line of introversion in the kinds of characters that you create?

Simard: Oh, yes I do because I'm always bringing myself to the characters. So, no matter how broad the brushstroke is, there are always fine brushstrokes inside. The defining brushstrokes to me are the introversion part. It might be imperceptible to an audience, but the best compliments I get are when someone says, "Oh, that's so subtle," or "that's so nuanced," and I think, "Oh, well that's probably that part of me."

Rob: As an introvert, how does the audience affect your work during the run of the show?

Simard: I love the feeling I get when it's cooking … it's firing on all cylinders, and I can tell they're with me. It's difficult if they're not going on the ride. I've learned along the way that, if they're not going along for the ride, you let them come to you. That's confidence in my introversion. I don't push. Even if it seems like I'm playing the broadest character, whether I've chosen to be that way or I'm directed to be that way or a combination of the two. It can seem like I'm the biggest clown in the world sometimes. But if they're not coming for the ride, I'm not going to push. There's always going to be some honesty and some calmness underneath the storm. Always.

Rob: How does your introversion impact your interpersonal relationships with crew and other actors?

Simard: I am an introvert. I have learned to act like an extrovert. I have to. If I were giving advice to someone in this business, I'd say it's such a social environment. If you're in a long run of a show, for example, you're going to see these people six out of seven days a week. It's not a job where you can isolate and write by yourselves. You have to learn how to play well with others. I do have some tools to help myself do that. One of which is, if I don't feel capable of doing the weekly social things that some people derive fun and energy from … such as bowling, I can't do that if I'm exhausting myself. That's just me. I know what I have to do to take care of myself. And it's not manipulation; it's knowing yourself and being kind to other people in ways that don't drain you. For example, it doesn't cost a whole lot of money to have a box of blank cards. One way I found to connect with people is to always try to remember to exhibit caring. If they have a birthday, or if they are an understudy, and it is their first time going on. If someone is going through something … whether it be a stagehand or a dresser or a wig person or the doorman. It doesn't cost a lot of money to be nice and polite.

Rob: I think what's interesting about that is it's an introverted way of connecting with people.

Simard: And it's a good tool people appreciate, but you're not being manipulative and inauthentic. It's almost more inauthentic to go out to a party just to fit in, if that's not who you are. It's better to do something quiet and one-on-one. Manners go a long way. One of the best compliments I got at *Hello, Dolly!* was from Bette's assistant, Jill Hattersley, who is so sweet. She always referred to me as Miss Manners. I never thought of it that way. I didn't do it for people to notice, but I guess people do. It makes them happy, and I've maintained the boundaries I need to do my job and be a happy person.

Rob: What do you love about your introversion related to acting?

Simard: I love that there's a great deal of self-acceptance and self-love I have for myself now that I can translate on a stage through my work, and hopefully give other people.

Rob: Because you have so much conversation with yourself as an introvert, you know yourself a little bit better?

Simard: Yes. I don't want to do a disservice to extroverts, who've done
           a lot of work. I think there's overlap with therapy, and that's
           not exclusive to whether you're an extrovert or introvert. But
           maybe there's a secret I've always had inside, and I feel confi-
           dent in exposing through my work.

Rob: What advice would you give to a young actor or student actor
           who's early in their training and who identifies as an intro-
           verted artist?

Simard: To practice self-love and acceptance and kindness. The more
           confident you are in who you are, the more people come to
           you. It's a case of the turtle and the hare. Don't try to be a hare
           when you're not. Usually, these things are a marathon and not
           a sprint. After a while, people are going to find out who you
           really are, and they're not going to like if you're faking it. So be
           who you are, love yourself. Let people come to you. And in
           going to other people, be kind. Don't seem desperate to get
           people to like you, but be kind. Be warm. Be human. Be an
           empath because if you are an introvert, I bet you already are.
           And do the work. You're there to do a job. It's wonderful to
           make friends, but this is your work. If you're always acting with
           love and kindness and being a good person, the other stuff just
           happens naturally, right?

Simard's interview contains great tips for the introverted actor, while also expanding on many of the themes of the earlier parts of this book. Her self-awareness and acceptance of her introversion as a professional actor offer ways for introverted actors to see themselves in this business. As she espouses, there are new ways to navigate the current system while also remaining authentic and introverted.

While Simard offers useful and often inspiring advice related to the business, the next chapter is about one of the hardest things for an intro-verted actor. In order to even ply their craft, actors must first navigate one of the most exhausting aspects of this business—the audition. The audi-tion can be overwhelming or even crippling for the introverted actor. This next chapter offers tips to turn the often negative experience of the audi-tion into a positive, and even successful, one.

NOTE

1. Simard, Jennifer. Personal interview. 13 April 2018.

REFERENCE

Simard, Jennifer. Personal interview. 13 April 2018.

CHAPTER 12

Auditioning

Be they introverted or extroverted, actors are brave. What other profession has almost daily job interviews? The environment of the audition space can breed anxiety and fear, even for the bravest actors; the chaos of the waiting room, where extroverts greet each other with boisterous conversation, the crowd of strangers within the audition room, inspecting the actor who stands alone on display; the introvert's inability to plan for the unexpected within the entire audition experience is sometimes paralyzing. Who knows how many introverts have skipped auditions based on fear of the unknown? The bravery required for auditioning can sometimes seem the domain of the extrovert. Psychology expert Dr. Richard Lucas points out that one important facet of extroversion is assertiveness: a determination to speak your mind and engage in self-promotion.[1] Introverted actors must summon the lesser-used trait of assertiveness within themselves in order to even begin to ply their craft. And they do, with an approach to communication that involves soft power. But this comes at more of a cost than it might for their extroverted counterparts. Due to their lower energy threshold, the act of auditioning can often be more taxing for introverts, and therefore, it requires examination.

As a way to weave a narrative of introversion in the acting profession, this section of the book about the professional world of acting relies on the transcripts of interviews with a corps of professional actors. We use this corps of professional actors' interviews to serve as a tapestry of experiences that creates a through line and represents a cross-section of introverted

© The Author(s) 2020
R. Roznowski et al., *The Introverted Actor*,
https://doi.org/10.1007/978-3-030-41607-2_12

actors working on stage or screen. The contributions of these trusted professionals are closely linked to and often reflected in our survey results. We hope their stories will model inspirational or aspirational ways in which introversion might affect and later empower artists in their chosen profession of acting. We will return to their interviews throughout this section of the book, so you may find a specific actor's story or point of view that resonates.

An audition is a high-pressure situation for anybody to walk into, and without effective coping mechanisms in place, it can seem the introverted actor is at a natural disadvantage. While not landing the gig is a natural part of the business, Dr. Brent Donnellan believes "extroverts have a propensity for positive emotions ... a reservoir to fall back on when things aren't going so well," whereas introverts, who might not so easily possess such "optimism in robust supply," can find the pitfalls of auditioning all the more challenging.[2] The introspective introvert's focus on details can lead to accurate, but rather damaging, analyses of each and every moment of the audition process.

Let's face it, the process of auditioning can set introverts up for failure. How then can introverts master and succeed at the art of auditioning, while still maintaining their authenticity? Donnellan concludes that no matter the personality type, anyone can be determined and driven. And many introverts are driven to audition well.

Certainly, introverts have been succeeding at auditions for years. They understand this part of the work is entirely necessary for success in their careers. They may have mastered the art of auditioning through trial and error or have created some tools of the trade to assist them in functioning within a system that works against their biogenetic disposition. Whatever their cultivated strategies, we know introverts succeed.

There are, in fact, some ways the audition can actually reward introverted proclivities. The preparation of material for an initial audition, where a monologue, song, or sides can be coached and crafted beforehand, can benefit the introvert's exacting process. The introvert can meticulously plan, as many like to do, for the setup and performance of the self-submission video they will send to a casting director. This is work an introverted actor can do to improve their audition experience.

STRUGGLES

But what happens when the source of the anxiety isn't the material of the audition itself, but the socialization aspect of the audition? In this regard, we find introverts at a disadvantage. In our next few chapters, we will include both a "Struggles" and a "Solutions" section for each of the potentially challenging elements of navigating the professional acting sphere so you can read first-hand how some professional actors have overcome common issues related to their introversion. Our goal is to allow you to find your own solutions to struggles you may be facing.

We begin by sharing some first-person accounts of the trials of introverted actors in the audition room. But don't fret; this section is followed by the ways in which those same people overcome their struggles in the audition process.

Michigan State University (MSU) Graduate student Sharon Combs has a severe case of audition anxiety.[3] She notes the audition situation is fraught with countless uncertainties. Even the notion of getting a callback, which is validation a director likes what they saw in the initial audition, causes consternation because, in her mind, "[c]allbacks favor extroverts who are more willing to make bold choices." These variables cause this student to question why she is an actor in the first place. Like so many, she looks for ways to reduce the anxiety caused by the unknown and find ways auditions might energize rather than exhaust her.

Professional actor Carol Schultz shared her own struggles with auditioning as an introvert when she first came to New York.[4] Despite having a strong professional resume, Schultz found no success auditioning. Following auditions, she retreated into conversations with herself. But rather than a catalogue of successes or even reviewing things to work on next time, she resorted to negative self-talk. She remembers obsessing over everything she perceived to have gone wrong in the audition and constantly second-guessing herself. So, in these times of challenge and lack of success, the introvert's focus on depth can become enemy, potentially negating any of the good work done at the audition.

While we've read several examples of how a strong connection to the interior life is a value for many introverts, it can sometimes be a detriment. Broadway actor Matthew Marks admits, "I'm the worst auditioner ... For most of my career, I was petrified about what the casting people were thinking of me. Am I coming off friendly enough? Am I coming off honest enough? Am I coming off talented and smart?"[5] The inability to silence deep thoughts can be a liability in the audition room. Marks continues, "Feeling comfortable in front of strangers is a basic [skill] lots of people in this business are great at, and I am not. That hurt me; the facade I put on didn't work in the audition room." The idea of creating an inauthentic, extroverted self is a common tactic for introverts that will be further examined in the Networking chapter. For now, Marks' dilemma of over-thinking while in the act of auditioning is a common problem for introverts.

Actor and educator Andy Head claims his introversion has often worked against him in an acting setting.[6] Head reports he tries to prepare and use strategies to counter his introverted qualities, but "knows" that when he gets in the room, he will not allow himself to take any risks. This self-defeating language has hurt Head in the past, no matter what he tried. He tries to tell himself things like "everyone else is nervous" or "do your best" or "you win some; you lose some." But in the end, these homilies offered him no real solace. His frustrations are real, and no amount of reasoning seems to dissuade him from that belief. He admits even if he receives a callback, reads something new, or makes an adjustment, there are still dragons in his head to slay because the luxury of time to prepare these new elements abbreviates his preferred, more lengthy analysis process. Head and other introverts report a trapped feeling of being uncomfortable in the moment when it is so necessary to showcase their most fearless work. Because they are often capable of much more than they are able to share in a quickly prepared reading, the function of the audition can be limiting for introverted actors.

SOLUTIONS

The feelings of boldness and fearlessness so essential to an audition are seen as extroverted traits by Michigan State University Master of Fine Arts (MFA) candidate Sharon Combs, who voiced her difficulty in immediately sharing big, bold choices in the room.[7] Combs' negative self-talk told her she wasn't as good as other people in the room, leading her to doubt whether or not she was even meant to do this kind of work. How did this actor summon the courage to overcome the self-imposed feelings of inadequacy? Combs mentions self-awareness as a way for her to vanquish those disturbing thoughts. It is through self-awareness that she embraced her introverted strengths.

Psychology expert Brent Donnellan notes self-awareness can offer a chance for introverts to use their processing skills and divine a way to get past the brutality of almost daily auditions, even when an audition doesn't go well.[8] He encourages, "Bouncing back after a busted audition probably isn't going to be as easy for introverts as it is for other people, but that doesn't mean it isn't possible for you to be successful." The awareness of who you are as an introverted actor can sometimes assuage the negative self-talk before, during, and after the audition. It is becoming aware of what you need in order to share your best work, and how much of those needs are within your control.

As we have noted, each actor's connection to and manifestations of introversion are unique. For Combs, her solution involved researching how anxiety affects her in order to find solutions to manage such anxiety. Combs reinforces the idea that research, reflection, and a healthy self-awareness are the actor's responsibility, and it can actually be very helpful for an introverted actor to take ownership of their needs, strengths, and challenges. Working publicly in the audition room on private dealings with anxiety can be difficult, but the actor reports increased awareness and researched solutions have helped her to improve her auditioning techniques. Combs acknowledges working on her anxiety "is hard to do in this business in particular, but there's a benefit to finding ways to navigate the anxiety in the moment it hits."

Carol Schultz, who talked about struggling in her first auditions in New York City because of the negative self-talk that consumed her, says she owes her turnaround to success in auditions to taking a class focused on the psychology of auditioning.[9] She shares:

> We had to journal everything we did from the moment we got the audition: 1) Everything before the audition: how we prepared, planned what we would wear, how we felt, and what we did; 2) What happened in the room at the audition, what we did and said, what the people at the table did and said; 3) What we did after the audition. Through this class, I learned I was auditioning to be liked as opposed to auditioning to get the job. All the constant rejection made me go into the room asking for approval instead of showing I could play the role.

There are several important ideas at play in this class example. First: engaging in mindful practice, as Dr. Lucas mentioned.[10] Second: creating a personal process for the actor that favors the introvert's propensity for analysis and a self-inventory to help identify patterns of behavior. Third:

remembering auditioning goes beyond simply landing the job. All three combine to offer the actor success in auditioning.

Schultz notes she was able to turn her struggles around by taking control of her auditions. Her process includes a complete devotion to preparation: know the script and all the characters; make bold choices; do your analysis; practice with a partner. As part of the preparation process, she also suggests researching the theatre and, if possible, the people who will be in the audition room. This can be invaluable help during the sometimes awkward interview or small-talk section of many auditions.

But Schultz understands no matter how much preparation is done, each audition is unique, and introverts can be derailed by something unexpected. She encourages introverted actors to try to be flexible and open to change. If the director asks for an adjustment on the spot, the actor can reframe the request from something unanticipated to something positive and exciting. She celebrates, "Hopefully you'll be given an adjustment from the director! It means you've already sold them and now you can show how flexible you are. This is where your research and careful preparation come into good use." Having deep analysis to fall back on can assist with the quick processing necessary at many auditions. Thanks to the implementation of these important strategies, Schultz, who was consumed by negative thoughts following auditions in the past, now has a much more positive outlook after her auditions.

Schultz offers several valuable suggestions, such as looking at auditions as a chance to return to your passion for acting. She suggests viewing the audition as a chance to play the role, describing each audition as your opening night, your run, and your closing of the show. She suggests acting the role the best way you know how and then leaving it there in the room; not thinking about it for another second. Schultz was inspired by Brian Cranston's autobiography *A Life in Parts*, where he recounts that, after auditions, he would place old scripts in a basket and be done with them. If there was a callback, he'd go back and fish it out, but the process of putting the script out of sight helped the actor leave the worries and second-guessing behind him.[11] Other strategies for overcoming negative self-talk for the actor can be found in Rob Roznowski's *Inner Monologue in Acting*, which offers tips for retraining the brain away from destructive thoughts.[12] Schultz's final suggestion involves resting to avoid post-audition stress. She suggests, "Immediately after the audition, dawdle time away with a latte and a magazine. Do something that will be pleasurable. It will set you up well for the next audition. Beating yourself up sets you up to fail the next audition." This is advice from an actor who reported real struggles with negative thoughts in the past. So, take solace introverts, change can happen.

Matthew Marks, the actor who struggled with thoughts of those behind the table judging him while singing, has also found success.[13] He admits this was a result of experimenting with lots of different strategies over time, focused on concern with his own work rather than distraction about what others might be thinking. If there were still lingering doubts, he also remembers using the life of the character to his advantage, walking into the audition room in character "to try to hide behind that character." Finally, he credits his recent success to therapy for self-awareness and Meisner's work for staying in the moment.

PASSION

If you are an introvert who struggles with the audition process, we have another suggestion to help rewrite the potential narrative of self-talk that might start to overwhelm you: remember why you became an actor in the first place; focus on what you love about getting on stage; and plying your craft. The thing you love about this profession is what should drive the act of auditioning. Your passion can overtake the challenges contained within the audition.

The same qualities of assertiveness and risk-taking that aid an extrovert in an audition can be channeled through love for what you do. This passion allows the actor to connect to their love of performance.

The process is ongoing, and because the act of auditioning is one an actor does so often, it is also a feature of their work with which they can constantly experiment to find new strategies and set new stretch goals. Dr. Donnellan feels most of the solutions people offer for experimentation won't necessarily work for the introverted actor.[14] He notes flawed ideas like "having a thick skin" or "not taking it personally" are going to backfire. However, each time an introverted actor auditions, it will get easier, as long as you remember your passion and your motivation for acting. Donnellan concludes, as with many things, it takes practice and hard work to establish a habit of confidence. With constant focus and continued experimentation, introverted actors can see results.

Dr. Rich Lucas, an extroversion expert, suggests a more traditional clinical approach to the work of repetition of auditions, approaching the practice in clear and careful stages: first auditioning in front of friends, then auditioning in front of your friends' friends, who might be a friendly audience but not quite as close.[15] And finally, getting closer and closer, modeling the behaviors of an audition that you know you can handle and are closer to the end result; this might allow you to gradually work up to success in the audition room. Lucas offers that approaching an audition through this use of stages provides some reinforcement for behavior. Introverted actors will see it's not a disaster, and things might go rather smoothly, so the next time it's done, it won't be quite as difficult. This is another form of mindful practice at which introverts excel.

Continual refinement of the auditioning technique combines with your passion to value your strengths and feel confident in the room. Embrace the process and let it unlock the product. Stretch to feel confident in what you are about to share. There are many ways to get there.

Preparation

Andy Head, who thought his introversion had stymied his acting, has created a personal process that has allowed him "to get out of his own way," a phrase often used by introverts when they perceive their introversion as something to overcome.[16] He begins as many introverts would, with preparation. Head notes this preparation is his most useful tool. If an actor knows they are prepared, they have no reason to worry. The transactional relationship between introversion and preparation is an interesting one that features the ongoing thought, "If I prepare, my introverted tendencies that sometimes hold me back might be assuaged." Head's preparation begins by researching a theatre company's season and preparing months in advance. He also practices a form of self-awareness in relationship to past successes. He tells himself, "I know these things flare up and hold me back from doing my best. I know I've been in scenes or plays when I've kept those things at bay. When I do, the work is so much better." As Head notes, he can succeed and achieve his best work when the performance or analysis distracts him from the negative thoughts. When he has practiced this ability, he more clearly understands it is his contribution to the audition process that needs attention, and this keeps his introversion from driving the audition. Head also trusts in the experience of having done it so many times and reports it gets easier the more you do it—another actor encouraged by mindful practice.

Callbacks that happen at the audition, or in the next day or so, pose another issue related to the quick turnaround in which to prepare. Since introverts can sometimes overthink a situation or analyze it past what may be necessary for this short timeframe, Head subverts that behavior by trusting his first instinct, saying, "My first choice is probably a good choice, and I don't need to block that." We can see this philosophy has many extroverted aspects of bold choices and immediate response, but Head has filtered those qualities through awareness of the pitfalls in the quick callback situation.

Actors, both professional and student, answered our survey on introversion in acting and offered some practical advice for fellow introverts who may struggle with auditions. Here is some of their advice related to preparation:

- Use breathing exercises and shaking-out. Focus on imagination exercises, so you won't focus on the possible failure.
- Create a routine to feel confident and comfortable, even in new environments. Without routine, new places and people can be stressful.
- Meditation is very helpful.
- Control the things you can control, like getting enough sleep, eating, and knowing your pieces.
- Come into the space hyper-prepared so you can be proud of your work. No matter the dynamic in the room, your work is a solid representation of yourself.
- Plan out your outfit, travel, and audition material well in advance, and reread all of the audition information to feel as "in the know" as possible. If you have questions about parking, the audition itself, or the building, send an email and ask.
- Preparation beforehand is key—fully rehearsed, vocally and physically prepared. Make creative work as strong as possible.
- Visualize every aspect of the audition space in your mind beforehand, from getting there, parking or walking, the waiting room, and the interview space, to leaving the room, getting home, and giving yourself a reward for auditioning!
- Plan your pieces with an extra one prepped in case you are asked to do more.
- Find a space to warm-up in private and meditate to feel centered. This helps to prepare mentally before going into a more social space.[17]

Hopefully one of these thoughtful suggestions may be something you can use at your next audition to help you do your best work. The work you are capable of.

Waiting Room Protocol

Even while there are a host of ways an introverted actor can prepare their own work, there is one variable that contributes to the atmosphere of the entire audition, an element over which the introverted actor has absolutely no control: the waiting room. The environment of the audition waiting room is often a beehive of activity that can actually cause more stress than auditioning itself, throwing all the introvert's hard work and preparation out of balance. In fact, it might even sabotage the process before it even begins. The waiting room has dynamic and enthusiastic energy before an audition—and why wouldn't it? It is a room populated by numerous people all competing for one job—a job that can offer needed money, attention, connections, and (currently in the United States) health insurance. It is also a room that can be ruled by the loudest voices.

Introversion expert Lisa Kaenzig advocates for finding simple ways to help the introverted actor feel comfortable with tips like arriving early or, if the space is new, checking it out prior to the audition.[18] These simple adjustments can reduce stress for the introvert, who may be thrown by the unknown. Patrick Midgely has put punctuality into practice with great success.[19] When attending an audition, he knows it will likely take place in a loud and lively environment, so he arrives early. Being one of the first to arrive in the space allows for the atmosphere to build up around you. For the introverted actor, this is often much easier to process than arriving in a loud and busy room, looking for a way to fit in. Several personality experts also suggest arriving early to any potentially loud or highly social event as a means to gradually acclimate the introvert to the environment rather than walking into the middle of the chaos all at once.

Broadway veteran Linda Mugleston has a strategy for success she has cultivated related to navigating the waiting room.[20] Even when entering an audition space where she knows several other attendees, Mugleston admits she still tends to find a space away from more frantic or intense energies in the room. The energies she describes are typically those of the more extroverted actors, who might alleviate their stress through friendly conversation, jokes, or loud vocal and physical warm-ups, all of which run counter to the needs of most introverts. Mugleston wears noise-canceling earphones because the noise gets to be too overwhelming. She stays prepared and focused on the task and takes the earphones out only when entering the room. She notes she uses the earphones quite often when walking around New York City because of the cacophony of the crowds and traffic.

The United Arab Emirates roundtable on introversion and acting yielded some passionate responses when asked about the time in the waiting room. There were even some contradictory points about how chatting with others can either calm or derail an audition, or how the extrovert's gregariousness can activate unwanted self-talk:

Actor 1: The worst thing about sitting outside a room is more people coming in, especially if you're the one nobody knows. There's chitchat going on, and you can't help listening as they talk about the last thing they did or the amazing play on Broadway or the West End … You're an outsider. I'm sure it's not on purpose, but they're making you feel uncomfortable.

Actor 2: As an extrovert, I think back to my last three professional auditions, thinking I was such a jerk to those three people because I was forcibly engaging them in conversation, and they wanted no part of it! Who the heck did I think I was doing that?! And it was only out of kindness that I was doing it! I was thinking, "Hey, you seem shy, let's talk."

Actor 3: At these cattle call auditions, there's a line of hundreds of people down the road. You're trying to stay focused on your pieces, preparing, doing some vocal warm-ups, and there are always people who want everybody to see them. It isn't fair. I hope we can teach the next generation of producers to be sensitive to the actors who are more introverted and need time alone to do their best work.

Actor 4: In an audition room, someone talking to me can help settle my nerves. I definitely need my quiet time and want to be alone to focus, but it helps my nerves if someone distracts me. We have a connection for a second that pulls away from what I'm there to do.

Actor 5: Often people in auditions are very stressed. Being introverted around all these extroverted actors, I have the benefit of being able to see stress and not let it affect me.[21]

The roundtable revealed a wide array of frustrations concerning the time in the waiting room. Minor and systematic changes to the waiting room dynamic can help both introverted and extroverted actors in this profession. Extroverts can try to read the energy in the room and gauge whether their more public ways of prepping for the audition might be impacting others. Introverts can advocate for themselves, requesting quiet time to share their best work. The lack of awareness of how one person's energy can affect another in the waiting room is an important conversation that can lead to real change.

The many actors and educators who took the time to complete the extensive survey have thoughtfully offered practical ways to help introverted actors succeed in the waiting room:

- Tune out others. Face away from the group. Focus on yourself and what you need to do to prepare.
- If someone is talking and you need to focus, go "use the restroom" to have some moments to yourself.
- Separate yourself from the main holding area during auditions and go to a corner or to the parking lot to get centered and focused.
- Listen to songs that boost your confidence.
- Appear calm and collected. Be friendly but don't engage in small talk unless someone engages you.
- Use meditation, mantras, and earphones to indicate "don't talk to me right now," even if you're not actually playing music!
- Arrive significantly early to new locations to observe and assess the space and your body's reaction to it.
- Have an audition routine that includes prep, before, during, assessment, and after/letting it go.
- Keep from looking over your material too much while at the audition. Greet people and make enough small talk to be friendly and polite and then focus on keeping your nerves down.[22]

These tips echo some of the other ideas mentioned in the chapter, and we thought it wise to include them, again simply based on their importance to this central issue of an actor's professional life.

In the Room

You enter the room. You introduce yourself and your material. You may have to chat for a bit ... and then finally, you can do what you do best. Act. Then it all feels much easier. An introverted actor might feel the anxiety fade as soon as the focus can be placed on the text and the scene partner. The freedom of acting returns you to your passion. You are in the room doing what you came to do and what you love, and the externals that favor the extrovert fade away. Joanne Magee, Director of Theatre at LREI in Manhattan, agrees, "The sooner the person can get to the acting, the better it is for them ... I don't know if there is any way an actor can cut to the chase, but my belief is, once they're acting, the proof is in the pudding. They're already delivering what the director wants to see."[23]

Another way to reduce audition nerves is temporarily shifting focus to another person—a scene partner or reader at the audition—the introvert can use their listening skills to escape their audition fears. The act of focusing on another can release the introvert from the over-stimulating environment. Introverts can thrive by mastering the acting methodology mantra of "putting their focus on the other." In a roundtable discussion with the Michigan State University Master of Fine Arts Acting candidates, Abbie Cathcart noted, "the focus on your scene partner is something I intellectually understand, but it's also something I'm realizing I haven't been doing. It's easy for introverts to be introspective, almost to a fault, because that's how they recharge."[24] The singular focus on the scene partner can assist with drawing the introspective introverts out of themselves. If there is no scene partner, say, in a monologue or song audition, the energy can be sent to the imagined scene partner.

Becoming aware of a tendency to turn inward, even to the point of excluding others, is what can set you free to build an Empathy Quotient (EQ) to others. EQ is a psychological self-reporting measure related to our ability to understand and empathize with others.[25] Being self-aware enough to recognize you are excluding others is already a positive indicator you are willing to increase your empathic qualities. Awareness can be a source of strength. It reveals a willingness to work outside your comfort zone in reaching out to others, trying to understand what it is to walk in their shoes. Your EQ is critical for you as an introvert. Examining when and why you turn inward reveals a healthy self-awareness of your social interactions as well as your capacity as an empathetic actor and scene partner. EQ is related to cultivated listening skills.

The challenge—or danger—is masking your true nature to the point of being fake, which can be exhausting to your physical and mental health. Midgely stopped trying to play an extrovert all the time so he could show people the real person they would be working with, trusting that, if the work was good, that was all that was needed.[26] Despite some struggle, he found success and confidence in embracing his introversion. Midgely notes, "the more I leaned into what my personality actually was, the more I found a better strategy on the whole. It requires a lot of self-confidence to be yourself."

Linda Mugleston has appeared in numerous Broadway musicals and advises that being comfortable in the auditioning room is about the real connections you make with others in the business and the experience that comes with many auditions.[27] She states, "I don't know if I'm necessarily introverted in the audition room...I'm quite relaxed. If I feel in tune with what's happening, who the character is, or I feel I'm particularly right for something, then I feel even more open." The feeling of openness in the audition room is one that many introverts envy. However, Mugleston confesses if she doesn't feel right for a role, she may be prone to self-doubt and overanalyzing.

LA actor and writer Emmanuelle Roumain-Yang focuses on relaxation before auditions.[28] She urges, "Relaxation is more important than people realize...I can do all the work in the world, and if I'm not relaxed, the work won't show." Roumain describes that when she truly connects with a character, she wants to tell this person's story. This desire makes the process much easier and transforms the audition into a character study. It alleviates her stress and makes for a better performance and a more enjoyable audition. This self-awareness is critical to the work of an actor, in that it supports the text, stays true to the story of the character, and allows the actor to share their authentic self with directors, auditors, and casting agents.

In addition to these applicable tips, there are some final things introverts may wish to consider to help de-stress the audition. Think about an anxiety scale between 1 and 10 where actors can identify what in the audition room is causing the most stress by rating them on a sliding scale, targeting a comfortable stretch in the 4–6 range. This can help the introvert know where to place their focus. Are the unknown variables of the interaction with the auditors causing you the most stress? If so, rehearse possible interactions and plan answers to the most common questions. At the very least, have a simple answer to the invitation, "So, tell me about yourself." This can reduce awkward interactions and fumbling answers.

Some other suggestions from the hundreds of actors who answered the survey regarding what to focus on when in the actual room include:

- Imagine you've known the people in the audition for years. If they are friends and colleagues, then it becomes a fun game. Remember they are rooting for you and want to be impressed.
- Be informed about what the director who runs the audition is asking for.
- Introverts might have trouble transitioning in and out of character quickly. Writing your own audition material can lead to higher success.
- You must get out of your comfort zone or you will lose opportunities.
- Use positive visualization prior to the audition. Imagine it being a success.
- Be open and thoughtful.
- Focus on your own audition and personal success instead of worrying about others and trying to mimic what they do.[29]

One of these tips may resonate with you related to your audition concerns. You may respond to the practical survey respondent who reminds you that you will lose opportunities if you don't push yourself. Or you may better align with the suggestion that being thoughtful could assist you in finding comfort in a stressful situation.

Changes to the Audition Process

For most of this section, we have been considering ways in which introverted actors can adjust their behaviors or reframe the audition in order to succeed. While the process of our auditions, in the United States at least, is often shaped around a highly extroverted model, it is not necessary for introverted actors to conform to this extrovert ideal. But introverted actors don't have to do all the work alone. There are a few ways those running the auditions can also help introverted actors succeed. Here are a few suggestions for those setting up the audition space:

1. Provide separate quiet spaces for actors to prepare pre-auditions, which allow both introverts and extroverts to do their best work.

2. If the extra space isn't possible, put up signage asking loud conversations or phone calls be held outside the waiting room.
3. If an anteroom is available, limit the number of actors in the immediate waiting room, or bring actors in small groups, to keep the space from feeling too oppressively crowded.
4. Provide a clear road map of what will happen in the audition room, including information about who is in the room and how the audition will run. These simple notes might include, "The director is seated in the third chair and will do a short interview before you present your material." Or, "Callbacks will be notified via email by the end of today." This information demystifies the process and is valuable to all auditioners, regardless of temperament.
5. On breaks, invite actors into the space to see the room to allow for introverts to feel comfortable.
6. Have the monitor ask the actors if they would like the interview portion of the audition to take place before or after they present their material. This can be easily communicated to the director and is a small modification that adds no extra time to the process.

These simple adjustments can offer reassuring evidence that producers acknowledge and respect both types of actors. It can begin the conversation related to how introverted actors are valued. It can also begin to erase the myth that all actors are extroverted. There are ways to embrace your introversion and succeed at auditions. Feel validated. Feel heard. Get out there and audition on your terms. Book the job.

Once you have booked the job, you get to play in the introvert's playground: the rehearsal process. For many, this is where introversion really pays off. Analysis, planning, and preparation all come together to the introvert's advantage. While we will look mostly at a typically theatrical model, the same freedom can also be cultivated for film work. In the next chapter, we will look at ways to make the already rich process of rehearsal even more enjoyable for introverts.

NOTES

1. Lucas, Richard. Personal interview. 15 Jan. 2019.
2. Donnellan, Brent. Personal interview. 1 Dec. 2018.
3. Combs, Sharon. Personal interview. 6 Dec. 2018.
4. Schultz, Carol. Personal interview. 20 Jan. 2019.

5. Marks, Matthew. Personal interview. 10 Jan. 2019.
6. Head, Andy. Personal interview. 15 Aug. 2018.
7. Combs, Sharon. Interview.
8. Donnellan, Brent. Interview.
9. Schultz, Carol. Interview.
10. Lucas, Richard. Interview.
11. Cranston, Bryan. *A Life in Parts*. Scribner, 2016.
12. Roznowski, Rob. *Inner Monologue in Acting*. Basingstoke: Palgrave Macmillan, 2013.
13. Marks, Matthew. Interview.
14. Donnellan, Brent. Interview.
15. Lucas, Richard. Interview.
16. Head, Andy. Interview.
17. Anonymous respondents. "Introversion Survey."
18. Kaenzig, Lisa. Personal interview. 15 Dec. 2018.
19. Midgely, Patrick. Personal interview. 23 Mar. 2019.
20. Mugleston, Linda. Personal interview. 15 Jan. 2019.
21. "Introversion and Acting." *American University of Sharjah Theatre Festival*. February 4, 2019.
22. Anonymous respondents. "Introversion Survey."
23. Magee, Joanna. Personal interview. 29 May 2019.
24. Cathcart, Abbie. Personal interview. 6 Dec. 2018.
25. Baron-Cohen, Ruggieri, Allison, Chakrabarti, and RA Hoekstra. "Empathy Quotient." Psychology Tools, January 1, 1970. https://psychology-tools.com/test/empathy-quotient
26. Midgely, Patrick. Interview.
27. Mugleston, Linda. Interview.
28. Roumain-Yang, Emmanuelle. Personal interview. 30 April 2019.
29. Anonymous respondents. "Introversion survey."

REFERENCES

Anonymous respondents. "Introversion Survey."
Baron-Cohen, Ruggieri, Allison, Chakrabarti, and RA Hoekstra. "Empathy Quotient." Psychology Tools, January 1, 1970. https://psychology-tools.com/test/empathy-quotient
Cathcart, Abbie. Personal interview. 6 Dec. 2018.
Combs, Sharon. Personal interview. 6 Dec. 2018.
Cranston, Bryan. *A Life in Parts*. Scribner, 2016.
Donnellan, Brent. Personal interview. 1 Dec. 2018.
Head, Andy. Personal interview. 15 Aug. 2018.

"Introversion and Acting." *American University of Sharjah Theatre Festival.* February 4, 2019.
Kaenzig, Lisa. Personal interview. 15 Dec. 2018.
Lucas, Richard. Personal interview. 15 Jan. 2019.
Magee, Joanna. Personal interview. 29 May 2019.
Marks, Matthew. Personal interview. 10 Jan. 2019.
Midgely, Patrick. Personal interview. 23 Mar. 2019.
Mugleston, Linda. Personal interview. 15 Jan. 2019.
Roznowski, Rob. *Inner Monologue in Acting.* Basingstoke: Palgrave Macmillan, 2013.
Roumain-Yang, Emmanuelle. Personal interview. 30 April 2019.
Schultz, Carol. Personal interview. 20 Jan. 2019.

CHAPTER 13

Rehearsals

Most theatrical rehearsals represent a small, safe community created with shared rules of engagement. A rehearsal hall is a place where the conversation is usually focused on a singular goal. It is an environment where analysis is rewarded and a schedule is distributed, so pre-planning can occur. All of these traditional elements of rehearsal support an introvert's strengths. Most introverts report loving rehearsals above almost any other part of the theatrical process. Rehearsal is where introverted actors can best showcase their passion.

Theatrical rehearsals traditionally operate under what we refer to as the Long Runway strategy, allowing a longer, more gradual processing time within a structure that prepares the actor for "take off" on opening night.[1] This gives introverts a chance to prepare and present their work in a structured fashion and allows for their temperament to be rewarded through focus and concentration, where many introverts excel. A rehearsal calendar also gives introverted actors a clue as to what scenes or moments in the play will be worked each day, giving them a chance to review specific parts of the script in advance to anticipate how they might contribute to the creative process once the room is full and the pressure is on. In a Long Runway approach to rehearsal, ideas are discussed and initiated, but there is also time to think, process, and reflect as choices and discoveries are made over a period of weeks. In a traditional theatrical structure, rehearsal seems designed for the introvert.

We do want to make a brief acknowledgment here of the difference between film and live theatre when it comes to rehearsal. Introverted film actors face some unique challenges, as time and budget constraints rarely prioritize extended rehearsals. Without the luxury of a lengthy and reflective rehearsal process, the introverted film actor may seem at a disadvantage to their extroverted counterparts so eager to immediately share their work. However, some of these same rehearsal strategies might benefit film actors as well. Film actors are given a list of shots for the day, so they can plan in advance for how they might approach their work. Some of the rehearsal aspects of film, such as shooting scenes out of sequence, can invite introverts to use their analytical and investigative skills, as they must always consider their character's given circumstances, through line, and moments before, even when approaching the story out of sequence. The repetition of getting shots from multiple angles gives introverted actors a way to gauge their work and look for growth. If scene partners are willing, there are often lengthy times between takes that can be used to mimic theatrical rehearsals with some private preparations.

As with auditions, considering and adapting the rehearsal space to honor the introverts as equally as the extroverts is a shared responsibility between both actor and director.

Struggles

In our research, we collected stories cataloging some of the struggles our corps of introverted actors have encountered in rehearsal and how they solved them.

New York-based actor Carol Schultz believes her introvert's processing time has impeded some rehearsals, noting she can't always openly express herself in the moment.[2] She admits, "If something is bothering me, it may take me until the next day to address it. Or, I'll speak privately with the director after rehearsal." This correlates to the expectation that an actor must make immediate adjustments that favor extroverted actors more comfortable with this spontaneity.

Broadway actor Matthew Marks revealed his stress regarding social interactions and his inability to connect with others at the start of rehearsal is related to his shyness.[3] There are major benefits to talking with new colleagues in a new rehearsal setting, and Marks says he often wishes this type of casual talk came more easily and quickly for his personality type. This introverted and admittedly shy actor wishes he was different in some way.

Like so many introverts, actor Patrick Midgely thrives on structure and finds he needs clear information in the process, and this may not always be a shared priority among the cast.[4] He notes, "I find my personality manifests in wanting to control more in the rehearsal room. I like to know what I'm going to be working on and how much of the text we're covering, so I can prepare." This actor's needs mirror many of the suggestions offered for directors to more openly acknowledge their introverted actors through detailed schedules. We'll check back in with these stories later in this chapter.

To the Director

Often directors choose their actors based on a brief audition or interview, but they don't know much about their work style or personality until rehearsals finally begin. You cast a new actor based on a solid audition and an interesting interview, but then you see them at rehearsal and they seem aloof; they don't seem to want to be part of the company or join the ensemble. Did you make a mistake? Do they even want to be here? More than likely, you have cast an introverted actor who works differently than participating in the enforced conviviality many directors cultivate in the rehearsal hall.

The culture of the rehearsal hall is a direct reflection of the way a director works. With just a few minor considerations and adjustments, rehearsal culture can include an understanding and respect of the introverted actor. This may simply mean a welcome speech that includes the mention of your understanding of temperament diversity and examples of how it will be respected in the process. It may be a short discussion about the importance of taking time to make discoveries. If you hire an introverted actor, they should be treated as such and not expected to conform to the extroverted model stereotype. And the conversation can begin on the first day of rehearsal.

Are you unintentionally promoting an extroverted ideal by modeling or encouraging a loud and boisterous atmosphere of constant laughter and conversation, or insisting on large group warm-ups or improv games to build ensemble? When an actor is quiet or self-isolating in rehearsal, do you assume resistance or take a moment to check in? Simple observations and a few thoughtful questions may be just the adjustments needed for a more inclusive process.

The favoritism toward the extroverted actor present in most rehearsals is most evident in the language directors often use when working with actors. Such seemingly inspirational phrases as "Take a risk" or "Make a bigger choice" or "Be brave" can inadvertently shame introverted actors, as they imply not only that these demands are simple, but that they can and should be applied immediately, whether that actor is prepared or not. These expectations can result in feelings of anxiety and inadequacy. Simple tweaks of language can have a major impact. For example, rather than "Make a bigger choice," try using the sliding scale method to describe a more measured build. You could say, "Right now, this moment is reading at about a five. How can we get it to a nine?" This not only acknowledges the goal as a gradual one, but that the processes for arriving there are collaborative rather than an immediate individual demand.

There are other minor adjustments that can enhance your rehearsal process and create a space where artists of all personality types feel equally valued. Allow equal time for quiet reflection as well as the loud moments. Offer time to process notes before expecting them to be applied to the next scene. Respect actors' recharging time on breaks when they need time alone. Designate areas for talking and areas for quiet in the rehearsal space and on breaks. Open up pathways for conversations about the ways in which actors like to work. Create and maintain a structure where introverts feel prepared to do their best work. Let actors know what is expected of them for the next day's rehearsal so that introverts can prepare. The unexpected aspects of rehearsal will certainly spring up and overturn the original schedule when a scene needs more attention than originally scheduled, but the base structure allows the introvert to do their best work.

Redefine what ensemble means in your rehearsal by understanding that introverts can offer unique strengths to what runs counter to traditionally extroverted expectations. Consider reframing ensemble exercises where all are asked to participate and contribute based on their strengths and their comfort—and not as a way to create what some actors view as a high-energy mob. Reexamine how you incorporate ice-breakers, group exercises, warm-ups, or improvisation to leave room for all different creative working styles.

Take a moment to assure all ensemble members that after-hours parties, dinners, or outings are not mandatory or even necessary. Actors do not have to socialize, interact, become friends with, or even like everyone in the ensemble/cast in order to connect and work successfully with them. A cast of professional actors is a group of working colleagues, just as in any job, and there will be varying levels of friendship and patience, but all work together to create the show.

Remember the actor from the Dubai roundtable who shared how directors have often misinterpreted his introverted processing as negativity or judgment? It is a common mistake that actors who aren't nodding their heads and smiling when getting notes are "being difficult." That actor has experienced what many introverted actors have—the misinterpretation of processing and reflection for impertinence or a lack of interest. This misunderstanding is further evidence of the ingrained bias that actors must behave a certain way, and often, that behavior seems based on the "extrovert ideal" traits such as vocal participation. The actor in the roundtable discussion has now become proactive and shares their processing habits with the director before that mischaracterization can occur. Having such conversations can facilitate a feeling of comfort for both director and actor.

In rehearsal, some of the actors' choices might not work or won't read as planned and have to be scrapped. In those moments, are directors considering the sensitivity to feedback some introverts can display? Are directors taking the time to check in, consider the failures, and acknowledge the incremental growth, even in the face of what seem like setbacks? This quick check in acknowledges the good work being done and helps pave the way for respectful collaboration in the future.

As we noted, actors are intrinsically brave, and their bravery is evident in many moments in the rehearsal room. One of the trademarks of many introverts is they do not like to take big risks in front of a group of people, but they are taking them in their minds all the time. This concept of risk is fundamental to acting work in rehearsal. While the term "risk" is common vocabulary when discussing acting, it actually encompasses several different points: visible risks, risks in sharing intellectual work, the vulnerability of connecting with another, and the risk of big physical or vocal choices. This vast array of risk raises many questions for the introverted actor: What is the definition of risk? How is risk embodied? How does risk-taking manifest itself in an introvert? How you facilitate and coach those moments of risk may be different for an introverted actor. The director may want to maintain high standards and expectations but celebrate incremental success. This can be showcased in the way you word and give notes, recognizing introverts might sting more from notes that expect immediate application. Make sure they understand what you are looking for and allow them time to take those notes away from the space to perfect the work.

A director can create a safe environment where vulnerability can be accessed freely. Examine how you allow actors to navigate vulnerability as they build from rehearsal to opening night. Certainly, you should encourage actors to work to the edge of their comfort zones, but that work can more readily occur in a safe environment. A safe environment might acknowledge and discuss empathy's connection to vulnerability or ask the actor how they might like to approach highly vulnerable moments.

The extroverted classroom bias already exposed in this and other research is just as detrimental in a rehearsal dynamic operating from the same extroverted bias. Regardless of temperament, the work of actors requires tremendous commitment, tenacity, and discipline, which opens them up to failure, and sometimes, this failure is public in its display. Inclusive rehearsals can reward bravery for all actors.

To the Actor: Overcoming Self-doubt

Okay actors, so you got the job. You are now a professional, working actor. For so many, this validation of your work from others is a cause for celebration. You are about to enter into rehearsal, where your passion and process come together in ways that allow you to share your work in a safe and controlled environment. A rehearsal process is a place where introverts thrive.

So, why then do some introverts experience a nagging feeling when heading into rehearsals that something isn't quite right? Is it disrupting an orderly life to live in a new city and meet new people? Is it that this director's process and expectations might be different from rehearsals they've experienced in the past? Is it that this new project might take them out of a known and comfortable daily structure? Or is it the classic introverted tendency to overthink, so despite getting the job, you don't know if you can handle the role? Is it the imposter syndrome that makes you imagine your castmates are skeptical or unsupportive of your work? Whatever the scenario, these feelings of self-doubt are valid and expected. A rehearsal process asks actors to work in ways beyond their control. For many, those fears can be allayed after a few days in the process, but the feeling of apprehension prior to entering the rehearsal hall and meeting your new company of actors can be overwhelming.

Just as a director can adapt their process, the introverted actor can take several, often simple measures to calm those fears. Perhaps it is by being upfront about your personality trait to those you are working with. You can let others know you aren't being rude, or difficult, or aloof. Simply tell them you are an introvert and need some alone time to recharge. This unapologetic mantra can become your response when asked to join others on the lunch break or have a drink after rehearsal. When a director asks for a major adjustment, don't be afraid to say, "I'm going to need a bit of time to process those notes, but I will bring in some great new stuff tomorrow." No matter the possible issue, honesty and education of others related to introversion can allay most of those fears. Additionally, adopting these responses can empower you to more clearly articulate your anxieties and embrace your introverted self.

But what happens when the fears go deeper than simply speaking up for yourself and the needs of your creative work? Actor and educator Andy Head discussed his favorite parts of the rehearsal related to his introversion and how he learned to remind himself that, out of all the introverted and extroverted actors who auditioned, he got the job.[5] They chose him, so despite any other lingering negative feelings, you always have this knowledge to combat them. Overcome your fears with the simple reminder of how lucky you are to be plying your craft by doing what you love.

You might find your fears and anxieties lessen as you move through the rehearsal process from first reading to tablework to scene work. Head admits he finds later rehearsals easier than early ones, as he has had time to more deeply develop the character. He advocates for frontloading preparation prior to rehearsals to also allow time to disregard any self-doubt. Reduce stress by reminding yourself every actor in the room is starting the process on the same footing. Especially with early rehearsals, there is no expectation that every choice and interpretation will be brilliant or even correct. It's perfectly fine, and even respectable and wise, to admit you don't have the answers and to ask questions. These simple reminders can assuage fears connected with the first few rehearsals.

An introvert can harness one of their greatest strengths—preparation—to counter the common resistance to making immediate adjustments. Head notes if he can come into rehearsal with numerous choices and ideas for scenes, then if a moment isn't working, he doesn't have to wait until the next rehearsal. Come to the scene with a list of ideas that might work and then the risk comes in trying them out, but you don't have the added stress of creating on the spot. For Broadway veteran Linda Mugleston the ability to remain invested in the character while also remaining free to follow impulses comes from preparation.[6] Full analysis and understanding of the character and memorization of the lines allow her to remain open and able to play with anything that comes her way. She notes, "I come in completely off-book, so I can free myself. I don't have to worry or stumble. I can think on my feet and go with whatever impulse is given to me." It's important to note that she must be completely off book to experience this level of freedom. Memorization and deep analysis are important work introverted actors can do in advance.

Our survey respondents have some advice and strategies related to successfully preparing for rehearsal:

- Mentally prepare by breathing through the anxiety.
- Don't be afraid to excuse yourself for a moment.
- Warm-up on your own to give yourself energy and get into the right headspace.
- In a show where the character experiences a heavier or more complex emotional journey, take time to think, focus, and recharge before going on stage. In shows that are lighter and higher energy, feed off the energy of conversing with castmates before going on stage and let that carry you through the scene(s).
- Find your own space in the room, usually away from the main group, a hub where you can relax and prepare for the next scene or run.
- Take copious notes and don't socialize too much so you have more time to prepare. Overprepare, then go with the flow.
- Take time to be alone and get into character, but check in with the ensemble beforehand to feel synchronized.
- Work extra hard outside of the allotted professional time. Then it's easier to get things done in professional spaces because the work is already done.[7]

These suggestions all seem to point to introverted actors advocating for themselves in the room for their comfort. They also suggest a highly attuned sense of self-awareness that understands what the individual actor needs. Most point to isolation in order to best prepare for the rehearsal. One may resonate most with your specific needs.

Even with preparation, rehearsals can be difficult when the actor feels they're not giving the director what they want or when the highly emotional work is draining and stressful. Lisa Kaenzig, an introversion expert, wants both introverts and extroverts to remember rehearsals are sometimes trying, but she acknowledges extroverted actors might have an advantage.[8] According to Kaenzig, "extroverts can almost work

themselves up to believing in themselves again, even if it's a fake belief."
An extrovert's predisposition to overcoming difficult situations might
help them in rehearsal, but the stress of self-doubt is not unique to introverts. At the moment when rehearsals inevitably become taxing, it is probably taxing for others as well. Both personality types might find this
challenging to overcome, but they can also benefit from a reminder that
they've practiced and done all the work in advance.

Break Time

So far, our focus has been on the work in the rehearsal room and how we
might find ways for the introverted actor to thrive and create in the
rehearsal process. Now we must call out the one part of the rehearsal that
so many introverts dread ... the mandated Equity break. This five- or ten-
minute break can seem like an eternity to introverts who want to resume
the rehearsal. Since extroverts can more easily drop in and out of character, for them, the break is often about socializing and shrugging off the
intense work in the rehearsal. For many introverts, who need more quiet
time to decompress and recharge, it is not that easy. Usually, they count
down the seconds so they can get back to work.

When asked what he does on break, Andy Head, like so many others,
reports, "I stay by myself and don't interact with people ... It's not a time
of hanging out for me. I'm there to work."[9] He has tried to interact on
breaks but admits these are usually halfhearted efforts, limited by nerves
and worry. The self-doubt so many introverted actors feel in rehearsal
might also keep them from reaching out or making a social effort. In this,
they might find themselves on the periphery of casual conversations but
not confident enough to contribute. The feeling of being an outsider is
enhanced in rehearsal breaks, where others might want to get you involved
or bring you into the conversation. An introvert can decide when and how
to get involved. Matthew Marks, who spoke of wanting to socialize more
but understands it is not his predisposition, has a few strategies.[10] He
describes, "I mind my own business ... I dive into my script or my phone
or go outside and sit by myself." While that could be perceived as antisocial, it is simply the introvert coping in a very public situation.

Breaks are sacred to actors, but for introverts to remove themselves
from draining social interactions requires some skillful solutions. Actor
Patrick Midgely shares his secret for maintaining his personal time while
also including a strictly limited social component:

I take break time literally and seriously, and I use it to my benefit. As soon as the break is called, I set a timer so I know exactly when I have to be back. Then, if I feel I haven't been warm enough or talked to folks enough, at two minutes left on the break, I go talk to them. I can be on a social clock for two minutes, and I enjoy it … people with introverted personalities often feel as though they are fighting against time and trying to get back to the quiet time they can have. Time is important, so I make sure I am in control of it as much as possible so I don't resent being in that moment. Instead, it's a moment I have chosen to be in.[11]

Midgely's strategy is the perfect example of a stretch goal as it applies to rehearsal. By investing in timed socialization, he is able to interact with the ensemble while also finding private recharging time.

Some of the hundreds of survey respondents offered sound advice for breaks. One of their numerous examples may resonate with you:

- Don't over-socialize.
- Check in on other people and their body language.
- Be completely focused and "in the room" when working and turn it all off on breaks and at the end of the day.
- Take time for yourself to daydream, stretch, or focus, so when you're back on, you're recharged to be fully present.
- Find a core group of common-minded people.
- Force yourself to get out of your shell and socialize, instead of always retreating to your script and notes. Try to have some fun in the dressing rooms and create a sense of play so you get out of yourself and warm up to the true spirit of play.
- Bargain with yourself to socialize. Not too much, but it's important to know your cast so you feel comfortable with them.
- Familiarize yourself with the performance space so you feel at home rather than anxious.[12]

You can see the tension between two possible options from these suggestions—using the break for yourself or using the break for others. Try both at different times or create your own hybrid of break strategies to help you find restorative time on the break, as well as maintaining a healthy relationship with the cast.

SOLUTIONS

We now return to the stories from some of our corps of actors who were struggling with various elements of rehearsal. If there is an issue or impediment in the rehearsal of a specific moment in the play keeping you from speaking out or fully committing, Carol Schultz advocates for ways to facilitate dialogue in a private setting, where introverts might feel more invited to talk.[13] This is especially useful in establishing a connection to ensemble members, where Schultz says she'll meet away from the rehearsal hall, in the dressing room or at a coffee shop, to chat about the impediments in the scene. She finds personal interactions can solve many blocks in the work, and most often, fellow cast members and scene partners are happy to meet outside of rehearsal to discuss and connect. This casual meeting can help both actors. She continues that, in spending this time alone together, "without the pressure of trying to be creative or perform or please anyone else, we'll find a deeper connection. We'll discuss the scene, run lines, and learn things about our own character as well as our partner." This kind of work will often create a bond that endures throughout rehearsals and the run of the show. By speaking in an unpressured and private setting in an intimate fashion, introverts can more easily express themselves.

Matthew Marks, who expressed wishing he could interact and socialize more in rehearsals, is also aware that this is not who he authentically is in his private or professional self.[14] But even as he values personal authenticity, Marks admits his most honest behavior has led to misunderstandings about who he is as a person. He notes, "People always thinks I'm a bitch when they first meet me because I am not a bubbly person." Where lighter social interactions might be easy for extroverted actors, introverts like Marks find them difficult. In these moments of stress, it's important to remember that socializing and friendship are not requirements of every cast or show, and introverts often put more value in fewer, deeper relationships, often away from the rehearsal hall. This is a common way introverts deal with the social expectations of their work. "To be less shy" seems like a stretch goal waiting to be tested.

Patrick Midgely, who thrives on structured rehearsals, finds value in creating some distance that still allows for his inclusion in rehearsals even when the schedule is not as clear.[15] While the director is working on other scenes that do not include him, Midgely sits in the back row of the rehearsal hall, waiting for his scenes, working on his lines and notes, and still keeping one ear on the work of the rehearsal, without expending the energy of being directly involved. Staking safe territory in a rehearsal hall is a tactic used by many introverts to help them prepare for and adapt to new situations or unexpected changes in the schedule. Midgely noted as he learned more about his personality, he was able to find ways he could temporarily recharge and remain open, spontaneous, and hungry for connection. Midgely has created a way of working that allows for freedom even without structure.

Our survey respondents have some advice for you as well, related to ways they have found success within rehearsals:

- Remind yourself the ensemble exercises will be over soon.
- Take a risk and make a bold choice so you know you can do it.
- Carve out time to be alone so you can prep and be ready to mix and react with others.
- If you are confident in what you're doing, you can ease into interacting on stage and making new choices.
- If you ask questions of the director first in private, this typically leads to more comfort in asking questions in front of the group and will hopefully keep you from feeling closed off or judged.
- Silently observe and think about what you can learn from the director, designers, or co-actors.
- Write down the moments that can improve your work and share it with the director or co-actors.
- Find and take your own space to work on character body or character building.
- It may take a while and cost a lot, but you will get heard.
- It's okay to react the next day to a previous day's problems.
- Ask a fellow actor to run lines in private. It offers a chance to talk about the scene and find out where the other person's coming from. It's usually enlightening and bonds actors together.[16]

These excellent hints may allay any fears the introvert has when heading into the rehearsal space. In each suggestion, you can see introverts using strengths such as analysis and observation to create real strategies for success. The respondents have offered their ways of finding success within the rehearsal, now it is up to you to find those strategies that allow you the freedom to do the work you know you are capable of doing.

Our final bit of advice is to not be intimidated by the social ease enjoyed by so many extroverted actors. Many of the actors we interviewed admitted to feeling a kind of envy or jealousy when it comes to observing the gregarious behavior of their extroverted castmates. Extroverted actors offer a valuable example of how to be comfortable in front of people, and it's easy to jump to a place of comparison and self-judgment. We hope to help introverted actors value the ways extroverts work without simultaneously devaluing their own. Know too that extroverts may envy many introverted qualities that allow their less outgoing castmates to thrive in rehearsal. An awareness of the complementary strengths of both types makes for the most compelling process.

In the next chapter, we offer transitional strategies for the introverted actor as they move from rehearsal into public performance. In this environment, the safety of the rehearsal room is stripped away and actors are asked to add a completely unknown element to their utopian rehearsals—the audience. The introverted actor must hold for laughs, accept applause, and find their light in order to work with their new "scene partner."

NOTES

1. Heinz, Amy. "Granting Kids the Time They Need to Socially Succeed." Quiet Revolution, June 20, 2017. https://www.quietrev.com/the-long-runway-granting-kids-the-time-they-need-to-socially-succeed/
2. Schultz, Carol. Personal interview. 20 Jan. 2019.
3. Marks, Mathew. Personal interview. 10 Jan. 2019.
4. Midgely, Patrick. Personal interview. 23 Mar. 2019.
5. Head, Andy. Personal interview. 15 Aug. 2018.
6. Mugleston, Linda. Personal interview. 15 Jan. 2019.
7. Anonymous respondents. "Introversion survey."
8. Kaenzig, Lisa. Personal interview. 15 Dec. 2018.
9. Head, Andy. Interview.
10. Marks, Matthew. Interview.
11. Midgely, Patrick. Interview.
12. Anonymous respondents. "Introversion survey."
13. Schultz, Carol. Interview.
14. Marks, Matthew. Interview.
15. Midgely, Patrick. Interview.
16. Anonymous respondents. "Introversion survey."

References

Anonymous respondents. "Introversion survey."

Head, Andy. Personal interview. 15 Aug. 2018.

Heinz, Amy. "Granting Kids the Time They Need to Socially Succeed." Quiet Revolution, June 20, 2017. https://www.quietrev.com/the-long-runway-granting-kids-the-time-they-need-to-socially-succeed/.

Kaenzig, Lisa. Personal interview. 15 Dec. 2018.

Marks, Mathew. Personal interview. 10 Jan. 2019.

Midgely, Patrick. Personal interview. 23 Mar. 2019.

Mugleston, Linda. Personal interview. 15 Jan. 2019.

Schultz, Carol. Personal interview. 20 Jan. 2019.

CHAPTER 14

Performance

Rehearsals are over and you are ready for opening night. This is what the auditions and long hours of analysis and preparation have all led to. This is a moment of transition when all the choices, connections, and work of rehearsal are now shared with an audience. This is where you now put yourself on public display, for public scrutiny. The combination of these pressures can add up to be an introvert's worst nightmare. Which reminds us of our essential question—why do introverts act?

Our survey results reveal an overwhelming number of introverts go into acting to transform themselves or become another through character creation. Many introverts can find playing another comforting, walking in the shoes of someone so different from themselves—the survey supports that introverts are truly transformative actors. Psychology expert Dr. Richard Lucas assures that being an introvert can be physically and emotionally exhausting, often because introverts are prone to sensory and social overload and weighing options before making decisions.[1] Lucas supports the notion that living—for a bit—as another might be liberating.

We have shared dozens of tips and suggestions to aid introverted actors in their work in rehearsals, but actors all realize the ultimate goal of rehearsal is to share the work with an audience. Despite hearing time and time again of an introvert's penchant for rehearsal over performance, it is our greatest hope that during rehearsals, the introvert has done the work to feel entirely prepared to perform. The rehearsal part of the work is done

© The Author(s) 2020
R. Roznowski et al., *The Introverted Actor*,
https://doi.org/10.1007/978-3-030-41607-2_14

and now is a chance to find confidence in the actuality of doing your job in front of an audience.

Again, we acknowledge this discussion skews toward the theatrical model of performance rather than toward film. While the idea of repetitive performance is more applicable to stage actors, concepts like "routine" and "preparation" can be easily transformed for the introverted screen actor and used on set in various ways.

Preparations and Routines

With the opening of a show, much of the uncertainty that may spring up in rehearsals is alleviated by a concrete production schedule. If you are lucky enough to be in a long-running show, a specific routine is created. A consistent routine is a boon for introverts, as it provides reliable patterns of when to arrive, when you will be done, what is expected of you, and who you will see. These dependable patterns help an introvert do their best work. Certainly, there will be moments of adjustment, when an understudy must go on or a prop goes missing, but the stable design provided by the run of a show is a place for introverts to thrive.

Introverted actors shared many of the personal routines they developed to help prepare for the demands of a performance. Arriving early, making rounds to greet everyone, finding alone time prior to performance, and creating motivational playlists to get into the right headspace were all popular suggestions. Actor Patrick Midgely's performance routine includes arriving at the theatre sometimes as much as thirty minutes prior to the assigned call time.[2] Early arrivals to potentially stressful environments allow introverts to gain a sense of control.

Linda Mugleston shared a Sunday routine for the Broadway performances of *Hello, Dolly!*[3] She reports, "Right before the show started, during the overture, everybody in the cast [was] up on deck, doing 'Soul Train Sunday', where everyone lined up on the sides and danced down the middle." This decidedly extroverted act is a common type of occurrence that casts may do backstage to energize the ensemble, but like many introverts, Mugleston found herself enjoying watching the warm-up from the sidelines, but was consistently hesitant when encouraged to participate herself. So often, introverts feel badly for not enthusiastically joining in with these public events. Like the engaged but quiet participant in an acting class, perhaps we can adjust these ensemble moments to include introverted actors by appreciating that standing on the sidelines, observing the group, and enjoying the action are all ways that introverts engage. Just because they don't actively join in does not mean they are not an important part of the shared group energy. Mugleston admits when she did join in, it had to be on her terms. Cajoling or pressuring introverted actors to join in and participate might actually work against the goal of the exercise to build an ensemble. Respecting an introvert's space can encourage them to feel comfortable with the group, and eventually, they might even join the dance. Providing introverted actors with the agency to decide when and how they participate in these group activities ensures that when they do take part, they will gain from the experience, rather than resent it.

Good acting (for an introvert or an extrovert) is taxing. It requires an ability to display, connect to, or portray a range of emotions that most outside this profession regularly subvert. This highly emotional terrain is what makes an actor unique, and after the curtain comes down or the cameras stop rolling, it is also what makes introverts exhausted. To prepare for such a job, introverted actors have described a range of strategies for preparation. This preparation is usually composed of solo activities like meditation, yoga, mindfulness, deep breathing, and other inwardly focused activities. Dr. Richard Lucas underscores the importance of an introverted actor's preparation, stating it often means "taking time alone, being able to hide for a little bit, and coming back with some reserve of energy that allows them to work again."[4] The isolated preparation is essential to the success of public performances.

Actor Patrick Midgely reports the actual time spent with other actors shifts significantly once performances begin.[5] He notes with performance, actors spend less time in the theatre and more time on their own. With most performances taking place in the evening and nighttime hours, introverts can create the day as they wish in order to prepare for the show by limiting their public interactions, making the moments of socialization and interaction often required at the theatre easier to navigate. Midgely fills his days with activities that allow him to perform at his best, and that preparation takes some time.

Some of our survey responses echo the concepts of routine and focus. They include:

- Find a quiet place to escape and warm up.
- Get there early to put on make-up or drink tea in silence, and give yourself plenty of time to put on your costume and check props.

- Meditate in the mornings and warm up privately before rehearsal ... center yourself first, then the nerves can't affect the performance.[6]

So, when it comes to performance, some introverts feel as though they have an advantage. They have routine to make them feel safe and time to prepare however they wish. They appear to be in complete control. But so far, we have only considered how an introverted actor might control their own preparation for performance. We must also consider the part beyond their control: the sea of unfamiliar faces that appears during every show to watch their work.

THE AUDIENCE

In a public performance environment, the safety of the rehearsal room is stripped away and the actor is asked to add a completely unknown element to their work—the audience. A nightly step into the unknown can intimidate some introverted performers. Others have found coping mechanisms that allow the introvert to succeed. Many of these strategies take them back to the strengths of their personality: reviewing the analysis and trusting the foundation of the work; blocking the audience out of their minds by focusing solely on their scene partner; using the literal fourth wall and the blinding lights to distract from the unknown; allowing time for reflection to examine why a moment didn't land or why a connection might feel different from one evening to the next.

In an episode of Susan Cain's *Quiet* podcast, screen and stage actor Molly Ringwald references the "light barrier" in order to give the introverted actor a more pronounced separation from the audience.[7] When an actor stands on stage, and the audience is out in the dark, an actor feels freedom in knowing there is an audience, but the audience cannot be seen—mastering the acting adage of being private in public. Additionally, on stage, there is a character and a script, which provide another barrier between an actor and the audience. Introverts can make constant adaptations and practice a variety of safety procedures to make this public profession work for them. What is the barrier you may need to "create" in order to feel safe when acting? Perhaps no barrier is needed?

Introversion expert Dr. Lisa Kaenzig speaks about another form of barrier to help introverts in the actual act of performing in front of an audience.[8] She notes it is all about perspective. In other words, it's not you performing; it's a presentation. This viewpoint employs what Kaenzig calls "the public mask," going on to explain, "there's a barrier [between] ... your public persona versus what you're like privately." Kaenzig's "public mask" is another way many introverts interviewed for this book keep themselves safe in performance.

No matter the tactic, the audience is still physically present, and they insinuate themselves into the work of the actor through applause, laughter, and shifts in energy. How does an introvert work within this unknown variable, when we know they might struggle with sudden changes or new experiences? Most interviewees replied the answer is in playing a character, and the character reacts appropriately. The nerves that arise in an introverted actor when they are asked to speak publicly or make small talk as themselves vanish in performance because the character is in this situation, not the actor. This phenomenon is entirely real and another reason introverts tend to thrive in scripted performance over extemporaneous speaking.

LA actor and writer Sean Patrick McGowan reminds us rehearsals serve as the foundation for performance, creating a sense of confidence and focus.[9] The rehearsal process has prepared everyone to do their jobs, and for McGowan, each member of the ensemble is "operating under the assumption it all goes well, so what is there to be afraid of? [The audience] wants you to do well." This attitude relies on the notion of the Long Runway, as the weeks of rehearsal prepare the introverted actor for the demands of opening night.[10] When asked how the audience's presence impacts his work, McGowan answers simply, "That is the point of all the work I've done, to share an experience with other people. This is my job; I'm not going to be afraid to do my job." Actor Andy Head agrees. By the time the curtain goes up, most of the work has been done; Head reports he is more able to socialize with cast and crew because the pressure he placed on himself in rehearsals is released in performances. Most of the questions have been answered and the choices have been made. Now, all an introverted actor must do is trust in the repetition of their work and focus on their partner.

However, Andy Head admits there is one element of performance that gives him pause.[11] Rather than the size of the audience, Head is more impacted by who populates it. He is not alone in this fear, as many introverts highlight this difference. Knowing who is in the audience transforms the faceless crowd into a place of possible judgment and unsolicited feedback. The introvert's propensity to overthink can spin into unwanted places by a simple alert that a friend, an agent, a critic, or a director is in the audience. Head continues, "If there are familiar people in the audience, I am more nervous than if I don't know anyone. I know they're there supporting me, and I want to do a good job for them." The pressure toward perfection is very real, and some introverts reported knowing someone in the audience can affect their performance. As an audience member, if you know a performer in the show is an introvert, you can ask in advance whether or not they want to know what night you are planning to attend the show. This can also be a question for stage managers or house managers, who often announce to actors who is in the audience. Rather than spur excitement, this information might hinder introverted members in the cast. Of course extroverts may react similarly. A simple solution is to ask first. This is another example of an easy and thoughtful question that can do a lot to alleviate nerves.

Related to the burden of overthinking, respected Indian actor Soumyabrata Choudhury[12] believes no matter their nationality, introverted actors tend to fixate on pleasing what might appear to be one disinterested member of the audience. The case of knowing who is in the audience might be one example. Choudhury offers this familiar scenario: There are fifteen people in the audience. Fourteen of them are enjoying the show. The fifteenth appears not to like it. Even though it's not a logical reaction, an actor will focus not on the fourteen enjoying themselves, but on the one audience members looking nonplussed. And while this behavior is not necessarily solely the property of the introvert, many introverts reported having a strong relationship with such behavior.

Choudhury suggests a way to assist the actor from this disproportionate anxiety. He posits the problem is that this introverted actor would otherwise be doing good work, but is overwhelmed by their concern for the audience. One can imagine extroverts also exhibiting such behavior. Choudhury describes this as an internal problem requiring an artistic solution. A solution is found in the discipline to train the mind toward acceptance rather than worry. The acceptance of a holistic and total craft, where the presence of others cannot distract the actor. Choudhury concludes, "The discipline of acting is not simply to overcome inhibitions … it is to sustain the work with a kind of discipline, both physical and spiritual, so [actors] are not subject to a kind of neurosis, a kind of continuous sense of being in the presence of others." He advocates that in order for the actor's career to have longevity, they should address their "need to please" and focus on the disciplined retraining of the mind for both the acting and the audience. It is a move away from fear toward mindfulness for the actor.

Mindfulness is a key concept in many of the comments below. Of course, mindfulness comes through a deep examination of self and an inquisitiveness our survey respondents shared:

- Fully get into character.
- Internalize the run of the show and how much fun and work it takes.
- Know the audience will have certain energy levels based on what you give them and vice versa.
- Develop a consistent routine for each show to prep and plan breaks during the run.
- Find ways to energize or ground yourself during performances and always look for new discoveries in performance to keep it fresh.[13]

In this last response, the respondent is urging the actors to take risks onstage by staying alive, alert, and fully invested in the work.

All of our interviewees share a pure sense of elation when sharing their work with an audience. The idea of showcasing their passion with eager audiences is what this whole process is about. The reciprocal energy received and shared between audience and actor is perhaps the most exhilarating part for an actor. Many introverts report this communion is more akin to their preferred one-on-one interactions. Many of the actors we interviewed described the energy and relationship shared between the performer and the audience as "private" and "holy," feeling the energy from the audience infect and affect their work. Many introverts find their time on stage, in front of an audience, freeing. That freedom is something an introvert can achieve, but it can be exhausting. Recharging post-show is vital.

Post-show

The show is over and the curtain has closed. Your job here is done, right? Not quite. There are still some major pitfalls introverts need to navigate. Two of the most common post-show interactions are greeting the audience and socializing with the cast. These two deceptively simple situations can cause major issues for introverted actors, and major misunderstandings between extroverted and introverted personalities.

Leaving the theatre can sometimes mean socializing with the cast or crew, as invitations to dinner, drinks, small gatherings, and cast parties all require additional energy and place demands on the introvert. And as we know, introverts usually wish to recharge alone after an intense experience like performing a show. Broadway actor Linda Mugleston confesses, "I'm very private, and people not understanding this has caused some friction. I like to be included in going out after a show, but I need to make the choice. I don't want to be pressured."[14] Again, it is necessary and respectful to allow the introvert to make the decision, rather than coercing them into an extroverted situation. As Mugleston points out, the invitation is often appreciated, but the pressure to attend isn't fair to the introverted actor, who needs to decompress.

Another post-show obligation that can feel overwhelming for an introvert may be greeting audience members after the show. Andy Head is one actor who has a strong opinion related to such activities: "After a show, I don't want to see the audience. Even though most people are going to say 'good job,' I don't want to be recognized. I think that plays into being an introvert."[15] Once the safety of the character is removed, the actor can become reconnected with their more introverted ways, leaving them feeling exposed, pressured, and unprepared to interact with others. Actor Patrick Midgely has the same response to seeing an audience and has tried different ways of dealing with this situation.[16] He alternates between two main strategies: he either rushes out of the building first, leaving the performance right away, even going so far as to have his personal items prepped and ready to get out of costume quickly to avoid the people outside; or he relaxes in the dressing room for 30–40 minutes before leaving to politely avoid a potentially uncomfortable interaction.

In these tactics, you can see an introverted actor adjusting potentially overwhelming social situations. We advocate for this level of self-awareness and ingenuity. Parts of this business will always continue to favor the extrovert, but how the introvert navigates these spaces can change.

One critical portion of the post-show process for the introverted actor is the important cool-down or recharge period. Introverts recharge in numerous ways, but this necessary time demands a personal solution. Dr. Richard Lucas notes the demands of performance are similar to any other exhausting experiences, and introverts must find enjoyable techniques to help them recover.[17] Whether it is reading a good book, taking a relaxing shower, exercising, watching television, meditating, or just taking a nap, you must find a strategy that works for you and allows you to rest and recharge because it all starts again tomorrow.

Entering into rehearsals and performances with a plan for alone time is key. Figuring out how to find time away from the group is important. When there is constant pressure to be outgoing and gregarious and dynamic, it is even more important to identify those quiet, recharge spaces in your environment. This work involves self-awareness and an unapologetic mantra of "I don't want to be social right now, and there is nothing wrong with that." The self-awareness piece is vital. Introverted actors might need to practice a kind of self-care that allows them to say, "I need my alone recharging time. I need to watch Netflix in my pajamas" (one of Susan Cain's favorite mantra), or "I need to go to the cubby and read a book," or "I need my alone time to recharge." After spending rehearsals or performances focusing on your scene partner, you must also allow some time to focus on yourself.

When examining how introverts and extroverts function differently within acting, there is a larger cultural piece to consider. Change can happen when an actor examines the nexus between self and community. The community also has a responsibility to understand different behaviors and needs for quiet. In communities like theatre that are set up around a very social mode, it can be difficult to remember the need for quiet space, for breathing, for time to be alone and to recharge, and to offer actors the assurance that this time is allowed and valued. With strategies like using headphones during breaks, or renting a car to get away from the group to recharge, or even simply taking a walk alone in nature, it is essential to identify the interchange of that nexus between self and community. Rehearsal halls, acting studios, and greenrooms can all benefit from normalizing a culture of quiet. There should be a self-awareness of when you need solitude and when you need social interaction, but this is reinforced by a community that understands and provides access to quiet time as well as public events.

Our survey respondents also reiterate the idea of both recharging and smaller gatherings, noting:

- Take quiet time for yourself to cool down and re-energize through music or other activities that "feed" you.
- Have dinner alone with one of your castmates. Getting to know them one on one helps with being in the show together.[18]

This last suggestion segues into the next, and sometimes most stressful, form of interaction for an introverted actor—the exhausting demands of networking. In a highly visible profession like acting, networking can make or break a career, and this forced intersection of business and pleasure is one area of this business many introverts loathe. Next, we hope to help you learn to appreciate and navigate networking—on your terms!

NOTES

1. Lucas, Richard. Personal interview. 15 Jan. 2019.
2. Midgely, Patrick. Personal interview. 23 March 2019.
3. Mugleston, Linda. Personal interview. 15 Jan. 2019.
4. Lucas, Richard. Interview.
5. Midgely, Patrick. Interview.
6. Anonymous respondents. "Introversion survey."
7. Ringwald, Molly, and Susan Cain. "QUIET PODCAST: Episode 7." *Quiet: The Power of Introverts with Susan Cain*, Panoply, podcasts podcasts.apple.com/us/podcast/episode-7-molly-ringwald-hollywoods-introvert/id1065074566?i=1000364998124
8. Kaenzig, Lisa. Personal interview. 15 Dec. 2018.
9. McGowan, Sean Patrick. Personal interview. 13 April 2019.
10. Heinz, Amy. "Granting Kids the Time They Need to Socially Succeed." Quiet Revolution, June 20, 2017. https://www.quietrev.com/the-long-runway-granting-kids-the-time-they-need-to-socially-succeed/
11. Head, Andy. Personal interview. 15 Aug. 2018.
12. Choudhury, Soumyabrata. Personal interview. 14 Feb. 2019.
13. Anonymous respondents. "Introversion survey."
14. Mugleston, Linda. Interview.
15. Head, Andy. Interview.
16. Midgely, Patrick. Interview.
17. Lucas, Richard. Interview.
18. Anonymous respondents. "Introversion survey."

REFERENCES

Anonymous respondents. "Introversion survey."

Choudhury, Soumyabrata. Personal interview. 14 Feb. 2019

Heinz, Amy. "Granting Kids the Time They Need to Socially Succeed." Quiet Revolution, June 20, 2017. https://www.quietrev.com/the-long-runway-granting-kids-the-time-they-need-to-socially-succeed/.

Head, Andy. Personal interview. 15 Aug. 2018.

Kaenzig, Lisa. Personal interview. 15 Dec. 2018.

Lucas, Richard. Personal interview. 15 Jan. 2019.

McGowan, Sean Patrick. Personal interview. 13 April 2019.

Midgely, Patrick. Personal interview. 23 March 2019.

Mugleston, Linda. Personal interview. 15 Jan. 2019.

Ringwald, Molly, and Susan Cain. "QUIET PODCAST: Episode 7." *Quiet: The Power of Introverts with Susan Cain*, Panoply, podcasts podcasts.apple.com/us/podcast/episode-7-molly-ringwald-hollywoods-introvert/id1065074566?i=1000364998124

CHAPTER 15

Networking

The crowds. The chatter. The din. The opening night party. The stage manager's birthday party. The one-month anniversary. The "Meet the Cast" potluck. The understudy's dog adoption party. The closing night party. Actors love a chance to celebrate. Well, not all actors. Networking events play to the social strengths of many extroverts. Extroverts are masters at these events and shine as they enviably and easily chat with numerous people. It appears extroverts charm and dazzle as they tell stories, make jokes, and put others at ease with their carefree and comfortable small talk. But for many introverts, the mental taxation and exhaustion engendered by these events is overwhelming and, in some cases, exactly why an actor might choose to leave the business. We purposely call the public events "get-togethers" because they are an important, inherently social, and often obligatory part of the business. While not usually part of the actor's actual contract, they are an unspoken and prevalent portion of the "contract" of this profession. And their implied and expected attendance is mandatory.

Sigh.

Yes, introverts, you have to go to the opening night party, the "meet and greet," the donor reception, the talkback, and the agent's holiday party. These are requirements of the business where merrymaking often leaves introverts feeling anything but merry. Of course, after the event, an introvert might reflect and think, "That wasn't so bad." But the very concept of the networking event, to many introverts, is debilitating. In the

© The Author(s) 2020
R. Roznowski et al., *The Introverted Actor*,
https://doi.org/10.1007/978-3-030-41607-2_15

book *200 Best Jobs for Introverts* (2008), author Laurence Shatkin asserts that for introverts, the steps required to get a job are often much more challenging than those needed to do the job well once it's secured.[1] Shatkin goes on to say, "The most effective way of finding a job – networking – is a technique that introverts may resist using because it involves so much social contact. Introverts can network successfully by concentrating on the strengths they bring to the task: their understanding of themselves, their ability to articulate their skills, and their ability to cultivate relationships over time" (17). Networking is not designed for what introverts do best—one-on-one, focused, and deep conversations. But these events aren't going anywhere, and if we want to be actors, we have to go. So the more valuable question becomes, how do we do it?

Networking is one of the few areas in our research not unique to actors; therefore, we urge you to seek out any of the numerous materials on the topic. Even as we examine new areas related to actor growth, the subject of networking has already been tackled in books like Frederica Balzano's *Why Should Extroverts Make All the Money?: Networking Made Easy for the Introvert* (2001)[2] and Devora Zack's *Networking for People Who Hate Networking: A Field Guide for Introverts, the Overwhelmed, and the Underconnected* (2019).[3] Where we devote only a few pages to the topic as it relates to actors, these books and others are focused on the intricacies of networking and offer more depth and strategies to help with this real dilemma. These sources advocate for numerous alterations to a person's way of interacting in a public setting and give tips for making interactions at such events more palatable. In short, they suggest how an introvert can manage these events more like an extrovert. Despite the plethora of materials out there helping introverts succeed at networking, as noted in our interviews and survey, introverted actors still report a high degree of stress related to networking.

In the book *Why Should Extroverts Make All the Money*, author Frederica Balzano makes an interesting observation about how modern technology has impacted our ideas about networking.[4] She opines that the world is becoming more introverted with the advent of isolating technology so that a worker might interact more with their computer than with their boss. However, she warns this trend is not happening so rapidly that an introvert can retreat into their shell and wait for the world to adapt to their preferences. Balzano notes networking remains a necessary and essential element in almost all business interactions. Of course, we can translate this sentiment to the actor's vocabulary with the growing popularity of tools like recorded audition self-submissions and Skype interviews, but based on the amount of time needed to devote to interactivity, an actor's life will likely remain a highly social one.

STRUGGLES

Several of our contributors shared their issues and struggles with networking. Even though they now enjoy successful professional acting careers, they have yet to completely shake the negative connotation of networking. Carol Schultz lamented, "Networking! I just can't go up to people at parties and network, not that I ever go to any parties if I can get out of it."[5] As we have noted, this attitude is a popular one.

Similarly, Matthew Marks reports, "I cannot walk up to casting people or music directors because I have nothing to say, and I assume they do not want to talk to me. Forcing myself to make a fake conversation with someone has never been easy, and I don't think it ever will."[6] You can see the introvert's overthinking in Marks' suggestion that others don't want to talk to him. The truth is that introverts can't guess what others at the party might be thinking, but negative self-talk often works against them.

Patrick Midgely notes he doesn't have an aggressive working mentality and rather trusts things will come along rather than chasing them.[7] He realizes he may have lost some opportunities because of his predisposition to introversion, but suggests if that is the case, the job might not have been a great fit anyway. The concept of "fit" for the introvert may actually be seeking simple respect for the introverted personality as part of a company's acting culture. This understanding of fit requires a keen self-awareness and acceptance of what is necessary for an introvert to feel most successful and in control. Midgely acknowledges the professional necessity of networking and considers the connections he's made at such events as one of the cornerstones of his career. Nevertheless, he admits, "I was never successful in large group networking situations. I recognized that right away. I didn't like them or the people who seemed to control them. I didn't respond well to them. So, I found ways to connect with people that I resonated with." Midgely has reformed his approach to large networking events through a useful self-awareness that highlights skills of deep connection, active listening, and authenticity.

"ACTING" LIKE AN EXTROVERT

You've heard it before: You're an actor; act like an extrovert! Quite a few of our experts offered this very same advice. Introverted actors are constantly faced with the outside perception that social events and casual interactions should be second nature to them simply because they are an actor. Actors are repeatedly volunteered to host talks, go to interviews, speak in public, or emcee events all because their job as actor implies they should enjoy these public and extroverted interactions. If only it were that easy. The concept of pretending to be a different personality is easy when we are playing a role guided by a script, but that safe mask of character is not present when we are ourselves at public events. However, experts in the field offered some advice that may help introverted actors as they attempt their personal portrayal of an extrovert.

Dr. Lisa Kaenzig, a self-described extrovert, has much to say on the subject:

> I always tell people you have to fake it. Pretend you're someone you know, who you think is comfortable at networking ... and pretend you are them. Ironically, for an actor, that might be a little easier. I was a master of networking, and I've continued those skills in [my current] job as Dean because I need it all the time.
>
> But it didn't come naturally to me in the beginning either, and I'm an extrovert. I had to pretend I was someone else who was comfortable with it. I would literally say that person's name in my head, and say I am this person. Then I'd go in and pretend I was them. So, though I don't have any formal acting experience, in order to learn how to be a good networker, I had to fake it for a few years and pretend I was somebody else. It took a while for it to feel authentic.
>
> An actor can be an extrovert when asked to. In this business, if a networking event causes anxiety because you know you're going to have to go and be on, what are the things that cause you stress in terms of the extroverted expectations? I'm not the best at networking. I struggle at those events. I have to gear myself up, and say, "It's only going to be a couple hours. Let's have a good time and chat with people. It's not life or death." It's okay to engage, and it's okay if you need to move on from someone. Just politely excuse yourself. I'm very empathic ... I'm subject to a lot of energies, so I can become overwhelmed with a lot of people. I do better on a smaller scale. Go and listen ... You're going to be drained by the end, but step up, have a good time, be light and bright and easy about it, and then rest later.[8]

In this passage, Dr. Kaenzig describes playing another from an extroverted point of view and explains quite a bit of the rational transactioning an introvert could do to play this part. But playing the role of an extroverted version of yourself veers a bit from the work an actor does in terms of the thought process of the character. In this "Act like an extrovert" hypothesis, there seems to be a reliance on personal and professional self and not on the thoughts and lines of a character. Can an introvert pretend to be an extroverted character when the character they are playing is just a different version of themselves? It may work for some, but many reported it could actually cause more stress.

In the article "Would Introverts Be Better Off If They Acted More Like Extraverts? Exploring Emotional and Cognitive Consequences of Counterdispositional Behavior" (2012) the authors (Zelenski et al.) experimented with both introverts and extroverts acting as their differing temperaments for controlled periods of time in a lab.[9] The results were both fascinating and surprising: "We conclude that dispositional introverts may indeed benefit from acting extraverted more often and caution that dispositional extraverts may want to adopt introverted behavior strategically, as it could induce cognitive costs or self-regulatory depletion more generally" (290). The authors mention their findings are relative to the length of time spent and the level of acting within the differing temperament and noted further study was necessary. They also acknowledged possible depletion of energy could occur for both groups, but the immediate benefits for introverts were that they reported feeling happier and more energized after brief, controlled stints as an extrovert. The authors conclude, "Such findings prompt the question, would introverts be better off if they acted more extraverted more often? This broad question is difficult to answer conclusively" (291).

Dr. Richard Lucas offers similar advice.[10] He notes simply, "Networking behaviors come naturally to extroverts; that's what makes them likable. It's not a bad idea to look at guides for doing those sorts of things. And to say, 'What is it that extroverts do that makes them comfortable in these situations?' Then plan to do those behaviors." But is it really that simple? So many of the safety nets an introverted actor relies on—the script, the character, the analysis and backstory, the structure of the rehearsal—are all gone when the actor must play themselves.

Despite the struggle between private and professional selves, introverted actors must learn how to navigate networking events. Dr. Brent Donnellan offers an examination of the nature of the necessity of networking in relation to professional success and explains, in many professions, the ability to network and make connections with other people for instrumental purposes may not come naturally to a lot of people, but those people who force themselves to do it end up being more successful.[11] Donnellan upholds the importance of understanding that networking is tied to professional obligations, and ultimately, to success. So, even if an introverted actor might feel inauthentic at a networking event, there is a validity to the practice for success in their chosen field. For even the most introverted actor, recalling the motivation for going into this business—passion—can rationalize networking and attendance as a necessity that comes along with the career you are working toward.

Like so many other public events, the demands of networking can become physically and emotionally costly to some introverts, and it is this cost that so drastically separates them from many of their extroverted colleagues. Donnellan understands networking "ends up being cognitively and emotionally demanding if it's not natural to you. You come away exhausted from it. A true extrovert wouldn't be exhausted. I think it's part of the liabilities we all have with some of our trades." He advocates for the use of self-talk, where introverted actors can create a specific list of what they need to do at the event, providing the kind of structure that allows an introverted actor to maintain a sense of control over an unpredictable situation. This list can include who you wish to chat with, topics for discussion, questions to ask, and even polite ways to exit a conversation if you feel the need to recharge alone. This organized self-talk can also highlight the importance of the event or how crucial it may be for your success or achievements. This drive for success and a return to passion for the craft can spur an introvert to find networking less taxing.

Actors must understand networking is part of the cultural script for their profession. Rather than adding an inauthentic layer of pretense by playing an extrovert, they could remain authentic. In the book *Why Should Extroverts Make All the Money?* Balzano notes introverts cannot force themselves to become extroverts and suggests trying to do so would likely result in disaster and a lack of temperament diversity.[12] The author understands that for introverts facing this dilemma, the issue of acting like an extrovert can be overwhelming. Balzano suggests identifying what communication habits are causing networking problems and deciding whether or not they need adjusting. The multiple, and sometimes contrasting, perspectives offered by the experts for how an introvert might best navigate the demands of networking reinforce that, in the field of acting, the study of introversion is still in its infancy. As we continue to explore and experiment with new strategies and practices, we will hopefully develop more consistent ideas for the introverted actor.

Unfortunately, no matter the amount of literature and strategies available, introverted actors still report great stress related to networking events and great concern that this professional obligation works against the advancement of their careers. At the United Arab Emirates conference roundtable, a group of introverts and extroverts shared their stories about networking. Their conversations revolved around the introvert's love of deeper conversation and an extrovert's ease in socializing. Here is a sampling of their feelings, experiences, and advice:

Actor 1: Networking is hideous. You have to push yourself to do it. Once I had the chance to meet a director from *The Globe*. My friend said I had to meet him because he'd heard of me. It took me everything to get there. And when I did, I saw so many actresses swarming, I [started] feeling sick and nauseated. I left. I couldn't do it.

Actor 2: Extroverts are lovely, chatting away and having fun, but when I do it, it's such an effort. I think it's not going to come across very well, so I generally leave. But you have to do it.

Actor 3: I'm infinitely jealous and envious of … introverts [who] seem to process information on a deeper level. If extroverts don't go someplace and meet a lot of people, it's a wash. My extroverted personality craves connection. But most extrovert connections don't have as deeply intertwined a thread as perhaps introverts do.

Actor 4: Maybe that makes a difference professionally, too because I do find I work with the same people over and over again. Maybe that's a byproduct of the fact that networking is so challenging.

Actor 5: That's me too! I've worked with the same directors, multiple times, and I make more connections, but it's more of a casual introduction. It's difficult to go out there and be yourself.

Actor 6: It becomes easier once you start making the first connections because you can use those to help make the next connections. They essentially do the job for you.

Actor 7: There's a set number of things [to discuss], and it's hard to know what to do when those shallow topics are over. You don't get to know someone on the deepest level possible or understand them at the core of their being. I don't feel comfortable expressing myself or talking about what I want to do unless I know who they are first. That can be hard when you have to process and understand things first.

Actor 8:   Networking events are created to not allow for deep conversations. They are cocktail chatter, and if you do have a moment, then sometimes topics get too deep, right? Suddenly you're monopolizing a conversation. Those personal topics can backfire.[13]

Interestingly, the extroverted actor in the preceding exchange shared their envy of the introvert for making deeper connections. That reciprocal appreciation of each other's strengths makes the collaboration of diverse personality types essential to what we do.

Perhaps the best advice comes from introversion expert Dr. Marti Laney Olsen in her book *The Introvert Advantage: How Quiet People Can Thrive in an Extrovert World* (Workman 2002), where she suggests rather than act the character of an extrovert, you can act "as if" you're a confident introverted guest.[14] She asks you to recall a time when you mingled with confidence and remember that behavior. The "as if" you are playing is already part of you. This suggestion respects the craft of acting and values individual authenticity by not asking an actor to play an extroverted character.

Solutions

If you, like Carol Schultz, often skip out on attending parties, you may employ one of her favorite tactics that also relies on one of the introvert's strengths—writing.[15] Schultz offers that even if you can talk to people at parties, that doesn't mean the conversation is over. Sending notes and emails is a less direct approach to asking questions and starting a dialogue. Schultz hails, "You can think things through clearly in email and try to make the right impression. I'd be awkward in person. I might say the wrong thing, and I'd beat myself up for whatever I did." Again, the actor's problem-solving for navigating social expectations is related to self-awareness and adaptation.

Matthew Marks uses a version of an earlier strategy related to time management.[16] He describes, "Every Christmas party I force myself to say 'Happy Holidays' and 'How are you?' to the director, choreographer, the original music director, the librettist, and the head producers. I make myself do that first." To the extroverts, this approach may seem quite simple, but to many introverts, it is a major investment. Marks' structuring of his networking interactions helps him prioritize his conversations, placing the most potentially uncomfortable exchanges first and hopefully eliminating stress for the remainder of the party. This is another example where a prepared list of comments, questions, and people to greet helps to guide the course of the evening, where the introvert has done his extroverted duties.

Actor Patrick Midgely, who admits he detests large business networking events, shares his idea for communicating on his terms: "I have [a business card] to give someone so I can set up a separate time to talk to them, get to know them, and express my interest in what they do, rather than do it spontaneously in a large group setting. That's been the best way for me to connect with someone and let them know they're important to me."[17] Midgely understands this is a necessary aspect of the business, but like most introverts, he prefers more intimate personal time. While there is always a risk a less extroverted actor might miss some opportunities, there is often a direct correlation between the number of people in the room and the willingness an introvert has to make a connection. The business card technique makes an introduction, provides information, and opens the door to a later, one-on-one interaction much more suited to the introverted actor's strengths.

Many comments from our survey respondents support both the struggles and the strategies shared throughout this chapter. The dread of networking is pervasive:

- The business side is hard for me as an introvert. Sharing opinions in unfamiliar groups, networking, promoting myself on social media … it is all too much.
- Of anything related to this business, networking is the most draining. The assumption that you are extroverted because you're an actor can be frustrating and make it more difficult to ask for what you need as an artist (space, alone time, etc.). It's often perceived as standoffish rather than an innate personality trait requiring certain self-care strategies.[18]

Both respondents write of being drained and overwhelmed. These seemingly low-key events can hold high stakes for many introverts.

In the next section, we offer some ways to lower the stakes. It is illuminating in one response that even the solo act of highlighting your social media presence (a sometimes solitary act) can be considered an extroverted affair. It is clear, whatever the platform, networking is a part of this business, and short of advocating for quiet rooms at such events (which may often be an unreasonable request), introverted actors may have to make some adjustments in order to attend and thrive in these demanding environments. If you fear you are missing out on opportunities because of your introversion, the management and mitigation of the dread brought on by these social gatherings might be an introverted actor's top priority. You can, as one contributor reported, make peace with networking.

COMMUNICATE

An actor's life is about communication. Communicating the story. Communicating the behaviors and psychology of the character. Communicating relationships. Communicating the circumstances of the world of the play. Communication is our specialty. Theoretically, these strengths can be cultivated and enhanced in networking sessions. Why then is communicating at these events so draining? How can you enhance these trained aspects of your personality that engage smaller venues to succeed in this larger one? Luckily, you can create stretch goals that allow you to communicate in ways that authentically represent your passion for what you do and who you are.

As we have pointed out, social behaviors of introverts are often mislabeled and misunderstood, and in a demanding networking situation, these misconceptions can have dire consequences. Theatre director at LREI and veteran educator Joanne Magee notes, "Introverted personality traits can often be completely misinterpreted by someone who is unaware of the ways in which introverts communicate."[19] Sometimes people will see a tilted head as a sign of nerves; having a firm handshake, making eye contact, or speaking in a higher volume can all be assets to the introverted actor. These are not qualities of playing another role, but rather simple adjustments of behavior that signal confidence and assertiveness.

VISUALIZE

Magee also encourages visualizing networking events as moments of potential growth and success. This mindfulness allows an introvert to mentally prepare for potentially stressful situations. Picture yourself going into the social event, interview, or audition. Envision how you behave, what you do, who you talk to, and even how you move through the space. If you can imagine yourself doing these things successfully, you can revise the script in your head that casts you in the role of the unsuccessful partygoer.

SCHEDULE IN ADVANCE

When a party is coming up, schedule some prior alone time to build up energy toward the event and take time after the event to recharge. Look ahead to the social demands of your schedule and work to find a balance between public and private energy. This is a strategy of self-care that upholds the idea that you cannot give of yourself if you don't first take care of yourself. Schedule thirty minutes of "you" time for every thirty minutes of "them" time. Managing your energy for the week or the month can help avoid feelings of nerves and breathlessness that often accompany anxiety. Schedule time in your week to prepare for what is to come and time to recover. Be kind to yourself. After you've gone to a socially demanding event, treat yourself to a reward.

ASK QUESTIONS

Introversion expert Lisa Kaenzig has a simple trick she often uses in social and networking arenas to calm her nerves: ask other people about themselves.[20] Whether introverted or extroverted, almost everyone enjoys talking about themselves and most of us struggle less when the topic is personal. Similar to an actor putting the focus on their scene partner, Kaenzig describes this shift as the quickest way to make yourself more comfortable and take the focus off of you. Introverts are excellent active listeners, and genuinely asking questions can highlight this quality in a way that is authentic and polite. While actors are often told they must market and sell themselves as a brand, this does not mean you need to constantly be talking about yourself. Inviting others to speak keeps you open to building new relationships and helps you learn more about the other influential people in the room. Once you are able to get the guests talking, all you have to do is listen.

You can also employ another introverted skill, research, to find out who is attending. This preparation can help you draw up two or three relevant questions you may want to ask. You can also utilize the functions of rehearsal by practicing the questions with friends to make sure they sound authentic. This kind of work may seem antithetical, but in these stressful situations, introverts can rely on mindful practice. Psychology professor Richard Lucas also suggests pre-planning some thoughtful or insightful questions that can put the focus on the other.[21] Not only does this take the pressure off of you to speak, but it can also boost your confidence through positive reinforcement. Lucas suggests, "It might not be as hard as you think … Hopefully, you get rewarded and it becomes easier to do over time." That reward might mean a later one-on-one meeting where you can chat on an even, introverted playing field. The reward might be simpler, but just as important: the confident self-awareness that you have found a strategy for enduring, and even enjoying and growing from, a stressful networking event.

In addition to a prepared list of questions, you can apply a similar concept to yourself. Inevitably, someone will ask you something about yourself and you want to be confident enough to answer. Simply prepare a few things to say about yourself and don't feel pressured to offer every detail of your resume. This idea of a scripted interaction should not sound rehearsed but contain a few quick sentences about who you are and what you're working on. It's also important to remember that often at these networking events, people don't want to talk exclusively about business. They want to get to know real people. This plays perfectly to many introverts' desire to be authentic. Having a quick, informal, personal story to pull out of your back pocket can be a life-saver.

TIMED CONTRACTS

Similar to a rehearsal calendar, introverts are more willing to participate when they know how their time will be spent. You can apply this same logic to the time you spend at social events. And you have control over how this time is dictated! When heading to a party, lower your anxiety by making a contract with yourself that you will stay for one hour. You can even break this down into numbers of conversations or laps around the room (e.g. "I will stay for exactly thirty minutes and talk to at least five separate people before I leave"). However you quantify your socializing, you can take comfort in knowing you will be able to leave in a manageable amount of time. And on a positive note, you can always add time if you find yourself in a great conversation. It happens often that an introvert who has dreaded attending a party is surprised to discover they are having a great time. In these happy moments, you can mentally extend the time you've contracted to stay.

WING PERSON

Introverts can adopt an age-old socializing custom by reimagining the role of the "wing person" to aid them in the demands of networking events. Find a trusted friend who understands your introverted tendencies and stick with that person at the party. Professor Lucas advises, "Grab an extrovert to lean on and plan your exit strategy when things get overwhelming."[22] A close extrovert can be an introvert's best friend at a social event. Ride the extrovert's energy and let them start the conversations you never would. Follow their lead and enjoy the sense of social ease extroverts so naturally create. An extroverted confidant can provide a secure base. They can help to read your signs of discomfort and check in with you periodically. Setting up this private communication between friends can be a valuable part of your pre-networking preparation. Checking in with these key people at appointed times can also break a stressful event up into manageable increments. Our survey respondents agreed, noting:

- As far as "networking" goes, I don't immediately grasp onto people and show who I am as a person. My extroverted, funny actor friends have an easier time networking with casting director.
- I've noticed extroverted actors tend to have an easier time networking and making professional connections. I hang with them.[23]

The suggestions from these respondents are also echoed in a book about networking and introversion. *The Successful Introvert: How to Enhance Your Job Search and Advance Your Career* (Happy About 2008) by Wendy Gelberg has a few other practical suggestions for introverts at large events.[24] She suggests volunteering for a task or finding a purpose so you can focus on a job rather than the mingling. She also suggests looking for other introverts to connect with at the event. And finally, she offers practical conversation starters related to the occasion, such as location, name tag information, visual clues, or topical subjects. These possible solutions may lead to the introvert finding they might actually enjoy the networking event.

FLOW

In the book *Why Should Extroverts Make All The Money?* Balzano notes introverts can become passionate when talking about their craft.[25] Networking events are often populated with people like you, creative people from the industry who have one very important thing in common—a passion for acting. You may find when you alight on the subject of acting, the networking anxieties dissipate as you get into the flow of discussing something you love.

In Tamara Girardi's chapter "Blatant Self-Promotion" from the book *An Introvert in an Extrovert World* (Cambridge Scholars 2015), she writes about this phenomenon of passion: "Extroverts might have the ease of attending three parties in one night and working the room, collecting a stack of business cards too large for their pockets, but an introvert might spend five hours sitting with three or four other writers, talking and building a relationship that will last far beyond that first interaction. Such a strength should not be underestimated; in fact, it should be embraced" (117).[26] Rather than playing into an extroverted version of the networking event, look for those like-minded folks who are willing to talk about what inspires you and share what inspires them.

If you want to hone your networking skills and make these events more palatable, apply and adapt the preceding and other quick approaches. There are many techniques available. Do some further research. The research can alleviate the dread.

LA actor and writer Sean Patrick McGowan has some final words of wisdom related to the subject of networking: networking is not acting but rather a *part* of becoming a *professional* actor.[27] It is helpful to disentangle these two. Take stock of how introversion is affecting your work and find the life and/or the market that allows you to do the work you want to do in the way you want to do it. McGowan suggests you can create a small network and learn how to put yourself in a position to have one-on-one interactions with people, rather than always going to large parties. He offers these encouraging words: "Being an actor and making your living through acting is not the same thing … No one needs to give you permission to be an actor."

In our next chapter, our contributors offer some final advice to help you understand, embrace, and claim your place in the acting profession as an introvert.

NOTES

1. Shatkin, Laurence. *200 Best Jobs for Introverts.* Indianapolis, IN: JIST Pub., 2008.
2. Balzano, Frederica J. *Why Should Extroverts Make All the Money?: Networking Made Easy for the Introvert.* Lincolnwood, IL: Contemporary, 2001.
3. Zack, Devora. *Networking for People Who Hate Networking: A Field Guide for Introverts, the Overwhelmed, and the Underconnected.* Oakland, CA: BK/Berrett-Koehler Publishers, Inc., 2019.
4. Balzano, Frederica. *Why Should Extroverts Make All the Money?*
5. Schultz, Carol. Personal interview. 20 Jan. 2019.
6. Marks, Matthew. Personal interview. 10 Jan. 2019.
7. Midgely, Patrick. Personal interview. 23 March 2019.
8. Kaenzig, Lisa. Personal interview. 15 Dec. 2018.
9. Zelenski, John M., Maya S. Santoro, and Deanna C. Whelan. "Would Introverts Be Better Off If They Acted More Like Extraverts? Exploring Emotional and Cognitive Consequences of Counterdispositional Behavior." *Emotion* 12, no. 2 (2012): 290–303. https://doi.org/10.1037/a0025169
10. Lucas, Richard. Personal interview. 15 Jan. 2019.
11. Donnellan, Brent. Personal interview. 1 Dec. 2018.
12. Balzano, Frederica. *Why Should Extroverts Make All the Money?*
13. "Introversion and Acting." *American University of Sharjah Theatre Festival.* February 4, 2019.
14. Laney, Marti Olsen. *The Introvert Advantage: How Quiet People Can Thrive in an Extrovert World.* New York: Workman Publishing, 2002.
15. Schultz, Carol. Interview.
16. Marks, Matthew. Interview.
17. Midgely, Patrick. Interview.
18. Anonymous respondents. "Introversion Survey." Qualtrics survey. Michigan State University, 2019
19. Magee, Joanne. Personal interview. 29 May 2019.
20. Kaenzig, Lisa. Interview.
21. Lucas, Richard. Interview.
22. Lucas, Richard. Interview.
23. Anonymous respondents. "Introversion survey."

24. Gelberg, Wendy. *Successful Introvert: How to Enhance Your Job Search and Advance Your Career.* Happy About, 2008.
25. Balzano, Frederica. *Why Should Introverts Make All the Money?*
26. Girardi, Tamara. "Blatant Self Promotion." *An Introvert in an Extrovert World: Essays on the Quiet Ones.* Ed. Myrna Santos. (UK: Cambridge Scholars Publishing, 2015), 117.
27. McGowan, Sean Patrick. Persona interview. 13 April 2019.

References

Anonymous respondents. "Introversion Survey." Qualtrics survey. Michigan State University, 2019

Balzano, Frederica J. *Why Should Extroverts Make All the Money?: Networking Made Easy for the Introvert.* Lincolnwood, IL: Contemporary, 2001.

Donnellan, Brent. Personal interview. 1 Dec. 2018.

Gelberg, Wendy. *Successful Introvert: How to Enhance Your Job Search and Advance Your Career.* Happy About, 2008.

Girardi, Tamara. "Blatant Self Promotion." *An Introvert in an Extrovert World: Essays on the quiet ones.* Ed. Myrna Santos. (UK: Cambridge Scholars Publishing, 2015), 117.

"Introversion and Acting." *American University of Sharjah Theatre Festival.* February 4, 2019.

Kaenzig, Lisa. Personal interview. 15 Dec. 2018.

Laney, Marti Olsen. *The Introvert Advantage: How Quiet People Can Thrive in an Extrovert World.* New York: Workman Publishing, 2002.

Lucas, Richard. Personal interview. 15 Jan. 2019.

Magee, Joanne. Personal interview. 29 May 2019.

Marks, Matthew. Personal interview. 10 Jan. 2019.

McGowan, Sean Patrick. Persona interview. 13 April 2019.

Midgely, Patrick. Personal interview. 23 March 2019.

Shatkin, Laurence. *200 Best Jobs for Introverts.* Indianapolis, IN: JIST Pub., 2008.

Schultz, Carol. Personal interview. 20 Jan. 2019.

Zack, Devora. *Networking for People Who Hate Networking: a Field Guide for Introverts, the Overwhelmed, and the Underconnected.* Oakland, CA: BK/ Berrett-Koehler Publishers, Inc., 2019.

Zelenski, John M., Maya S. Santoro, and Deanna C. Whelan. "Would Introverts Be Better off If They Acted More like Extraverts? Exploring Emotional and Cognitive Consequences of Counterdispositional Behavior." *Emotion* 12, no. 2 (2012): 290–303. https://doi.org/10.1037/a0025169.

CHAPTER 16

A Call to Action

Why does an introvert want to act? We have returned to the question numerous times, but in our last chapter we give the final word to clinical psychologist Dr. Chris Hopwood: "Introverts attracted to acting feel it affords them an opportunity to let themselves out a bit because the formal trappings of the performance create enough distance that they don't feel the pressure of a typical conversation. This is amplified by the fact that the actor-audience relationship is not mutual."[1] Rather, this essential relationship is one-sided; the introvert has the script and the audience listens. Hopwood goes on to share the enlightening fact that "[p]art of the reason introverts are reticent is that human beings tend to let you down, but to a certain degree, the actor has more control over an audience, who is scripted to respond positively to a good performance, and it doesn't go beyond that. [Acting] may be an outlet for the natural need to commune that we all share, but that introverts don't easily find elsewhere." The reticence described is then transformed into ease when an actor is on public display. This interesting conundrum is what makes introverted actors so enigmatic. Hopwood understands the counterintuitive nature of the relationship. He describes introverts as individuals who "tend to like personal and deep interactions and dislike superficial ones. Even if the content of a script is superficial, acting as performance is always serious in the sense that it has to be done well in order to work, it is also a way to avoid the frivolous flavor inevitable in many interactions." Introverted actors take their work very seriously. Their drive for perfection, their deliberate practice,

© The Author(s) 2020
R. Roznowski et al., *The Introverted Actor*,
https://doi.org/10.1007/978-3-030-41607-2_16

and their tireless work ethic all create an actor who commands attention, even when not speaking.

In our introduction, we wrote about the various audiences for this book, and now, the time has come for those audiences, whether they be introverts, extroverts, ambiverts, or those who prefer not identify with such a label, to begin to make changes in the classroom, the rehearsal hall, and at auditions. It is time to launch a dialogue about introversion and extroversion, where we work to normalize the conversation and talk openly about unconscious biases. It is time to empower introverted actors to proudly say, "I am an introverted actor, and as such, I am ultimately more sensitive to stimulation from the outside world than an extrovert. There is nothing wrong with that. I was born this way. This is my neurobiology." From there, imagine the mutual respect that can create great acting from an inclusive atmosphere. We've got to start talking about it. It's a larger cultural conversation, and it can begin to happen in the realm of acting, thanks to all of you.

To Actors

If this book provides nothing else, we hope you know, as an introverted actor, you are not alone. There are many of you out there. Value your introversion. Play to your strengths and understand that some training and roles require you to work outside your comfort zone. It is there you will find your work goes to unexpected places. Be excited about the adventure.

One question we asked of all our contributors, regardless of their role, profession, or level of experience, was what advice they would give to introverted actors, who often feel they are alone in struggling with the contradiction of their passion and their personality. What follows is a collection of aphorisms and advice from many of the voices we have followed throughout our discussion on introversion and acting that will hopefully empower both the introverted actor and the actor educator. Whether in the classroom, the audition space, or the rehearsal hall, these affirmations are meant to inspire actors, directors, and educators.

From New York City Veteran Actor Carol Schultz

> Advice? The theatre is exactly the place for you! Introversion is welcome here! But you have to want and need and be able to do the work. It takes incredible discipline to be a good actor. Be the best you can be. Study, learn

how to make your voice work. Learn how to make your body work. Research. Watch actors you admire. Learn everything you can.[2]

We support Schultz's advice of learning all that you can and adapting what may be extrovertedly biased training into what resonates with you. The holistic approach to acting is something introverts can always work toward. Connecting your over-active brain with your body is a struggle for some introverts, but it can be done. Allow your voice to be heard … when you want it to be.

From LA Actor and Writer Sean Patrick McGowan

When it comes to acting, as an introvert, the best thing is to pay attention to how your body and your psychology respond to all the different circumstances you are in … often, part of the dark side of being an introvert can sometimes be feeling there's something wrong with you or you should be different to satisfy an idea of what it means to be socially successful or well-liked. At least in the way certain pieces of media tell [introverts] we ought to be well-liked. The more you pay attention to where your motivation comes from, how you fill your time, and how you perform your actions, the more respect and appreciation you will have for the uniqueness of who you are, as opposed to blinding yourself to your own behavior, thinking you have certain traits that are defective and will be fixed someday.[3]

As McGowan notes, there is no need for introverts to be "fixed." They are not broken. However, there is a need for more inclusive training practices to allow introverts to thrive on the stage or in front of the camera. As McGowan suggests, connect to your passion. Remind yourself why you must act. No adjustments are required.

From Broadway Actor Matthew Marks

Accepting that I am [an introvert] has made me a better auditioner. I don't think it's made me better in a holding room full of 45 people, but at that point, you should be focusing on your script or sides anyway. Stay honest. It never works for me to be fake. People can see right through it … it's tough to be fake. It drains you and impedes your performance, your audition, and your interview. Try to fall in love with yourself and who you are.[4]

The concept of knowing yourself and knowing where you thrive is entirely important to introvert or extrovert. But that is a process. That takes time. And self-awareness.

From Actor and Educator Patrick Midgley

Remember why you're there in the first place. Think about why you want to be an artist and why that is something you're not willing to compromise. Why you can't live any other kind of life. If you always put the work first, everything else can fade into details. The details are still important, of course, so as you're dealing with those doubts and frustrations, don't fake it. Find ways to continue to be yourself and let yourself shine through to other people. Make connections with other people that are genuine. Don't push or feel you have to perform for other people in professional settings. Introverted people, myself included, combine introverted with self-conscious. Learning how to let go of some of that self-consciousness and instead develop a self-confidence is a trick. It takes a lot of practice and exposure to the environment that makes you uncomfortable. The more you are in it and gradually increase your exposure, and the less you ghost out or do your hermit stuff, the more confidence you gain.[5]

Transforming self-consciousness to self-confidence is extremely difficult. Using the power of observation and empathy so prevalent in self-consciousness to find self-actualization is liberating for the personal and professional self.

From Actor and Educator Andy Head

There is a lot to be said about your effort. It's easy to run from things you're scared of, but if you give them a try, it's usually not that bad. Even if my feelings are saying something different, logically I know, in most cases, if I just do something, it's probably going to end up being a good thing. Even my fifteen-year-old high school self realized that, and that's why I did theatre in the first place. But, I still have to reinforce that a lot. I don't always feel that way, but I do believe it. Once you believe that, it makes it easier to fight the nerves and fears that come along with being an introvert. Also, preparing helps me feel ready for situations that are uncomfortable because of being an introvert. In situations you know you have to do, even if you don't want to, just put on your biggest smile and fake it ....[6]

The theme of "faking it" versus an introvert's need for authenticity appears in the last three quotes, with some experts advising against it and others acknowledging it might have its use. Many introverted actors subscribe to the concept of pretending to be an extrovert in order to fit into the prescribed notion that an actor must be theatrical. As mentioned earlier, "theatrical," in its very definition, is an extroverted notion. That actors must be histrionic and performative is the very bias this book hopes to debunk. These actors found solace and comfort in their own authentic and quiet voices. Their contribution to their craft is now honest and honored.

While we know the extrovert ideal is much more common and expected in American theatres and acting classrooms, international parallels exist and are worth remembering. Here are some encouraging words from some of our international interview subjects.

From Indian Actor Student Kavya Misra

You will be amazing on stage. You're a gem already because you function better in solitude ... and acting will only refine you. A self-immersed personality can give a lot to the multitude. You don't necessarily have to become an extrovert and be the center of attraction. Just be the thinking human you are, and enjoy the whole phase. I know you don't like listening to your voice a lot; I know you get those shivers when you start speaking; I know your hands tremble and you want the whole thing to end as soon as it can. But the secret is that it will. The end is inevitable. So, push the pull door and pull the push door. Don't be hard on yourself by abiding by all the rules. I'm glad you are working on a topic like this, which so many relate to but don't even know how to accept. They care so little about personalities and take them for granted, as if only a new birth can cure a distorted personality. But drama really works as therapy for many.[7]

From Indian Actor and Graduate Student Shafali Jarial

It is only you who can help yourself. If you have a dream, push yourself every day to make it happen. Take baby steps if you can because deep down, you know what you are made of and your potential, even if the world disagrees with you. Do it for the dream.[8]

In this advice, we see the concepts of reminding yourself of your passion along with stretch goals. These two concepts are key takeaways from this book.

From Indian Actor and Director Soumyabrata Choudhury

Make relaxation an important, fundamental enjoyment of the work. Relaxation is neither laziness nor is it something purely internal. Relaxation is a sense of comfort, yes, but also alertness to the possibilities of a congregation of people when they're together. The sense of invention to something we can do together, something new we can create together, but not from a point of view which is already hyper-energetic. Those people who are always, "Hey, I'm an actor, I'm an actor. Look at me!" That is precisely not an actor. An actor is someone who is not recognized, and then you do the first bit of acting and someone says, "Oh, God, this is an actor."[9]

For the introverted actor, relaxation is key. While extroverts may be loud outwardly, conversely, may the introvert be loud internally. Relaxation can bring balance to the inside and outside worlds.

Finally, some of the many actors attending the Introverted Actors' roundtable discussion in the United Arab Emirates have some final words of advice for introverted actors:

Actor 1:   There's a lot of pressure to put yourself in the American ideal of the extroverted actor. That's the way it should go because that's what everybody else is doing. But because everybody else is doing it, you bring something special and unique to the table. It's individual to you. It's okay to embrace that and allow that to be part of your process because that's something different you bring to the table from everybody else. Sometimes you need extroverts, and sometimes you need introverts … those complementary traits make for a balanced and productive class or rehearsal room.

Actor 2:   Quite often it takes introverted actors a little longer to get seen in a room, and it takes a little bit longer to get to the point where they feel allowed to work. Trust your process is your strength and what makes you unique and special, and that process inside the rehearsal room is going to make that final product valuable. Yes, it takes a while to get to the point where you're allowed to have your process, so be patient, but trust your process is what makes you valuable.[10]

The concept of trusting oneself can only come through understanding that there are so many others like you in this profession, even as each introverted actor is unique and brings something special to the studio:

Actor 3:   I assume, but shouldn't assume, all directors are looking for an actor who is able to open their heart when given the opportunity. Whether they are an introvert or an extrovert, we want honesty. As a director, that's what I'm hoping for. I try to give every actor the opportunity to give that when they come into the room.

Actor 4:   Being an actor is about learning how to be in the moment, open yourself up, and be vulnerable. It's sometimes painful to do. You've got to go there to be successful.

Actor 5:   Being vulnerable on stage, especially to an introvert, ironically enough, gives you power. On stage, when you're open to judgment, you don't care anymore. It gives you a kind of power. Honestly, the joy of acting is that a person can have the worst day, and come to two hours of your performance, and you can change their mood. That's all I want.[11]

The theme of vulnerability has been an important one throughout our examination of introversion. Above all else in acting, the authors of this book value vulnerability. Actors who allow themselves to be affected and thus affect others. Introverts can do that. Their capacity for empathy links so closely to the vulnerability required for acting.

To Directors and Educators

There is a special place in the creative process for quiet, for stillness, for thinking, and for reflection. So often we are driven by producing the product—finish the show, put up the art—and we are sometimes made nervous or uncomfortable by silence or stillness or a perceived lack of productivity. But there is a tremendous value in the act of stepping back as a part of the process. In the writing process, this is the step of incubation, the step of allowing the ideas to continue percolating in the back of the mind without actively pursuing them. Because we so often are dealing with truncated rehearsal calendars, this is a step of the process that can often go neglected when it comes to acting or rehearsal. If we are looking at reinventing the structure of theatre in regard to introverted actors, can't we also advocate for silence and stillness in the process? There is a value to allowing space for silence, whether that is space in the room, space on the calendar, or space in the day. In our need to produce the work, we might be neglecting a valuable element of the creative process when it comes to quiet.

The next two pieces of advice are aimed squarely at directors and educators. Either on set or in rehearsal, directors must make some adjustments to their expectations that they are working only with extroverts. Simple and respectful changes can be easily achieved.

From LA Actor and Writer Emmanuelle Roumain

> Exercises to help actors get to know each other are important because, especially when dealing with more vulnerable and heavy material, the actor should be in as comfortable an environment as possible and know what the other actors they are working with are comfortable with too. I'm often introduced to actors I'm working with in the hair and make-up trailer. Introducing the actors beforehand and encouraging rehearsals so they can build a rapport would be really helpful.
>
> The relationship between the director and the actor is extremely important, and in television, it's rare that the director will connect with the actor before the shoot. It helps to be able to talk to the director about the character and how they fit into the story. Most of the time, you book the part, and you have to figure out your character as best as possible on your own. Because there is so much money on the line, and productions are working on tight deadlines, it often limits the amount of attention given to the actor's process. If communication were made more possible between the actor and the director, it would really benefit the project.[12]

Starting production on a level and respectful playing field can yield dividends in the shooting of the film. Finding ways to work with actors of various temperaments can be embraced as a way to not only be fair but to get the best work out of actors. Isn't it time to make these simple changes to your process to reach all actors, not only those similar or pretending to be similar to the actors you normally work with?

From Director Joanne Magee

> Directors need to know there is a large population of incredible actors who are confident and skilled, and who may well be missed and overlooked merely because the theatre industry often listens to the loudest, brightest, "bubbliest" person in the room. Perhaps directors and casting directors need to think less about the sparkle an actor comes in with, and focus instead on what the actor does on stage or in the scene. We need to be respectful of the diversity of personalities.[13]

Such respect for the diversity of temperaments can balance the playing field for all actors. Educators and directors can modify any training practices that are inherently extrovert-based. New ways to create ensemble and warm-up will be created. And introverts can feel welcome, safe, and included in studios and rehearsal halls.

LET THE CHANGE BEGIN QUIETLY

So, there you have it ...You have sound advice and encouragement from all over the world. You have the knowledge and comfort of knowing you are not alone as an introverted actor or educator of students of diverse temperaments.

You have tips and strategies for every major demand of your craft, and tools to advocate for what you need to do your best work. Rule the rehearsal room with quiet leadership. Set the pace in classes through in-depth analysis. Network on your terms. Model the practices and techniques that honor your personality. And set stretch goals that help you grow—with authenticity and vulnerability.

To us introverted actors, let's change the perception that all actors are extroverts by advocating for what we need. Being honest when we feel excluded. And educating others' who believe that this is an exclusively extroverted field. The introverted actor has unique strengths that allow them to create extraordinary work. So, share your skills and strengths as an introverted actor on your terms. Challenge stereotypes. Change the script. And own your unique and quiet voice.

NOTES

1. Hopwood, Christopher. Personal interview. 17 May 2019.
2. Schultz, Carol. Personal interview. 20 Jan. 2018.
3. McGowan, Sean Patrick. Personal interview. 13 April 2019.
4. Marks, Matthew. Personal interview. 10 Jan. 2019.
5. Midgely, Patrick. Personal interview. 23 March 2019.
6. Head, Andy. Personal interview. 15 Aug. 2018.
7. Misra, Kavya. Personal interview. 10 Feb. 2019.
8. Jarial, Shafali. Personal interview. 15 Feb. 2019.
9. Choudhury, Soumyabrata. Personal interview. 14 Feb. 2019.
10. "Introversion and Acting." *American University of Sharjah Theatre Festival.* February 4, 2019.
11. "Introversion and Acting" Sharjah.
12. Roumain-Yang, Emmanuelle. Personal interview. 30 April 2019.
13. Magee, Joanne. Personal interview. 29 May 2019.

REFERENCES

Choudhury, Soumyabrata. Personal interview. 14 Feb. 2019.
Head, Andy. Personal interview. 15 Aug. 2018.
Hopwood, Christopher. Personal interview. 17 May 2019
"Introversion and Acting." *American University of Sharjah Theatre Festival.* February 4, 2019.
Jarial, Shafali. Personal interview. 15 Feb. 2019.
McGowan, Sean Patrick. Personal interview. 13 April 2019.
Marks, Matthew. Personal interview. 10 Jan. 2019
Midgely, Patrick. Personal interview. 23 March 2019.
Misra, Kavya. Personal interview. 10 Feb. 2019.
Magee, Joanne. Personal interview. 29 May 2019.
Roumain-Yang, Emmanuelle. Personal interview. 30 April 2019.
Schultz, Carol. Personal interview. 20 Jan. 2018.

CONTRIBUTOR BIOS

The following professional actors and educators graciously donated their time and expertise to assist us with this book. Their experiences and opinions formulated much of the book's structure and suggestions.

John Baxter is the Head of Movement at LAMDA. He trained at LAMDA as an actor. John has worked with the RSC, the NT, Shared Experience, and the Almeida Theatre, to name a few, as well as in television and film. As a director, he has worked for the Royal Opera, the Queens Theatre, the National Gallery, and the National Youth Theatre, among others. He has led workshops and masterclasses in London, Paris, at the Ancient site of Epidauvros, and for Welsh National Opera.

Benil Biswas is a performer, director, and scholar. He is an assistant professor at the School of Culture and Creative Expressions, Ambedkar University Delhi.

Cameron Michael Chase is an MFA Candidate in Acting at Michigan State University. He has been a professional actor for the past 15 years and is also certified in The LoVetri Somatic Voicework.

Soumyabrata Choudhury is a well-known Indian actor and educator who currently teaches at Jawaharlal Nehru University.

Rodney Cottier is head of the drama school division at the London Academy of Music & Dramatic Art. He has 39 years' experience as a stage director and teacher of stage combat, acting, and text at LAMDA, where he has directed 26 plays from Shakespeare's canon.

© The Author(s) 2020
R. Roznowski et al., *The Introverted Actor*,
https://doi.org/10.1007/978-3-030-41607-2

As a fight director, Cottier has worked at Shakespeare's Globe as Master-of-Fight, choreographing several productions including Mark Rylance's Hamlet, as well as the Royal Opera House, English and Welsh National Opera, the National Theatre Studio, and many regional theatres.

Brent Donnellan is a professor of Psychology, and he investigates research questions at the intersections of personality psychology, developmental psychology, and psychological assessment.

Maria Frangi is a Greek theatre director and a faculty member at the University of Patras in Greece.

Andy Head is a professional actor and an assistant professor with the Department of Performing Arts and Visual Culture at the Rochester Institute of Technology.

Sarah Hendrickson is Assistant Professor of Acting and Improv at Michigan State University and professional improviser, actress, instructor, and producer in Chicago performing with many theatres, including The Second City.

Chris Hopwood is Associate Professor of Psychology at the University of California, Davis, and his research sits at the interface of clinical and personality psychology.

Lisa Kaenzig is the dean at Hobart and William Smith Colleges in Geneva, New York. A frequently invited speaker on issues relating to gifted and introverted learners, Kaenzig's acclaimed research on the topic, "Introversion: The often forgotten factor affecting the gifted," is cited as one of the most influential early references in the field.

Shafali Jarial is an MA Performance Studies major at Ambedkar University Delhi.

Richard Lucas is Professor of Psychology at Michigan State University and one of his research areas is extraversion.

Matthew Marks is an actor currently in *The Book of Mormon* on Broadway. Before that, he has been in many other productions such as *Priscilla, Queen of the Desert, West Side Story, Gypsy,* and *Fiddler on the Roof.*

Joanne Magee is a tenured drama teacher and theatre director at LREI, a leader in progressive education since 1921 in New York City. She trained at the Royal Central School of Speech and Drama in London, England, and has 25 years of teaching and directing experience both in London and New York.

Sean Patrick McGowan is an LA actor and writer, known for *Townmouse, Face to Face Time,* and *The French Teacher.*

Patrick Midgely is a professional actor who has worked with numerous classical companies devoted to the works of Shakespeare and holds a PhD in Theatre from Texas Tech University.

Kavya Misra is an Indian student and actor currently studying for an MA in Theatre.

Linda Mugleston has appeared in nearly a dozen Broadway shows including *My Fair Lady, Hello, Dolly!, Beautiful: The Carole King Musical, Cinderella,* and *Young Frankenstein.*

Emmanuelle Roumain is an actress and writer known for *Hawaii Five-0, 90210, This Is Family,* and *Criminal Minds.*

Carol Schultz is an NYC based actor who has worked extensively in regional theatres throughout the country and has been a company member of the Pearl Theatre in NYC, as well as the Cleveland Play House and CSC Rep.

Jennifer Simard is a Tony, four-time Drama Desk, two-time Drama League and Lucille Lortel Award nominee. Broadway credits include *Disaster!* (Sister Mary Downey, Tony nomination); *Hello, Dolly!* (Ernestina); *Company, Mean Girls, The 25th Annual Putnam County Spelling Bee* (Rona); and the original companies of *Sister Act* and *Shrek the Musical.*

Andy Sloey is a graduate of both the iO Training Center and Second City Conservatory in Chicago and is currently an adjunct professor at Webster University's Conservatory of Theatre Arts. He is a teacher, performer, and general manager at The Improv Shop in St. Louis, MO.

Capital City Improv Roundtable Participants
Eric Flick
Al Nimpson
Alexsis Page
Drew Stroud
Carla Wilson

Dubai Roundtable Participants
Mohammed Abdulsalam
Karan Ahfid
Maegan M. Azar
Jason Culbreth
Jason Dernay
Hassan Haliyah
Michael Long
Patrick Midgely

Rodney Omar
Rachana Pillamari
Anthony Tassa
Collin Vosbeck
Austin Wilson
Elie George Yazigi
Student Respondents from Chap. 10
Eric Balamucki
Molly Bennett
Grant Cleaveland
Lydia Cotner
Sarah Davis
Shelby Eppich
Peter James Florian
Evan Houdek
Brandon Drap
Jala Jackson
Elise Jorgensen
Paige King
Hongwen Lu
Kallie Marrison
Mack Marshall
Taylor McPhail
Madison Moylan
Taylor Mueller
DJ Shafer
Camiile Thomas
Brandon Townsend
Sara Weldon
Michigan State University Master of Fine Arts Candidate Actors
Ryan Adolph
Abbie Cathcart
Sharon Combs
Kevin Craig
Darah Donaher
Eloy Gómez Orfila
Claire Wilcher

Index[1]

[1] Note: Page numbers followed by 'n' refer to notes.

© The Author(s) 2020
R. Roznowski et al., *The Introverted Actor*,
https://doi.org/10.1007/978-3-030-41607-2